COCONUT

COCONUT

FLORENCE Ọ̀LÁJÍDÉ

Thread

Published by Thread in 2021

An imprint of Storyfire Ltd.
Carmelite House
50 Victoria Embankment
London EC4Y 0DZ

www.thread-books.com

ISBN: 978-1-80019-466-3
eBook ISBN: 978-1-80019-465-6

For all those who walk between two paths.
May you find a torch to light your way.

BROWN SHELL

CHAPTER ONE

My Earliest Memories

Somewhere between the ages of four and five, I realised I was different. Everyone around me flaunted skin as pink as candyfloss, hair as soft as silk and eyes the colour of the sea, or perhaps the occasional brown like mine. In contrast, my walnut skin stood in sharp relief and there was nothing remotely silky about my wiry hair. Those early memories whizz in and out of my mind like clouds on a breezy day. Some, I remember with a vagueness that suggests they were not real. Others are so stark, I don't doubt their authenticity.

I lived with Nan and her family. Nan was old enough to be my grandmother, although she wasn't. She was my foster mother, someone my parents paid to look after me while they studied during the day and worked at night. My parents were from Nigeria, a former British colony that had only recently got its independence from Britain. They were studying in England to get the qualifications needed to man the post-independence jobs vacated by British expatriates. Most African students of their generation could not afford live-in childcare. Hence, a private fostering industry mushroomed in England and beyond, whereby, for a fee, Black children resided with white families.

I saw my parents when they visited me at Nan's, or I went to them at weekends. Dad was a handsome man with toffee-coloured skin. His hooded eyes bore a slight hint of the orient, although as far as we knew there were no Asians in the family tree. Of slender build, he was shorter than most men. Yet, he walked with a jaunt that belied his compact frame. By the time he hit his thirtieth birthday, he was already half-bald, which meant whenever in public, he always wore a tweedy flat cap. Soft-spoken, but vivacious, Dad loved socialising with friends over a pint.

At five-foot one, Mum was slender and almost as tall as Dad. Her skin tone was much darker than Dad's, a flawless mocha that gleamed in the sun. What made people stop was the irresistible draw in her smile. Mum was hardworking and liked to be busy. If something needed doing, Mum was your woman. Like Dad, she loved company and both of them enjoyed a large circle of friends. When people met us, they said I sported my father's face and my mother's skin tone. I thought I was a delightful mix of both.

Before I lived with Nan, I had two prior carers. The first, a childminder, looked after me while Mum worked. One day, my mother missed her train home. She turned up an hour late, and to her dismay found me lying in my cot in the minder's back garden. The minder's husband had arrived back from work earlier than usual. He didn't like Black people and didn't want a Black baby squalling in his home, so she put me in the garden. That it was the middle of one of the coldest winters since British records began and I was only three months old, didn't seem to matter.

Mum stopped working and searched for another carer. The first one she found, willing to foster me full time, lived in Norfolk, so off I went. A few weeks later, my parents received an unexpected visit from a health visitor querying my whereabouts. The Norfolk health services had contacted their London counterparts when my foster mother had tried to organise my next vaccination. While sympathetic to my parents' plight, the health visitor frowned on the arrangement because the distance reduced the opportunities for visits, especially in the winter. She advised Mum and Dad to find an alternative placement.

So, aged one, I came to live with Nan. Mum's best friend had introduced her to Nan. Nan had fostered children before, the last one being a Nigerian girl, whose parents had spirited her away in the dead of night, breaking Nan's heart in the process. Because of this, Nan only wanted to offer day-care services. My parents and Nan both lived in London, but the distance between them made a daily commute impractical. Somehow, they convinced Nan to meet me before deciding. I had just started walking, and at our first meeting I toddled into Nan's arms and she fell in love.

*

If the eyes are the window to the soul, Nan's spoke of kindness. Her crow's feet and the dimples embedded in her square jaw were a testament to her sunny disposition. Hugs were her speciality: tight ones, cuddly ones, pick you off the ground and swirl you around ones. Nan kept her ash brown, curly hair trimmed, a fortunate thing, because her fingers never strayed from it, especially when she engaged in a good old natter. Nan spoke the Queen's English mixed with a smattering of cockney, her favourite cockney word being 'ain't'.

'May I have some sweets, Nan?' I'd ask.

'No, you may not,' she'd say. 'It ain't time.' Sweets were for after dinner, not before.

Nan's short and cuddly frame belied the speed at which she whizzed about like a tornado, duster in hand, apron tied around her waist. In the living room, she would lift the vase with its beautiful arrangement of fresh flowers and dust underneath. Next it was the turn of the snow globe, filled with tiny fake magnolias. Finally, she would dust the garland of dried flowers surrounding the fireplace mantle, before settling down to a cuppa in her dainty, floral, fine china, teacup and saucer. Yes, Nan loved all things flowered, dresses and aprons included. She also loved playing bingo and never missed her weekly outing to the local club. Nan had no artifice. Quick to the point, she ruled our happy household.

I called Nan's husband Pop. I never did find out his name, and no one called him anything else. The two couldn't have been more different, Pop's tall and thin frame a direct contrast to Nan's more rotund figure. Pop never said much unless arguing about football. In the summer, he loved nothing better than sleeping in his favourite deckchair in the garden. He often perched his eyeglasses over his forehead and covered his head with a newspaper to block the sun's glare from his balding patch. Sometimes, he'd have a tobacco pipe resting on a stool right next to his deckchair, and every so often, he'd take a puff. In the winter, you could find him pottering in his tool shed at the back of the garden. I never knew what he did in there because it was out of bounds.

Nan and Pop had grown-up children, Phil, Julie and Tom. I remember little about Phil. He didn't live with us, and we rarely saw him. Julie lived with us for a while, then she got married, leaving Tom, the youngest of Nan and Pop's three children and Dee, my younger playmate. Like the rest of the family, Dee's pale white skin, wispy blond hair and blue eyes set us apart. He was another one of Nan's foster kids. I believe many had come and gone before us. Dee visited his parents almost weekly, which meant that I was often by myself, but when he was around, he was fun.

Every few weeks, Tom would take me and Dee out for a special treat. We'd skip behind his extra-long legs, down the road to the fish and chips shop at the corner of Priory Road and Middle Lane. We'd watch as the shop owner lowered a basket of battered cod into the sizzling oil.

'And what comes next?' Tom would ask, peering at us through rimmed glasses that made him appear much older than his twenty-seven years.

'Snap, Crackle and Pop!' we'd both chorus, before bursting into uncontrollable giggles. The sound of the sizzling oil reminded us of eating Kellogg's Rice Krispies at breakfast. Wide-eyed, we'd ogle the shop owner as he emptied the hot food into large sheets of newspaper.

'Can we have some extra salt and vinegar?' I'd ask.

'Of course, you can,' the shopkeeper would say, before sprinkling the food with a liberal dusting of the two condiments. To this day, I'm still partial to salt and vinegar.

*

We lived at 144a Middle Lane, a Victorian structure on a typical North London street. The house was four storeys tall with both a basement and an attic. From the street, a steep flight of steps led to the first floor, which housed the living room and kitchen. More stairs led to bedrooms on the middle floor and to the attic where old Mrs Smith, a lodger, lived. An external flight of stairs behind the kitchen led down to the back garden. I have no recollection of who lived in the basement.

The house made a perfect backdrop to our favourite game, Batman. Dee and I spent hours in dress-up costumes, racing each other around the old, rambling house, up one flight of stairs, down a corridor, up another flight. I was Batman, and he was my faithful Robin. Now and then, Pop or Tom would yell 'Oi, slow down!' as we whisked past on our mission to save yet another imaginary victim.

When Dee and I weren't playing Batman, Nan could find us in the garden on our tricycles. The garden was generous, with a rectangular lawn and a riot of perennials and annuals dotted along the fence separating us from the neighbours. The heady scent of sweet peas, lavender and peonies made it an attractive place to be in the spring and summer. A paved area, our racing track, separated the flowerbeds from the lawn. Pop loved his backyard and hated us racing in it; his major fear was that we would run the wheels of our trikes over his favourite plants and ruin them. Often, he'd pop up from beneath his newspaper shade and check that we were behaving ourselves, before going back to sleep.

Most afternoons, it was my job to take old Mrs Smith's tea up to her. Nan would pack it into a small picnic basket. On tiptoe, I would clutch the banister as I crept up the stairs, pulse racing, all the while casting furtive glances over my shoulder. I wasn't sure what I was expecting to jump out at me, but climbing the dark stairwell alone was nerve-racking. This was despite Mrs Smith rewarding the effort with a handful of sweets. I had a sweet tooth, and it almost made the fear and trepidation worth it. But Nan always made me share the sweets with Dee and that just didn't seem right.

In the mornings, I would wake to the tantalising wafts of bacon signalling breakfast was cooking. I would skip into the kitchen where Nan would greet me with a 'Good morning, Ann, how are we today?' before placing a cup of milk in front of me. Then she would pause as she waited for my reply, twinkles at the ready. She would follow my 'I am fine, Nan. Thank you' with a quick peck on the forehead. Then she'd scoop whatever we were having for breakfast onto my plate before settling down to eat hers.

Bedtimes were special. Nan would bathe each child in succession and watch us brush our teeth before helping us into our pyjamas. Then she would settle Dee into bed before coming into my room. First, we would read a chapter out of my favourite story of the hour, before saying my prayers. Next came the game of 'Which hug is it?' as I tried to guess what kind of hug I was about to receive. Would it be tight and squishy or warm and fuzzy? Or would it be the bear hug? With eyes closed, I'd wait for arms to envelop me and I revelled in the comfort they gave. After another peck to the forehead, I would settle down to sleep. Nan would tiptoe out of my room, leaving the door wide open.

Darkness, in any form, gave me the chills, and I never slept with the door closed. Nan kept a single light on in the corridor. With the door open, it beamed through into my room. Although paltry, I found its orange glow soothing as I lulled myself to dreamland. One evening, I struggled to sleep despite the hot mug of cocoa Nan gave me. Deciding that I needed a distraction, Nan gave me a handkerchief. She showed me how to fold a corner into a tongue and tickle my left hand with it until I fell asleep. From then on, I went to bed with my handkerchief as my faithful companion.

CHAPTER TWO

It Does Matter If You're White or Black

Just before my fourth birthday, Dad picked me up from Nan's so I could celebrate it with him and Mum. We got off the bus close to home, and I held Dad's hand, skipping alongside his wide strides. Dad turned and his eyes crinkled as he slowed his pace to match mine. 'I have a B-I-G surprise for you at home,' he said.

My eyes lit up. 'Oh, goody! Will I have cake with my candy?'

Dad shook his head, 'Maybe, but that's not the surprise.'

'Did you buy me a birthday present? A doll?'

'No, it's bigger than that.'

'I can't guess it, Daddy, please tell me.'

'Just wait. It's a lovely surprise, I promise.'

As our house came into view, I scrunched my nose, wondering what could be bigger than a doll.

Dad and Mum lived in a one-bedroom, first-floor flat on Seven Sisters Road in Haringey, London. It was so much smaller than Nan's house, but the rooms were spacious with high ceilings. The living room's focal point, the striking bay window and its comfy window seat, overlooked the street below. It was my favourite place to perch and gaze at the world going by. The room was sparsely furnished with a black, leather, three-seater sofa which doubled up as my bed whenever I visited. Mum often covered it in pastel-coloured cushions which softened the black and brought some life to the otherwise plain, cream walls. A coffee table and Dad's radiogram, a contraption that combined a radio with a record player, completed the furniture.

As soon as we entered the flat, Dad led me to the living area where I found a smiling Mum sitting on the sofa with two bundles in her arms. I paused, but Dad tugged me closer. I peered at the sleeping bundles, then looked up at Dad in wonder.

'You've got a new brother and sister,' he said. I looked closer, and he continued.

'The one dressed in pink is a girl. Her name is Taiwo. The other one, dressed in blue, is a boy and his name is Kehinde.'

Mum's welcoming face held an amused grin. Intrigued, I peered at the girl. She had hair like mine. 'You can touch her but be gentle,' Mum said.

I reached out and touched the girl's cheek with the tip of my finger. She squirmed and yawned. I snatched my hand back. 'How did they get here?'

Mum and Dad shared a smile. 'The storks brought them,' Dad said.

Dad led me to one of the walls, now decorated with two round plates. I studied the plates, noticing that they each had a gold-rimmed, scalloped edge. Just inside the edge of each plate was a patterned circular band, blue on one plate, pink on the other. The white centre of each plate depicted an enormous bird with legs that looked like stilts. Each bird had a baby wrapped in a bundle dangling from its extra-long beak. A curious thought entered my head.

'Did a stork bring me too?'

Dad nodded in response before leading me to a third pink plate mounted on the other side of the room. For now, the explanation satisfied my curiosity and Dad let out the breath he had been holding. I skipped back to Mum.

'Can I play with the babies, Mummy?'

'No, sweetheart. They are still too little. Wait until they get bigger.'

After supper, Dad brought out my birthday cake, and my parents both sang Happy Birthday before letting me blow out the candles. Satiated and happy, I settled on the sofa-bed ready to sleep. Then I remembered my special hankie, the one I soothed myself with. Mum was busy with the twins, so I asked Dad.

'Dad, can I have my hankie please.'

'What hankie?'

'The one I tickle my hand with before I go to sleep. Nan packed it in my bag.'

'Okay, let's have a look.'

Dad crossed the room to the bag cosseted in a corner. After a few minutes of rummaging, he lifted his head. 'I can't find it, are you sure it's here?'

'Nan promised she'd pack it.'

Dad turned the bag upside down and emptied the entire contents. Out tumbled knickers, socks and dresses, but no handkerchief.

'Nan must have forgotten to pack it,' Dad said.

Tears welled. 'I need it to sleep. Please, can I have another one, Daddy?'

Dad took in the down-turned corners of my mouth and the glistening pools in my eyes.

'Okay, let me talk to your mummy.'

Dad padded off to the bedroom and returned moments later. 'Sorry, Funmi, Mummy doesn't have any clean hankies right now.'

'But I can't sleep without it!'

Dad lifted a finger to his lip. 'Shh! You don't want to wake the babies. They take ages to fall asleep.'

The tears fell, and I hiccupped into my pillow. Dad knelt beside the sofa, put a calming hand on my back and rubbed it in circles. When I stopped heaving, he kissed my forehead, pulled a blanket over my shoulders and said good night. To my relief, he left the bedroom door open, so a faint light wafted into the darkness.

When I returned to Nan's, I told her all about the babies and my missing handkerchief. Nan had a clever solution. She showed me how to twist the edge of my pyjama top and shape it like a tongue. If I ever found myself without a handkerchief when I needed one, I now knew what to do.

*

Nan and Pop started planning Julie's wedding. It would be a grand affair and Nan said I could be a bridesmaid. On the wedding day, the house teemed with people. All the bridesmaids were getting dressed at Nan's and travelling to the church together in a fancy car. After breakfast, the excitement moved to a bedroom. The girls squealed as an adult handed out the dresses. Soon silence reigned as we concentrated on slipping into our outfits.

A few minutes later, I realised something wasn't right. The three girls around me busy pulling the tulles of fabric over their heads had one thing in common. Their pink, satin dresses reached down to their ankles, but my dress was white and only came down to my knees. With their fluffy white hair bands and cute pink slippers, the other girls resembled little princesses while I looked like a ballerina. *Why the difference when I was supposed to be a bridesmaid too?* When I asked the adults helping us get dressed, they just smiled and told me how beautiful I looked. The other bridesmaids, not so kind, whispered and giggled. I couldn't help it; my lips pouted and wobbled.

I went in search of Nan and found her in her bedroom. Eyes glistening, I held the skirt up. 'My dress is all wrong!'

As always, she pulled me into a hug before leading me to her full-length swivel mirror. 'See how beautiful you are!' she said. I gazed silently at my reflection. Okay, my outfit was different from the other girls'. Still, it was the most beautiful dress I had ever worn. I didn't have the headband, but it probably wouldn't have worked with my woolly pigtails. I had the same slippers though, albeit in white, to match my dress.

'You've always wanted to have a ballerina outfit. Now you do and…' Nan leaned in to whisper her secret, 'you are the only ballerina in the room.'

I cocked my head and watched myself in the mirror. I twirled and the skirt of my dress ballooned and swirled with me. A slow grin spread across my face and I twirled once more. Nan handed me over to Tom so she could finish getting ready.

I had the most wonderful time dancing the night away with Tom and Pop as my ever-constant companions. After the wedding, we took a long-deserved holiday to Blackpool. I struck a pose on the sandy beach in my blue bikini and straw hat and Pop took my picture. It was to last for posterity. There were no other girls like me around, but it didn't matter because I ran and built proper sandcastles to my heart's content. In my little world, all was well, and I was happy, just the way a child should be.

*

Whenever Dee visited his parents and I had no one to play with, Tom let me tag along on his walks in Priory Park. He would also sneak me a sweet or two when Nan wasn't looking, which made him my favourite of Nan's children. One Sunday afternoon, with Dee away and Tom unavailable, Nan allowed me to go up the hill to meet some friends from Sunday school.

We always met at Susan's house. Her mum was a member of the church Nan attended sporadically. It had been a normal afternoon of board games followed by skipping in the garden. Tired from the physical exertion, we took a break when Susan's mum offered us chilled drinks and cookies, before retiring to another part of the house. Waving her hands, Susan started talking. 'I have a brand-new doll! She's got beautiful eyes and eyelashes that move. When I press her belly, she cries, and tears fall from her eyes.' The girls gasped, pressing in to hear more. 'Wait here, I'll get her,' Susan said, before dashing upstairs to retrieve the doll.

In Susan's absence, the girls chattered. The doll sounded marvellous and none of them had seen one that could cry. In record time, Susan reappeared, doll in tow. My eyes lit up when I saw it, my sneaky suspicion confirmed. Nan had given me the exact doll as a Christmas present, and it was the closest thing to an actual baby that I had ever seen.

Susan settled the doll into the crook of her arm. 'Look,' she said, 'she's got her own water bottle and I can feed her!' She stuck the miniature bottle between the doll's heart-shaped lips. She lifted the doll's knitted dress and pointed to one of the two buttons on its belly. 'Afterwards, you press this, button and she pees!'

The girls crowded round, jostling for a better glimpse. 'It's just like the one Nan bought me for Christmas,' I said from the back. A hushed silence descended as all the heads in the room swivelled a full ninety degrees before six pairs of eyes settled on me.

Susan glowered. 'What do you mean, it's just like yours?'

The heads all swivelled in the opposite direction. I opened my mouth to explain further, then snapped my lips shut. With her arms crossed over her chest and the two frown lines marring her pretty face, Susan wasn't expecting me to answer that question. In fact, I could tell that she would much rather I recanted. Susan was the kingpin in our group, and she hated the thought of others owning things she did.

'I have the same doll,' I said, feeling the need to stand my ground.

Susan's neck grew pink. The other girls, sensing the coming onslaught, edged back a little.

'No, you don't. You are just a copycat.'

My nostrils flared. 'Yes, I do. And why would I copy you?'

My reply only seemed to enrage her more. Her face turned crimson. Planting her feet wide apart, she pointed. 'You are not my friend anymore, get out of my house!'

My skin flushed with heat. I knew what that meant. If I wasn't Susan's friend anymore, then none of the others could be my friend. I eyeballed the girls. A few held my gaze, and I read the pity in their eyes. Others squirmed, refusing to look at me altogether. While sympathetic, they didn't have the guts to stand up to Susan. With jerky movements, I turned around and flounced through the house, heading for the front door. As I bounded down the stairs leading to the pavement, I realised too late that I had left my jacket behind. Still, I wasn't about to ruin my dramatic exit, so I kept walking.

Moments later, Susan came running after me. 'Don't forget your stupid jacket, you black monkey!' She flung the offending clothing at me. I stiffened as I felt my blood boil. Unable to contain my outrage, I swivelled back around, body rigid and eyed my ex-friend. Ruddy-faced, eyes glaring, she was in full fight mode. I took in a deep breath and bellowed, 'I am not a monkey!'

'Yes, you are. Why is your skin so dark if you're not?'

Before I could respond, 'Hoo, hoo, hoo…' she chanted, stamping each foot from side to side, her fists beating her chest in synchronised rhythm. I presumed she was mimicking a monkey. I looked up towards the house. Susan's mum was nowhere to be seen. The other children had gathered at the front door to watch the fight. They picked up the chant.

'Hoo, hoo, hoo…'

Mortified and shaken, I felt my hands clench and unclench. It was one against six. Picking up my jacket, I turned around and stormed home. I couldn't believe Susan had called me a monkey. I vowed I would never go back to her house.

*

I was pensive that evening, unable to get Susan's words out of my head. I wasn't a monkey. That much I knew. They didn't talk or walk like people, and they lived in trees. Still, Susan had a point. Why was my skin so dark? At bedtime, Nan tucked Dee, back from his day trip, into bed before coming into my room. We went through the usual routine, but my heart wasn't in it. As if she could sense something troubled me, she gave me an extra-long hug, before turning the lights out. Just as she was about to step through the doorway, I whispered, 'Nan?'

She paused, 'Uh-huh.'

'Why am I not white like everybody else?'

Nan came and sat on the edge of my bed. 'What do you mean?' A tender finger brushed against my cheek.

'Well, everyone in this house, at school and even Sunday school is white. Why am I Black?'

Nan enveloped me in her arms and rocked us both back and forth in silence. Finally, she coughed. 'Ann,' she began, 'God made different people, coloured and white. You are coloured, I am white. That's just the way God likes it. The world has loads of coloured people like your mum and dad, and they have coloured babies.'

I pondered her response for a moment. 'Nan, if I scrub very hard, can I wash the Black skin off?'

I felt the warm arms wrapped around me go rigid. With a finger under my chin, she lifted my tear-stained face.

'You will do no such thing.' Her voice, firm and sure, continued. 'Like you, another boy once thought the same. He scrubbed hard, hoping to get his skin off. He made himself bleed so much that his parents had to take him to hospital. We wouldn't want that, would we?'

I pictured the bloody scene in my mind with revulsion. I nodded, confirming we definitely didn't want that. Nan wiped my tears with the corner of her apron. With another tight squeeze and a kiss to my forehead, she headed out for the last time. I settled down to sleep with the questions still pounding in my head. *Why was I here, a Black girl in a world full of white people? Where were all the Black folk Nan was talking about, and why wasn't I living among them?*

*

That year, I became more aware of the differences between living at Nan's and my parents' place. Mum and Dad shared their garden with other tenants, and they never allowed me in it alone. I therefore spent a lot of my time indoors. With the birth of the twins, the flat felt more cramped. With the double pram parked in the hallway, the highchairs and day cot in the living room, you couldn't move around without bumping into something or someone.

I also noticed major differences in the food I ate. Mum always cooked Nigerian meals, especially *eba* and stew. You moulded the *eba*, a thick, glutinous substance, into little balls with your fingers before dipping it into the stew. I wasn't keen on *eba*. It tasted like sawdust, and when you chewed, it smeared your teeth. However, I loved the stew, made of chillies, tomato and okra – sometimes called lady's fingers. The way Mum cooked okra, it had a gloopy, slimy consistency, I suspect to help the balls of *eba* glide smoothly down your throat. I started swallowing the balls rather than chewing them. It made a colossal difference. I could savour the stew without tasting the *eba*.

Like spaghetti, you could tell when I'd had *eba* and okra. It always left me looking as if a slug had crawled all over my front leaving behind an orange maze. I soon learned the trick of eating it without covering my hands and arms in a slimy trail. First, you dipped the *eba* in the okra stew. Next, you cupped your hand to keep the contents from falling out, before gently swirling it around, until the trail of okra broke. Then you lobbed it all into your mouth in one swift motion. The skill required some practice, but Mum cooked it so often, I soon got the hang of it.

The dish became a firm favourite, and I wanted Nan to make me some when I returned, the only problem being I couldn't remember its name. 'Nan,' I said one afternoon, 'can I have some of that stuff Mum makes for dinner?'

'What stuff?'

'The stuff that goes like this...' I stopped speaking, cupped my right hand, swirled it around twice, before lobbing the imaginary food into my mouth.

Nan stared, perplexed. She called Pop over. 'Come on Ann, show Pop.'

I repeated my actions. They looked at each other, then simultaneously burst into laughter.

'What's funny?' I asked. That only made them laugh louder. Soon, their laughter triggered my own, and we all laughed together. When Nan's mirth subsided, she asked me the name of the food. I shrugged my response. 'I don't know.' That set off more hysterics. Nan promised to find out the next time Dad visited. For now, I had to settle for English beef stew, and although I liked it well enough, it was nowhere near as nice as okra stew.

I started school when I turned five, but for some unfathomable reason, I have very little recollection of it. I have flashbacks of being locked in the girls' toilets with other girls and screaming our heads off, but in excitement rather than fear, and that's pretty much it.

On their next visit, Mum and Dad talked about leaving England and going home to Nigeria, where I would meet lots of new cousins, uncles, aunts and my grandparents. I hadn't a clue where Nigeria was, but it sounded exciting until I saw the sadness on Nan's face. After my parents left, I overheard Nan and Pop discussing the war going on in Nigeria. According to them, it wasn't safe. I didn't know what 'war' meant, but given Nan's expression, it wasn't anything good. Nan's unhappiness distressed me, and I didn't want to leave her if it made her so sad.

The next time I visited Mum and Dad, I heard them talking again about the trip back to Nigeria. 'When are we going?' I asked.

'Soon,' Mum said.

'Nan said there's a war there. It's not safe. I don't want to go.'

In the deafening silence that followed, my parents exchanged a look I didn't understand. They kept conversations about Nigeria out of earshot from then on. My visit ended, and I headed back to Nan's.

CHAPTER THREE

The Separation

I visited my parents often after the birth of the twins, yet when the stork brought another baby two years later, it still caught me by surprise. My new sister was named Idowu, and a fourth plaque joined the three on the wall. With four children in it, the one-bedroom flat felt confined. The twins didn't enjoy vying with the baby for Mum's attention, and they wept incessantly when she carried the newborn. Dad was out working all day long. Mum did her best, but even with the little help I provided fetching things for her, it all seemed too much. For once in my life, I longed for quiet and couldn't wait to get back to Nan's.

A week later, I hadn't returned to Nan's, and I started asking questions. But on every occasion, Mum or Dad gave me a funny look followed by silence. Eventually, one evening, they both sat with me. My gaze flipped from one to the other. *Uh-oh, I'm in trouble. What did I do?* I bit my lip, waiting for them to speak.

'Olu.' Mum's use of my Nigerian pet name made me pay attention. It usually signalled she was happy, except this time, the emotions on her face contradicted this. 'You are not going back to your nanny,' she said.

I squished my eyebrows together and searched their faces. They were not making any sense. 'But why?'

'We are going to Nigeria soon.'

'But I don't want to go to Nigeria, I want to go back to Nan's!'

Dad put a heavy hand on my head and turned my face to his. 'We are a family. We love you and can't leave you behind.' His voice was resolute in its stillness.

'Can't I stay with Nan until we leave?' My voice trembled as my eyes filled with tears.

'We need to get used to being together as a family, us, you and your brother and sisters.'

My voice hitched, 'But I didn't say goodbye!'

'We're sorry about that, but you will get to see Nan again someday.'

Hope renewed, my heart fluttered. 'When? Can I see her next week?'

Dad shook his head, his eyes soulful. Not one to give up, I pushed, fists clenched, tears falling fast. 'What about all my clothes and toys? What about school?'

'We'll pick your things up soon. You will go to a new school until we travel.'

My shoulders drooped in defeat. I couldn't imagine never seeing Nan again, and although Dad promised I would, I didn't trust him, because he wouldn't tell me when. I turned and shuffled to the sofa. Arms hugging my middle, I sobbed. My parents let me cry for a while, then tried to cajole me out of my misery with dinner. But I wasn't hungry, and I just pushed the food around on my plate. At bedtime, I cried myself to sleep while tickling my hand with the hem of my pyjamas. Remembering Nan had shown me how to do this made me weep even more.

I moped around for days. Mum tried to cheer me up with stories of Nigeria. At every opportunity, I tried to coax Dad into letting me visit Nan. He wouldn't let me but repeated his promise that I would see her again someday. I couldn't understand why they wouldn't just let me stay at Nan's until the move. Then one evening, I overhead them talking when they both thought I was fast asleep. 'My dear, do you think we are being too hard on her?' Mum said.

'Possibly, but we can't take the risk of a court battle with her nan. The last time that happened, the courts awarded custody to the foster parents. As you know, she's already suggested keeping her until the civil war is over. If we leave her behind, there's a good chance, we'll never get her back.'

There was a lengthy silence before Mum spoke again. 'Have you thought about what going back will mean? Despite our best efforts, we haven't saved much. Until we both have jobs in Lagos, maintaining the family might be harder than we think.'

'That's true, but what other option is there? We can't stay here and be treated like dogs for the rest of our lives. Even with my diploma in sales and marketing, I'm still filling empty shelves in a supermarket. I'm not living like that when I know I can do far better back at home.'

I didn't hear Mum's reply as I drifted off to sleep, but I sensed my parents struggled with their decision as much as I did.

*

With Mum at home with the babies, Dad worked all hours, so he could buy all the household goods we would need in Nigeria. One evening, Mum put the baby and toddlers to bed before sitting beside me on the sofa. 'You are starting school on Monday.' She wrapped an arm around my shoulder and gave me a sideways hug. *Yippee! It would be nice to get out of the flat.* 'How will I get there?'

'Dad will take you to a childminder on his way to work. She will take you to school and pick you up. Dad or I will bring you home later in the day. You'll like Mrs Brown. She is Black like us and she has two children who are a little older than you.'

My ears perked at the news that they were Black. It would be awesome having Black friends for a change.

Mrs Brown was from the West Indies. She was a stout woman with a booming voice and a cackle that made me wince from the sheer loudness of it. Her twins, Benton, a boy, and Briana, a girl, both attended my new school. I thought our flat was small, but Mrs Brown's entire apartment comprised one multi-functional bedroom, living room, kitchen rolled into one, and a tiny bathroom. Dad dropped me off so early he often woke up the household. Mrs Brown hated Dad seeing her cluttered living space and bemoaned the fact daily, although never in his presence.

My hopes of becoming friends with Benton and Briana vanished before they could even germinate. The Brown twins, or the Nasties as I called them, took an instant dislike to me, and the feeling became mutual. On the way to school, Mrs Brown always walked ahead holding my hand, while the twins brought up the rear. Every few minutes, one of them pulled my hair or poked my back. When I turned round, they pulled faces, stuck out their tongue, or sniggered. If Mrs Brown noticed anything, she didn't say. At school, they got their friends to join in their cruel games and, together, made my life a misery. African monkey, fuzzy and golliwog became my new nicknames. I did my best to avoid them. Sometimes I was lucky, and I succeeded. However, I still had to go home with them. Soon, the bullying became intolerable, and I was desperate to find a solution to it.

One Saturday morning, Mum and I walked to the shops, and she took a route we had never taken before. 'That's my school, Mum,' I squealed, as we walked past the school gates.

'That it is,' she replied.

Just then, an idea bloomed in my head. I hoped Mum would take the same route home and my chest drummed when she did.

As soon as we got to the school gates, I paid extra attention to the rest of the way home.

At school on Monday, I worked hard at dodging the twins. After lunch, I slipped back into class and went up to Miss Simpson, my teacher. 'Miss, can I be teacher's little helper today?' I flashed her a megawatt smile when she said yes. It meant I would avoid the playground misery. At home time, I hid in the toilets and waited until the hubbub of children's voices died. Hoping the twins were long gone, I made my way out of the toilet cubicle. Determined to get home by myself, I walked out of the school gates and turned left. A few yards up the road I heard a voice that sounded suspiciously like Briana's. I paused and ducked behind a lamppost. It was definitely the twins explaining to their mother how they'd searched for me. Slowly, their footsteps faded away.

Breathing a sigh of relief, I walked to the traffic lights and as Nan taught me, waited for the little green man before crossing. I turned right and continued up the busy road. While I found the thought of going home alone daunting, the Nasties terrified me more. I was certain of the way. I just had to keep going on this road until I saw our door, the only one with a dark, olive green colour. Sure enough, a few minutes later I saw our house just up the road. Proud of my accomplishment, I strolled up to the doorstep and pressed the flat's doorbell. No one answered. I tried again. Still no answer. *Mum and the babies must be out.* Tired, I plonked myself down on the doorstep to wait.

Mum came home soon after and found me fast asleep outside. Later that evening, she and I had a long chat about my first big adventure. I explained why I ran away from the Browns. I don't know if she had a word with Mrs Brown after that, but for the next few weeks the Nasties were less nasty.

*

A week after I ran away from the Browns, Mum started taking me to school and picking me up herself. It was quite a task for her to get all four children ready in the morning for the trek, but I was thankful that I no longer had to deal with the Nasties. Weeks had gone by and despite my pleas, Dad still wouldn't let me see Nan. He had collected all my stuff from her and to show how much she cared, Nan sent me two beautiful, knitted hats, one white and one red. I loved my hats and although it wasn't winter yet, I wanted to wear them every day because they made me feel close to Nan. Fortunately, Mum let me.

One day, Mum was late in picking me up after school, so Miss Simpson told me to wait outside the headteacher's office. On my way, I ran into two much older boys and before I knew what was happening, one of them snatched my hat off my head and ran away. Mimicking Tom and Pop, 'Oi, give it back,' I yelled, running after him as fast as my little legs would go, while his friend jeered behind us. But no matter how hard I tried, I could not catch up with the hat snatcher. He weaved and bobbed, ducking all my attempts to clutch his coat.

After five minutes of fruitless chasing, I gave up, breathless. With slumped shoulders, I shuffled back to the head's office, fat, twin rivulets leaking from my eyes. I arrived just in time to see Mum and the headteacher walk out.

'We were just about to... Why are you crying? What happened?' Mum bent to wipe the tears off my face, but that made me want to cry harder.

I opened my mouth and heaved out the words. 'My hat. A boy took it!' I broke into a fresh bout. The headteacher looked at Mum, a worried look plastered across his face.

'It's a special hat, a present from someone close,' Mum said.

'Oh dear,' he said, understanding dawning in his eyes.

Just then a girl strolled up. 'Are you talking about a hat? I saw a white one floating in a toilet bowl in the girls' toilets.'

As the import of the revelation hit me, I dissolved into an incoherent flood.

'Come on, let's go home, we'll get a new hat,' Mum said.

'No! I don't want to go home, not without my hat.'

Now that I had started, I couldn't stop myself. I heaved out great hacking sobs, one after the other, only stopping in between to gulp a breath. The twins, who had hitherto been silent, whimpered. Afraid they would wake the baby and she'd end up with four squalling kids, Mum raised helpless eyes to the headteacher. The headteacher took my hand and drew me into his office, leaving Mum to pacify the toddlers. He spoke to me gently, telling me how sorry he was about what happened. Slowly, my sobs transformed into quiet hiccups, until they disappeared into a sigh.

Mum popped her head into the office and exchanged a grateful look with the headteacher. She turned to me. 'Come now. Let's get going before the baby gets hungry. We can buy a new hat, and remember, Nan gave you two. You still have the red one at home, but I don't think you should wear it to school anymore, just in case.'

I had cried so hard that now my head hurt. I rubbed my eyes furiously and sniffled. Bone tired, I was more than ready to go home and sleep off the trauma. I nodded and limped after my mother.

Soon after the hat saga, Mum and Dad began packing for the return to Nigeria. Then one day, a huge van appeared outside the front door and two men spent the entire day hoisting trunks containing everything we owned into it. That evening, I had a final surprise. I was playing with my doll when the doorbell rang. Over the previous days, my parents had seen lots of visitors, friends who came to bid farewell, so I thought nothing of it until I heard a familiar voice. I could not contain my joy as I flew into Nan's arms. Dad had graciously allowed her to come by and say goodbye. We spent a lot of time kissing and hugging. She brought a gift. I unravelled the wrapping paper, and two beautiful dresses fell into my lap. After more cuddles, Dad made that promise once more, this time to both of us. One day in the distant future, he would let me come back to visit Nan.

CHAPTER FOUR

New Beginnings

Three days after Nan's visit, we boarded a plane from Heathrow Airport and flew to Liverpool. From there, we embarked on a huge ship and sailed to Nigeria. I only have vague memories of scuttling around long and narrow corridors as I amused myself with the other children on board. Two weeks later, in the last week of October 1968, the ship docked at our destination, Apapa in Lagos. Carrying the baby, Mum led us out, with me sandwiched in the middle and Dad bringing up the rear, a twin in each hand. As we stepped onto the ship's gangway to disembark, a blast of heat struck me as if I'd fallen headlong into a furnace. I turned to Dad behind me. 'It's boiling!'

His grin split his face in half. 'Welcome to Africa!'

I fanned the air, trying to cool myself to minor effect. Even dressed as I was in short sleeves, the heat was stifling, and I could feel the sweat beading on my collarbone.

We emerged from the immigration desks into the arrivals lounge in the Port Authority building. My steps faltered at the welcome from dozens of clamouring voices. I gaped at the sea of Black faces, with not a single white one in sight, and remembered Nan's story about how God made people of different colours. *This must be where all the Black people lived, where I belonged.* I sniffed and scrunched my nose. The smells were strange, a suffocating mixture of humid air, earth and sweat.

A host of relatives welcomed the family home from England. They spoke in a language I could not comprehend. Even their clothing was different, with the ladies draped in technicoloured fabrics, skirts that bunched at the waist and roomy tops whose sleeves could have happily accommodated several more arms. The men wore long flowing gowns with baggy trousers underneath. Some older women had huge scars carved into each cheek. I wondered if they'd all been in the same accident.

The women surrounded Mum and enveloped us in a group hug. '*Eku abo!*' they trilled. Overwhelmed, I clung to Mum like a limpet. Then the ladies transferred their attention to us kids. One lady relieved Mum of the baby. Another one detached me from Mum's skirt, looked me over, patted my cheeks and said, '*Oyinbo*,' before passing me to the next relative. I wondered what she meant. One by one, they manhandled me and my siblings, repeating the mantra *Oyinbo*, until the twins burst into tears and Dad came to their rescue.

The welcoming party led us to the cars waiting to take us home. 'Beep-beep, beep-beep.' The incessant sound of horns filled the air as if the drivers were deliberately composing discordant music. I turned, wondering what the emergency was, but the adults kept on moving, oblivious to the racket. *Was this normal?* Soon, we reached the fleet of cars belonging to our entourage. Dad climbed into the passenger front seat with Kehinde on his lap. Another relative holding Taiwo clambered into the back. Mum urged me into the middle before climbing in with the baby. Exhausted from the day's events I settled in between the grown-ups and, lulled by the car's motion, drifted off to sleep.

*

Mum jostled me awake. We had arrived at our new home. I climbed out of the car, arched my back and stifled a yawn as I stretched my achy muscles. It was dark, and I couldn't see much, as a relative led us up a flight of stairs and knocked on a door. Someone opened it, squealed and pulled us into the room with a joyous hug. Inside, more relatives congregated. Once more, they handed me like a parcel from relative to relative as they patted my head, shoulders, or any part they could reach, all the time singing '*Oyinbo!*' I tolerated the attention for a while until I needed the bathroom.

Deftly disengaging from a would-be admirer, I crossed the room to Dad. 'Here's your grandmother, my mum,' he said. I hung back shyly but looked at her. She smiled, and I noticed she had scars on her cheeks too. *Golly! How many people were injured in this accident?*

'Dad,' I tapped his side and tiptoed, trying to reach his ear. He bent down, and I whispered, 'I need the toilet.'

His eyes grew wide. 'Ooh! Let's get your mum.' He led me to another room where Mum sat on a bed, feeding the baby. 'She needs the toilet,' Dad said, as Mum looked up.

'Oh dear,' Mum replied, 'get one of the relatives.'

I frowned at both of them. *What was the problem?* Dad disappeared, and two minutes later a lady's head popped round the door. She and Mum had a brief conversation in the foreign language, then she signalled that I should follow her. I glanced at Mum, who gave a nod of approval. As I swung round, Mum said, 'Stop, do you need toilet paper?' I nodded. She rummaged through her bag before stuffing a wad of tissue in my hands. I took the lady's hand and followed her out.

Just as we re-entered the living room, it went dark and everyone groaned, 'NEPA!' I grasped the hand holding mine tightly, uncomfortable being in the dark amid a bunch of strangers.

Within a few seconds, a candlelight flickered in the corner, and my relative moved towards it. There we found my grandmother. After a brief exchange between them, my grandmother reached behind the sofa and pulled out a potty. The relative took it and led me out of another door onto a balcony. She put the potty on the floor and signalled that I should use it.

I shrank back in surprise. *Me, use a potty in the open air with a stranger looking on?* But by now I was squeezing my legs together and couldn't hold it for much longer. I darted a quick look around. It was pitch black apart from the light from our candle, which was threatening to die any minute. I suppressed a sigh, pulled my knickers down and squatted over the potty. The deed done, I stood up and looked at my relative. With no qualms she bent down, picked up the potty and led me indoors.

We walked through the much quieter living room, many of the guests having left while I attended to my toileting needs. The candles remained the only light source. The bedroom, where I found my parents, glowed from an amber flame flickering behind a glass-shaded lamp. I yawned at the sight of the twins fast asleep atop the bed, envy blazing in my eyes. As if reading my thoughts, Mum signalled, and I scrambled up into a nook next to my siblings and closed my eyes. My life in Nigeria was about to begin, and life as I had known it was relegated to the annals of history.

*

I stirred out of my slumber the following morning with a pervading ache all over. I had dreamed about using a potty on a balcony. My eyes snapped open. *Wait! That wasn't a dream, it really happened.* I squirmed a little. *Why was I so uncomfortable?* Slowly, I looked around. I was lying on the floor in the living room. Well, not quite, but on a mat on the floor, surrounded by the twins, two other children, my grandmother and the lady who helped me use the potty, all fast asleep. I eased myself up and ran a palm over the criss-crossed imprint of the mat on my tingling cheek. I pressed my fingers against my face, gently easing out the lines.

Eyes wide open, I looked around our new abode. The sizable living room where I just woke led to the inter-connecting bedroom where I fell asleep the night before. I could see no bathroom or kitchen. *That explained the previous night's saga on the balcony.* I wondered how we would manage without both. The answer came later that morning once the household awoke. Mum rolled a towel and toiletries inside some newspaper and gave it to me to hold. Then she picked up a small wooden stool, a plastic basin and a bucket before leading me out of the door. 'Where is the bathroom, Mum?' I asked, as she opened another door which brought us on to an outdoor landing with an iron staircase. She led me down the stairs, into the enormous courtyard. She pointed to the bathrooms. 'Over there.' My eyes widened.

As we approached, I eyed the two tiny huts, made of corrugated iron, standing side by side at the back of the courtyard. Three sheets formed walls and the fourth a make-shift roof, leaving a gaping opening in front. Mum took the toiletries from me and set them down on the newspaper on the floor, adding a small plastic bowl from the bucket. With the larger basin and the bucket, which had a rope tied around its handle, she walked to a cylindrical concrete wall nearby. I watched, fascinated, as she lowered the bucket into the cylinder, swished the rope around like she was lassoing a horse, then pulled it up. I gasped as the bucket reappeared, heaving and splashing water. Seeing my surprise, she said, 'This is a well where all our water comes from.' I moved forward to inspect it, but she stopped me. 'No, don't come any closer, it's dangerous. You must never go near it.' She stopped and made sure she had eye contact. 'Do you understand?'

'Yes, Mum.'

Mum poured the water into the basin, picked it up, moved a few paces and placed it on the bathroom floor. 'Right, take off your clothes and fold them on the newspapers,' she said. I looked around the courtyard. It wasn't busy, but there were women and children in another outbuilding. The adults concentrated on their cooking, but the children gawked at us.

I pointed to the open bathroom. 'Um, Mum, there are people here and no door.'

'It doesn't matter, hurry, I have yet to wash your brother and sisters.'

Heat rushed to my cheeks as I lifted the hem of my nightgown and pulled it off. I cast a glance at the children. Yes, they were still gawking. Ignoring them, I stepped up to the flat concrete slab which made the bathroom's floor. Mum dipped the small plastic bowl into the water, scooped some and poured it over my shoulders. 'Arghh!' I hopped from one foot to the other. The water was frigid. My body stiffened and tiny goosebumps flooded the surface of my skin. Mum ignored the faint protest, picked up the soap and sponge and started to scrub my back. The second splash of water didn't feel so bad, and I relaxed into the wash.

While Mum washed me, I looked around. The bathroom's raised floor allowed water to run off into the bushes behind the huts. Where the door should have been, a thin pole hung, secured at both ends with a nail. The three-storey structure housing our dwelling appeared massive, the iron staircase running all the way to the top floor. Our rooms were on the first floor. Sandwiched between the outdoor kitchen and the bathrooms, but set further back, sat two additional huts with doors.

As Mum finished my ablutions, another woman exited the building with a bucket and bowl and headed to the well, just as Mum had. I towelled myself dry and picked up my nightgown, pulling it over my head just in time to see the woman move into the other bathroom. I watched avidly, curious to know if she would take a bath in full view of everyone. Instead, she pulled out a wide sheet and draped it over the pole hanging across the doorway. *So that's what it's for!*

*

Life in Nigeria couldn't have been more different from my former existence. Our new home in Mushin, the same size as our London one, felt crowded sheltering nine people. My paternal grandmother, whom everyone called Mama, had come to stay along with her niece, Sola, and another child, Wasiu. Both children were younger than me. Mum, Dad and the baby slept in the bedroom while the rest of us, including Mama, slept on mats on the living room floor. I didn't like it one bit. The floor was hard, there were no pillows, and every morning I woke up with the mat's herringbone weave etched temporarily into my cheeks. I missed Nan, and I missed my old, comfortable bed.

With only two bathrooms servicing the building, people going to work rose early to queue for them. Younger children didn't and instead bathed naked, out in the open next to the huts. I soon overcame my initial unwillingness to bathe publicly and in no time was bathing myself under Mama's watchful eye. It wasn't long before the foam sponge Mum brought from London disintegrated. Mum replaced it with the local sponge made of pounded raffia. The problem was, it made me itch, leaving huge welts where I'd scratched. 'Don't worry about it,' Mum said, as she coated my skin in Vaseline. 'You will soon get used to it.'

For toilets, the children used the potty day or night. Then the adults removed and emptied them. Curious about the adults, I asked Dad.

'Haha,' he said, 'the two huts between the kitchen and the bathrooms are pit latrines.'

'How are they different from toilets?' I asked.

'On the inside of each latrine there's a wooden platform with a hole in the middle. People squat over the hole to do their business, and a large metal bucket underneath the platform collects the waste.'

My eyes rounded. 'What happens when it fills up?'

'At midnight, men with faces masked with bandannas come and empty the waste into giant trucks and take it away.'

'What's a bandanna?'

Dad chuckled. 'It's a triangular scarf which they tie around their nose and mouth, so nobody recognises them.'

I chewed on that for a moment. *I suppose I wouldn't want anyone recognising me if I was carrying poo.*

'Can I use the latrine too?' The potty made me feel like a baby.

'No, not yet, I'm afraid. Perhaps when you are bigger.'

*

Besides the large, outdoor communal kitchen, the building had kitchenettes on each floor, in an outer lobby, just before the stairwell. Here, some tenants kept their own cooking stoves. Fed up with being cooped indoors all day, I stood at the entrance to the kitchenette and watched Mum prepare supper. Four kerosene stoves, all the same identical forest-green colour, sat on a waist-high wooden bench placed along the left side of the rectangular room.

'How do you know which one is yours,' I asked.

'Come over here.'

I shuffled closer and Mum pointed out her initials etched into the base of her stove. Mum struck a match and dropped it into the central aperture in the stove. Within seconds, a bright yellow flame sprung out, and I watched, transfixed, as the uneven flames licked the bottom of the pot Mum lowered over it. In places, the flame was sky-blue, in others, orange-black. The orange-black flames left a trail of soot all around the outside of the pot, but the blue ones didn't.

While Mum cut green vegetables and put them into the pot, I studied the rest of the kitchenette. A square opening with steel rods, in the wall opposite the door, served as a window and provided the only ventilation. It made the room resemble a prison cell. The blackened wall behind the bench created a contrast with the other dirty cream walls. Pondering the difference, I ran a finger along the black side. It left a trail behind. I looked at my finger, now coated in soot and realised it wasn't black paint at all.

As Mum continued cooking, the room darkened into a smoky haze. The piquant aroma of the tomato and pepper stew mingled with the acrid smell from the cooker's flames. I blinked rapidly, covered my nose and whined. 'Mum, my eyes and nose sting.'

'That's the fumes from the kerosene,' she said. 'Let me turn the wick down. See if that helps.' The fire tongues became smaller, and the odour dissipated somewhat. 'The food will take longer to cook with a lower flame, she said.' *No wonder I was almost always starving by the time family meals were ready.*

I helped Mum take the prepared meal inside, and as we settled down to eat, the lights went off. The collective groan 'NEPA!' resounded through the entire neighbourhood. NEPA was the acronym for the National Electricity Power Authority, although locals translated it to 'Never Expect Power Again'. I was getting used to the frequent blackouts. We rarely had electricity for long, and most evenings, candles or kerosene lamps provided light. We had only eaten a few morsels when the electricity returned. A resounding, welcoming cheer thundered through the building. 'What was that noise for?' I asked Mum.

'People are just so thankful the electricity came back so quickly.'

'Why do they keep taking it away?'

'I don't really know. They say there isn't enough to go round, so we all get a little now and then.'

None of it made sense. People in England had electricity all the time. Why was it so different here?

*

Life was settling into a rhythm, but all my toys, including my beautiful life-sized doll, stayed in the trunks. 'Why can't I play with my toys?' I asked for the nth time. Mum's response remained the same. 'You would have to share them with Wasiu and Sola. They would destroy them in minutes, and I can't afford to replace them.' I didn't understand Mum's logic. *What was the point of a toy you couldn't play with?*

My one remaining red hat and the matching pair of shoes that Mum bought before we left England also stayed in the trunk. And no, Mum hadn't replaced the hat that ended up in the loo. I understood why I couldn't use the hat. It was far too warm for the balmy Lagos weather, but my shoes! When Mum eventually brought them out at Christmas, they were way too small for my feet.

Although Nan had called me Ann, my parents called me Funmi and Mama called me Keji. 'Why does each person I know call me by a different name?' I asked Dad.

'Actually, Ann's not your name at all.'

That baffled me. 'It's not? How come Nan called me that?'

Dad paused, as if deciding whether to speak. 'Well, before Nan had you, she looked after another girl. Her name was Ann.'

I mulled over this piece of information. 'So, Nan called me Ann to remember the other girl?'

'Maybe, or maybe she just liked the name Ann.'

An awkward silence followed, then Dad brightened up. 'The name Mum and I gave you is special. It means God gave us you to cherish.'

A smile broke across my face. I liked the sound of that. 'What does Keji mean?'

'I am Mama's only child. Keji means second. You, my little one, are Mama's second child.'

'So, I have three names?'

Dad tittered. I peered at him. *What was so amusing?*

'You have thirteen names.'

'Thirteen!'

'Yes. When a couple has their first child, family elders get overexcited and they each give the baby a name. That's why you have so many.'

'Do you know what they all are?'

'Some, and your mum can tell you the rest.'

'Is *Oyinbo* one of them?'

Dad couldn't contain himself. He roared with laughter.

'What's so funny?'

He coughed and spluttered, merriment still dancing in his eyes. 'No, *Oyinbo* is not one of your names.'

'What does it mean? The day we arrived, everybody called me that. I remember.'

'That's true, but it's not your name. It means "white person".'

My brows furrowed. 'But I'm not white.'

'I know. Let me tell you some of your other names. Your other grandmother named you Tokunbo. That means you came from overseas. Your grandfather named you…'

As Dad reeled off unpronounceable names, my mind slipped back to what he said earlier. *Why did my relatives call me a white person when I was as Black as they were?*

CHAPTER FIVE

The Wonder of It All

Now that we were all living under the same roof, it was the perfect chance to get closer to my siblings. However, the twins were happy playing with each other and there was a limit to how I, at the grand old age of six, could interact with two-year-olds. The baby, well she was a baby. There wasn't much I could do with her since she was strapped to Mama's back like a parcel when Mum wasn't carrying her. I had a lot of free time to amuse myself and I spent it mostly alone, observing the comings and goings around me.

The first time I saw the baby on Mama's back, my eyes nearly exploded. All I saw was the baby plastered to Mama's back, her head sticking out, her body shrouded under a cloth which held her by the neck. Heart racing, I sprinted to Mum's bedroom.

'Mama is strangling the baby!'

Mum stopped what she was doing. 'What do you mean?'

'Come quickly!' I dashed back to the living room, beckoning her to follow. Mum entered the living room, took one look at Mama and collapsed in giggles. That brought me up short. I seemed to be forever amusing my parents.

'The baby is okay. That's how Africans carry their babies. There are no prams here.'

She went over to Mama and released the baby. 'See for yourself. She's okay.'

I peered closer, just to be sure. The baby squirmed and, without opening her eyes, went straight back to sleep. Mama adjusted the cloth previously tied around her chest to her waist. Only then did I realise that the outfit I saw on the ladies who welcomed us home, which I thought was a skirt, wasn't a skirt at all. It was a traditional, rectangular piece of cloth called a wrapper or *iro*, which Mama wrapped around her waist, before tucking the loose ends into the waist fold. *How on earth did she keep the cloth up without a zip or buttons or even tying the ends into a knot?*

I hadn't learned to speak the local language, Yoruba, but I recognised some words. Mama or Baba meant mother or father. Since I now knew Yoruba names had meaning, I asked Mum about my siblings' names.

'Their names reflect their birth,' she said. 'Taiwo means "the one who tried the world first" and Kehinde means "the one who came after". Idowu is the name given to the next child born after twins.' I marvelled at all the additional things I was learning and wondered if English names had meaning too.

*

The Nigerian civil war, which started in 1967, was still raging and my parents never allowed me out of the flat. I didn't go to school either. For the first few weeks after our arrival, Dad and I spent copious amounts of time reading the books I brought from England. However, it wasn't long before he got a job, limiting our contact. Mum had her hands full with my siblings. This restricted my lessons to the evenings when Dad returned from work.

I relished my sessions with Dad. They gave me the chance to get to know him better, and it was the only time in the day when an adult paid me much heed. At Nan's, I was the centre of everyone's attention. Here in Lagos, besides me, Mum had the twins, the baby, Sola and Wasiu to look out for. By now, I had read through the half-dozen books we brought from England more times than I cared to remember. Every so often, Dad would come home with a book he had picked up from a bookshop. After eating supper, he and I would settle down on the sofa, and he'd tuck me under his arm. I would read through each page and as I got to the end, he would turn the page over. Thus, our learning partnership began.

Dad, I found, was a jovial character. Friendly and charismatic, he had more close friends than I could count. We had a constant stream of visitors who often stayed late into the evening. It was a cultural norm that if you visited a friend, on departure you would bless your host's children with gifts of money. Dad's penchant for gathering people around him was very lucrative for my growing piggy bank, which Mum promised I could spend at Christmas.

Dad couldn't buy books as fast as I read them. So, we devoted some of my learning sessions to writing letters to Nan. First, Dad would help me draft the letter in a notepad. Then, when we were both happy with the draft, I would transcribe it in my best handwriting into a sky-blue, airmail letter, which Dad posted. Every month, I wrote lengthy letters, telling Nan about my new life, letting her know I was safe and missing her, but I did not get a single reply. Dad reckoned this was because of the poor postal infrastructure, further compromised by the ongoing war. But he encouraged me to keep writing, anyway.

Then, about ten months after our arrival, Dad came home from work one day with a gleam in his eyes. 'Can you guess what I got today?' he asked. I took one look at his face and just knew. I skipped and hopped, begging him for the letter he was hiding somewhere in his suit. Mum gave me an indulgent smile from the corner where she was feeding the baby. Dad took his jacket off, one arm at a time, exaggerating each movement and prolonging the melodrama. Then he pulled out not one, but two letters. Both had arrived the same day.

'I told you not to give up and to keep writing. See?' he said.

Dad and I settled down to read Nan's letters. I was overjoyed to hear that she was well and missing me too. From the text in the letter, it was clear she hadn't received all of my letters. I wondered where the missing letters had disappeared to. Receiving Nan's letters was most comforting. It reassured me that the distance hadn't broken our link.

*

One night, I woke to panic-stricken screams of '*Ole, Ole!*' I rubbed the sleep from my eyes and observed Mum and Mama in the living room, beside themselves, echoing the word over and over like a mantra. Mum flapped her arms about, and Mama scuttled from one corner of the room to the other. Frightened, and with no idea of what was going on, I pulled my knees into my chest and rocked on the spot while the adults went berserk. Dad came out of his bedroom and tried to calm Mum down. Then came loud knocks on the door. Mum had woken the neighbours.

Mum eventually calmed down and told everyone the story of a would-be burglar, who had climbed through the open window. His foot had landed smack between my parents' heads, waking Mum. She had screamed in fright, causing the thief to scramble back to the adjacent balcony and run. It took a while for the excitement to die down and for everyone to go back to bed, but it left a lasting impression on me. *Feet through the window and on your pillow. Imagine that!* I couldn't wait to write my next letter to Nan.

*

A year after arriving, the family moved from Mushin to Morocco Road in Shomolu. Dad rented three rooms in a property type called a 'face me, face you' – single or multi-storey structures with several rooms flanking both sides of a central corridor. Tenants simply rented as many rooms as they could afford. As with our previous dwelling, tenants had access to a communal kitchen and bathroom. Mum and Dad used one room as their parlour, a general living area. The other two were interconnecting bedrooms, one for Mum and Dad, one for Mama and us children.

I noticed that few of the adults were ever called by their given names, even by their friends. Most adults were called the mother or father of their firstborn if they were parents. Although a few people addressed Mum as Mama Funmi and Dad as Baba Funmi, most people preferred to call them Mama or Baba Ibeji, meaning mother or father of twins. It seemed having twins trumped having one child at a time. I learned it was disrespectful to call my elders by their first name. I had to address anyone who looked old enough to be my mum or dad as Mama, Baba, or the English equivalents of mummy and daddy. If they looked much younger than Mum and Dad, but were at least two years older than me, I had to preface their name with uncle, auntie, brother, or sister.

The only people I could call by their first names were children my age and younger. When meeting someone new, I had to figure out the proper form of address, to avoid causing offence. In addition, whenever an elder called me, I had to respond with 'Yes, ma,' if the caller was a woman, or 'Yes, sir,' if a man. With so much extra stuff to learn, I wondered if I would ever manage it all.

*

To distinguish between each elder, younger family members often named them after their professions or the location where they lived. My paternal grandmother spent a significant part of her adult life living near a new road construction. This earned her the nickname Mama New Road, which was eventually shortened to

Nurodu. Yorubas preferred their words to end on a vowel sound, hence the additional 'u'. While older family members called her Nurodu, all the children called her Mama.

Mama was of medium build and height. Her oblong face bore a strong resemblance to Dad's, so she must have been beautiful in her youth, even with the three faint, vertical welts carved into each cheek. Her mocha skin was smooth with barely a wrinkle in sight. Only her salt and pepper hair, usually styled into two traditional braids that started from the front of her head and ended at the nape, alluded to her age.

Mama had an unusual sense of dress. Most of the time, she was naked from the waist up, with just a wrapper and underskirt around her middle to cover her nudity. The first time I saw her that way, my eyes nearly popped out of their sockets, but nobody else batted an eyelid. 'Why isn't Mama wearing a top?' I asked Dad.

'That's how elderly women dress in the villages,' he said. When we had visitors, Mama untied her wrapper and hitched it higher, so it covered her bosoms. Otherwise, it stayed at her waist.

Mum and Dad both had jobs now. Every day, they went to work leaving Mama in charge. Mama had serious concerns about my usefulness. I couldn't speak Yoruba, couldn't wash clothes, fetch, or carry, and she had to do something about it. Although I didn't know it yet, Mama's great mission was to ensure that I grew into a biddable woman who would find a suitable husband, stay married and not bring disgrace on my family.

When two of Dad's teenage cousins came to visit during their school holidays, Mama assigned them the task of teaching me to speak Yoruba. They sat me down on a wooden stool before them. One held a stick in her hand and the other said, 'Repeat after me, bah, bey, beh, bee, bo, bau, bu.'

'Bah, bey, bah…' The stick descended and hit my leg.

'Ow!' I moaned.

'*Oya* [alright], back to the beginning,' my cousin said. 'Bah, bey, beh, bee, bo, bau, bu.'

I chanted repeatedly and every time I got it wrong, the other one hit me with the stick. It was my first introduction to caning, something that would become an integral part of my childhood and an excellent incentive to learn the Yoruba alphabet quickly.

At weekends, Dad had other cousins who came to visit. They would drink until they were merry, and their conversations descended into riotous banter. On one such occasion, Dad's cousins teased Mum, telling her she was lucky Dad had married her, a village bumpkin, given that he was from royalty in a sizeable town. Mum took the insolence in her stride. 'Really,' she said, 'no one else would have him. If I hadn't taken pity on him and married him, he would still be single.' One cousin noticed me in a corner of the room and called me over.

'Of which place are you prouder?' he asked. 'Your mum's tiny village, which only has ten houses, or your dad's town, which is very large?'

I paused and looked at Mum, then Dad. Both had amused smiles on their faces. I could tell this was just a game and my answer wasn't really going to offend either. Still, I felt I needed to defend Mum. 'Mum's village,' I said. Mum's grin widened and the other adults groaned. I turned to return to the corner where I was playing and caught Mama's malevolent glare. I knew instinctively that I had made the wrong choice. Once Dad's cousins left and the family retired to the bedrooms, Mama called me over. She planted both hands on her hips and brought her face within a whisker's hair of mine. In a stony voice she said, 'If you ever choose your Mum's village again, you will see…'

The word Mama had left hanging at the end of her sentence was 'trouble' and that usually meant the cane. I sensed Mama didn't like me or Mum much, and from that moment on, I feared her.

*

My first experience of acute trauma came one sunny afternoon. All the children and Dad's teenage cousins, who were still around, congregated in Mama's room. Mama kept a small kerosene stove in the room for cooking snacks and small meals. One cousin wanted to eat boiled eggs, so Mama added some to a kettle and placed it on the stove. Once the eggs boiled, Mama turned the stove off, removed them from the kettle and continued chatting while her fingers peeled their shells.

With the adults engrossed in conversation, no one paid much attention to my baby sister Idowu, now a crawling toddler. The kettle had caught her eye, and she made a beeline for it with speed and determination. She'd almost reached it when one of the teenagers swooped her off the ground. But she was much quicker on her knees than anyone gave her credit for, and one of her feet caught the kettle, anyway. Before anyone could stop it, the scalding water came pouring all over my thigh.

I screamed in agony and shot off the floor. Almost at once everybody panicked, except Mama, who swung into action, grabbing some raw eggs and breaking them over my legs. The moisture from the eggs was meant to cool my skin down, although I couldn't feel the effect. My screams brought Mum, Dad and half of the building's residents running. Still screaming, I tried to rub my thighs, hoping to ease the pain, but the adults held on to my hands, preventing me from doing so. Mum held me close, consoling me while Mama broke more eggs over my skin. Aeons after someone gave me some aspirin, the burning eased, and my screams quietened.

Within an hour, several blisters formed all over my thigh. Mum covered them with petroleum jelly to protect them. It took two weeks before they dried out, and the healing process both fascinated and repulsed me. As my skin healed, the blisters turned paper thin, before drying and peeling like a snake shedding its skin. The pink skin beneath my burns intrigued me. I remembered the conversation with Nan, about scrubbing my skin off so I could become white. Having had my first taste of genuine pain, I was absolutely certain I didn't want a skin peel. I wondered if the burned patches would stay pink. I tried to help by picking at the dead skin, at which point Mama smacked my hands away. Over time, the pink patches turned brown, my skin returned to normal and I was glad the incident left no permanent scars.

However, there was more distress to come. A few weeks after my accident, I woke in the middle of the night to the sound of Mum's blood-curdling screams. I dashed through the interconnecting door to my parents' bedroom to find Idowu's stiff body jerking in Mum's arms, while Dad hovered anxiously. 'Don't let her teeth or jaw lock, otherwise she might die,' Mama said. Mum tried to stick her fingers between the toddler's teeth but couldn't prise them apart. 'We need to wedge a metal spoon between her teeth.' Mama issued the instruction above Mum's sobs. Dad found a spoon and inserted it between the toddler's locked jaw. The next few minutes stretched as Mum kept chanting my sister's name over and over, like a mantra, willing her to open her eyes.

Soon I was crying along with my terrified siblings. Mama left the room and returned moments later with a bowl of water. She dipped her fingers in the bowl before sprinkling the water over Idowu's head. Eventually, Idowu's rigid profile relaxed. She opened her eyes and cried. Everyone heaved a sigh of relief. Only then did the adults register our presence in the room. Dad shooed us back to bed, but as I settled back on the mat, Mum's screams kept ringing in my head. I hoped I'd never hear that sound again. Unfortunately, this wish would not come true.

CHAPTER SIX

The Wedding

We moved once more, to an address just down the road. The landlord and his family, who occupied the flat above ours, would exert a noticeable influence on my future. Our new flat had an extra bedroom, and I wondered if it would be mine. But two male, teenage cousins, Brother Segun and Brother Femi, came to stay, and Dad gave them the room. The rest of us slept on the floor with Mama.

The civil war was drawing to a close. Because my parents kept me indoors most of the time, I had no sense of the impact of the war. However, that was about to change. Our new house had an expansive front yard, with a curved drive-through, large enough to accommodate several vehicles. In the middle of the yard, a dwarf-walled patio, heavily shaded by two almond trees, provided shelter and a place to sit and enjoy the evening breeze.

To earn her own income and with the landlord's permission, Mama set up a petty trading stall comprising a table and stool on the patio. From here she sold a variety of minor items, mainly cigarettes, matches, sweets, stationery and canned food. Our landlord ran a public transport business and owned a fleet of buses. In the evenings, his drivers congregated in front of the house and brought him their daily takings. These were Mama's clients.

One afternoon while I was manning the stall with Mama, pandemonium broke out. Panicked shouts of '*Soja, soja!*' followed by a stampede running towards us on Morocco Road grabbed Mama's attention. Mama's hand snaked around my wrist. Hearts pounding, we sprinted indoors. When things quietened a little, Mama headed outdoors to check her stall, and I sneaked quietly behind her. It turned out that one of the landlord's bus drivers had challenged a soldier over an unpaid bus fare. The soldier attacked the driver, beating him to a pulp. When the injured driver's comrades tried to carry him to the landlord's house for help, they were chased by more soldiers.

By the time Mama and I ventured back outside, the soldiers had left, but their handiwork was visible. The injured driver lay on the floor, his eyes swollen shut, head ballooned to twice its size. His semi-conscious form barely moved while the landlord's family debated how to get him to hospital. The bloodied shirt and the dark bruises all over his body highlighted the savagery of the attack. I had never seen the impact of such violence before. Although the memory dimmed in time, I would always view men in uniform with more than a little trepidation.

*

Not too long after the incident with the soldiers, the family began preparing for travel to visit Mum's parents in their village and attend a wedding. The journey seemed to take forever. I remember little of it, having slept most of the way. However, as we neared the village, the excited chatter of the adults in the bus woke me up. Remembering Dad's cousin's banter, I stretched my neck, trying to see if there were only ten houses in the village. My diligent counting soon put that question to rest, and I realised Dad's cousins had been joking.

The rural village posed a stark contrast to Lagos, with plenty of vegetation, including an abundance of banana trees, surrounding each house. As we drove past, I noticed a variety of dwellings. Thatched mud houses, ancient-looking red clay bricked bungalows with tin roofs, interspersed with a smattering of modern two-storey structures. The latter were built by the more affluent sons and daughters of villagers, who lived in the major cities. None of the roads were tarred, and the wheels of the bus kicked up a dust storm, as they bounced up and down potholes large enough to swallow a chicken. When the vehicle's axle scraped the road's surface, the shock waves travelled right through to my core, bouncing me about on my seat.

The bus stopped in front of one of the older buildings and, within seconds, out flew a small, wiry woman. This was my other grandmother. As soon as she saw me, she picked me up, swung me about, then enveloped me in the biggest hug I had received since leaving England. Her three sisters came out too, and in no time, a throng of welcoming villagers engulfed our entourage. In between more chants of *Oyinbo*, they called me *Tokunbo*. I guessed these were some of the relatives who had the privilege of naming me at birth.

My grandmother, Mama Iwaya, led us through a courtyard to an adjacent building, down a narrow corridor, to the room where my grandfather lived. As we entered his room, Baba rose from his lying position and sat upright on his wooden bed. Mum knelt and Dad prostrated himself before him. I followed my parents' cue, copying Mum. Baba drew us each into his arms one at a time, his lined face, a wreath of smiles. After the greetings, Baba sat back on his bed and pulled out his most coveted possession, his Yoruba Bible, from beneath his pillow. He read out a Bible passage, after which all the adults sang hymns and gave thanks for my parents' safe return from their sojourn.

Once the singing and prayers were over, the grown-ups offered the children food in another room, but I wanted to stay with Baba. Just as an adult was about to whisk me away, Baba stopped her. He stretched out his hand and invited me to sit beside him. Without hesitation, I clambered next to him, and his large palms took hold of mine. I stared at Baba's ancient face, the speckled grey on his chin and the criss-crossed lines on his face a testament to his longevity. Even the hairs on the back of his gnarled fingers were grey. He fascinated me, and he was the only grandfather I had.

I was still pondering Baba's age, when he asked in a deep, gravelly voice, 'So, how is the Queen?' I gasped and almost fell off the bed. Baba spoke perfect English. I assumed he was talking about the Queen of England. All the eyes in the room were trained on me, waiting for my answer, although I had never met her.

'I think she is fine.' Everyone laughed.

Obsidian eyes bored into mine. 'How are you liking Nigeria?'

The man was shrewd. I squirmed. He patted my head. 'Don't worry, it will grow on you.'

By now, the news had spread that Baba's daughter had returned home from overseas and more villagers trooped into the compound to congratulate him. This prompted Baba to move from his bedroom to his parlour to receive them. Baba settled into a rickety cane chair covered in an assortment of rugs. The other elders in the room planted themselves on wooden chairs and benches. The visiting men bowed or prostrated themselves, while the women knelt. This was the traditional way to greet one's elders, and it seemed Baba was older than almost everyone in the village.

A smell as ancient as Baba, a cross between citrus, incense and camphor, permeated the room. Other than a small centre table and heavy curtains, which came down to the window ledge, the parlour was devoid of furnishings. The pelmets from which the curtains hung doubled up as a shelf for pictures of each of Baba's fourteen children and their families. I scanned each one, recognising some faces. My eyes landed on a picture of my family. It must have been taken just before we left England. Dad stood with a hand on each of the twins' heads, as if to keep them from running off, with me beside the twins and Mum with the baby.

The conversations in the room shifted around the adults, and when they encouraged me to eat a second time, I did not hesitate. Through the window, the orange glow of the sky hanging low on the horizon, the darkening room and my renewed hunger pangs, told me it was way past dinner time.

The following morning, I noticed that my maternal grand-parents had the same scarring on their cheek as Mama Nurodu. This had to be more than an accident. 'Why do the elders have three cuts on each cheek?' I asked Dad at the first opportunity. He was the only one who never seemed exhausted by my incessant questioning.

'These are tribal marks that people used to identify others from the same tribe. In the olden days, they allowed villagers to recognise strangers who raided their villages to capture people and sell them to the white man.'

My eyes rounded at the concept of selling people. I was about to ask more questions, when I caught Dad's eye. Yoruba elders spoke with looks and I had become a quick study. The one on Dad's face said now was not the time. I shelved my questions for later.

*

The traditional wedding, a grand and loud affair, took place outside my grandfather's house under a vast tent. The guests arrived dressed in an assortment of colourful outfits. Women wearing tall head-pieces, twisted into three dimensional masterpieces, sat next to men in tunics with intricate designs embroidered along the neck and front. Mum's relatives had gathered and were seated around tables, with my grandparents, my siblings and I centred in front of them. Mum and Dad were absent, but Dad's family stood several yards away in front of a group of women – wives who had married into Mum's family.

Dad's family were led by another group of wives from their side. They sang and danced and tried to inch forward, but the other party blocked their path. A spokesperson for Mum's side jeered. 'Is this how you dance? You are not ready to come in.' Dad's side responded by passing a thick envelope full of cash to the spokesperson and dancing harder. After much banter, they were allowed near and took their seats opposite Mum's family. Before they sat, the women knelt to greet Mum's relatives, while the men bowed. The spokeswoman from Mum's group introduced herself as Madam Olayinka, welcomed Dad's family and asked what business brought them to my grandfather's home.

A spokeswoman for Dad's family came forward and introduced herself as Madam Iretiola. She began telling a fascinating tale: 'One day, our son, Ladi, walked to the river to fetch some water. On his way, he saw a flower with beauty so captivating, he wanted to pluck it. He knew he had to do so with care but didn't know how. He came back home, but his mind would not rest. Soon, we noticed he would neither eat nor sleep. All he could think and speak of was the beautiful flower. To help our son, we inquired from the elders. We found out the flower belonged to your family. That is why we are here to ask if you would part with your flower.'

Madam Iretiola handed over a silver tray containing a letter and an envelope full of money covered by a pretty lace handkerchief. Madam Olayinka thanked Dad's family for coming to enquire about the flower. 'What is the name of this flower you speak of,' she asked. The entire group on Dad's side chorused Mum's name. Up to this point, fascinated by the exchanges, I hadn't realised they were talking about my mother. I found out later that although my parents had married legally in England, Yoruba custom did not recognise their marriage without the traditional ceremony between their families.

Madam Olayinka nodded. 'The flower is indeed beautiful. Wait, let me pass your message to her family.' She knelt in front of my grandparents and whispered in their ears. After a few seconds, my grandparents nodded. Madam Olayinka smiled and returned to the other side. 'You are in luck,' she said. 'The family has agreed to part with their flower.' A loud cheer rose, followed by more singing and dancing.

A pause in the singing allowed Madam Olayinka to request the groom's presence. Minutes later, a group of young-looking men and women led Dad into the tent. Dad cut a dashing figure, dressed in a traditional outfit made of shimmering damask. The cap on his head had two flaps that mimicked a dog's ears. When he held out his arms and danced, his outfit resembled a parachute. On reaching the front, the dancing ladies disappeared, leaving Dad and his male friends standing. Dad and his friends paid homage to my grandparents, prostrating themselves with their faces mere inches from the ground.

Once the greetings had finished, Madam Olayinka led Dad to a beautiful throne-like chair in the centre of the tent. Then she came back to his friends and lined them up in a row. Like an army sergeant, she marched them to the back of the gathering to the guffaws of everyone around. I noticed the empty chair right next to Dad, and I wondered when Mum would join the ceremony.

Next, led by Madam Iretiola, Dad's family offered the gifts they had brought for Mum and her family. These included food and drinks for the family and clothing and jewellery for the bride. After the exchange, Madam Iretiola asked if Dad's family could see their flower. 'Ah, that would be difficult,' Madam Olayinka explained. 'We need money for an aeroplane to get her.' More laughter and banter followed. Dad's family handed over an envelope and Madam Olayinka disappeared into the courtyard. Moments later, out came a group of beautiful young women, all dressed in similar clothing. Right in the middle, under a shawl which covered her from head to toe, the bride danced. The women sang and danced as they moved forward, extolling the bride's beauty. When they got to the centre of the tent, they stopped.

Madam Olayinka came forward and addressed Dad's family. 'Here is your precious flower. Please treat her well.'

'No, no, no,' Madam Iretiola shook her head. 'Why are you treating us this way? Look,' she pointed to the feet of the woman under the shroud, 'our flower doesn't have crooked toes like that!' Laughter erupted.

'What do you mean?' Madam Olayinka countered. 'That is your flower; at least it's the one you paid for.'

'No, this is not our flower. Our flower is a beautiful rose.' Madam Iretiola removed the shawl and revealed a woman who was not Mum. Dad's family groaned while Mum's relatives chuckled. 'All right,' Madam Olayinka conceded, 'but we need money to get a boat to where the real flower is.' Out came a white envelope. Madam Olayinka took it and disappeared into the courtyard with the group of women.

After one more round of the fake bride escapade, more haggling and passing of envelopes, Madam Olayinka appeared finally with the actual bride. I knew it was Mum this time because she was wearing the shoes I had seen on her earlier. Everyone beamed and the dancing and singing increased. The ladies led Mum to Dad's family where she knelt, greeting them all before sitting next to Dad.

My siblings and I joined my parents, and the family elders on both sides prayed for us. The ceremony concluded with more feasting and dancing. When my parents moved to the dance floor, all their relatives joined them, one by one, pasting one-pound bank notes on their foreheads. My parents removed the money and passed it to two of my aunts, who tucked the banknotes into a bag for safekeeping. Captivated, I moved to the dance floor, started dancing and wondered what would happen. As I wriggled my hips like all the ladies, to my delight, my very amused relatives pasted banknotes on my forehead. I don't recall how much money I collected, but I went to bed ecstatic.

On the way back to Lagos, as the gentle rumbling of the bus's engine lulled me into a feeling of contentment, I marvelled over the weekend's events. Julie's wedding in England had been fun, but it paled compared to the vibrancy of Mum and Dad's. Like all my experiences so far, the differences were stark. I had noticed the wives in Mum's family counting bags of money when they were not dancing. Mum said the money given to them by relatives was their reward for doing all the cooking for the wedding. I didn't know it yet, but preparation for becoming a wife would be a central theme influencing how the grown-ups in my life would parent me.

CHAPTER SEVEN

Family Life

In Lagos, life settled into a rhythm. Mum and Dad became shadowy figures who left for work in the morning and came home in the evenings, except at weekends when we saw more of them. They employed a maid to help Mama with the baby and the twins. She was in her late teens and more than a few years older than me. I called her Auntie Kike.

Mama took charge when Mum and Dad went to work. Mama loved the cane, and she beat us for every offence, real or imagined. Long and fat at one end, thin and willowy at the other, Mama's canes came direct from the village. When Mama caned, you danced. The trick was to stand far away enough from Mama to catch the cane right in the middle of your palm. This was important with new canes, otherwise, the wispy end of the cane left little, tell-tale bruises all over your skin. But doing so was difficult, as Mama liked to lunge forward with every stroke. Failure to catch the cane was not an option. That only incensed Mama and resulted in double the number of strokes intended. I preferred a beating when the cane was worn down to the middle. This part of the cane was thicker and rounder and meant you got it in the palm of your hand; no near misses. My parents, I suspect, were ignorant of how much Mama caned us, and Mama kept it that way with threats of more beatings.

Saturday mornings saw a frenzy of house-cleaning, overseen by Mum. In the afternoons, she plaited the girls' hair in readiness for the following week. Mum didn't converse with us much. It was not the way of adults. She would, however, hold animated conversations with Mama and other adults as she plaited. We could listen, but never take part. Once, I interjected a conversation. The adults all stopped at once, and Mama directed her full glare at me. 'Who is talking to you? Adults are speaking, and you are speaking. Ehn?'

I stared back, surprised at the admonishment. 'Eh, I am talking to you and you are looking me in the eye?'

I dropped my gaze to the floor.

'She doesn't know better; she is still learning. Don't be cross, Mama,' Mum said, then she turned to me. 'Oya, kneel down and tell Mama you are sorry.' I did what I was told.

Saturday evenings provided some fun time with Dad. Once we had cleaned up after dinner, he would turn on his pride and joy, the radiogram. All of the children would pile into the parlour and dance to our hearts' content, or until Mama broke up the show and sent us to bed.

Dad, being kind and good-natured, rarely beat us. However, he had one golden rule: Thou shalt not fight. Breaking this rule invited his displeasure. Dad thought he was like the wise King Solomon in the Bible, and when any of the children fought, he held court. He would call a family meeting, which everyone, except Mama, had to attend. After listening to each child's version, Dad would question them carefully and he was skilled at telling when one was lying. He would point out each person's mistakes and ask them what they should have done instead. Once that was all sorted, Dad would pronounce the punishment due to each child.

Instead of doing it himself, Dad made the culprits cane each other and only interfered if they were being too kind. That happened once with Brother Segun and Brother Femi. Dad sprung out of his seat, took the cane from Brother Segun and said, 'Let me show you how to do it.' The next stroke had him yelping in pain and dancing on his toes. Dad gave the cane back to him and said, 'Now give Femi the rest.' After this incident, we all got the message, and although we'd squabble, full-blown fights were a rarity.

On Sundays, Mum would wake us up early so we could wash, eat and get ready for church. While Dad and Mama stayed home, Mum led the troops to church. Dad came along occasionally, but Mama only ever visited church thrice a year: Christmas Day, New Year's Eve and New Year's Day. 'Why don't Dad and Mama go to church more often?' I asked Mum once.

'Don't mind your dad's family,' she said, 'they are all heathens.'

*

Living in Nigeria was affecting my health. I had no immunity against the mosquito-borne malaria fever. Mosquitoes were pesky little things. Sometimes, the buzzing sound as they whizzed by alerted me to their presence. However, most of the time, the sharp pain as they pierced my skin was the only warning I got. No amount of arm-waving seemed to deter them from having a go. If I tried swatting them, they moved before the slap landed and I ended up slapping myself for nothing. While I was still nursing the site of the self-inflicted pain, the same mosquito would take a bite elsewhere. The family joked that the mosquitoes could smell my British blood from a mile away and much preferred that to their usual local delicacy.

Smoke coils, which kept the mosquitoes at bay, were our only defence. Mama would light one just before bedtime. However, the coils burned out halfway through the night, and then the mosquitoes would feast to their hearts' delight. The insects left little bite marks, which swelled and itched like mad. The inevitable scratching left me with scabs and the occasional scar. But often, I got malaria, at which point Mama's herbal medicinal knowledge kicked in. As a family, we rarely used conventional medicine beyond analgesics. Doctors and medicines cost money. Herbs were much cheaper, and Mama knew exactly which ones to concoct for different ailments.

With the leaves of the Neem tree, which the Yoruba called *Dongoyaro*, as her base medicine, Mama would mix a variety of leaves and barks from different plants. She would simmer these for hours in a large clay cauldron, before dishing out the resulting broth. My first sip had me gagging as the bitter flavour exploded all over my palate. From then on, I would only drink the broth with Mama standing over me, stick in hand as an incentive to swallow the dreadful stuff. It often took three days to recover from a malaria-induced fever. If I was still bedridden after the third day, then my parents would consider using conventional medicine as an alternative.

Besides malaria, I suffered a constant stream of infections, including boils, ringworm and scalp lesions. Mum treated the lesions with camphor and sulphur oil, which stung and left me reeking. The boils were more difficult to treat. Mama left them alone for days until they ripened and came to a head. Then she prepared a hot poultice out of *eba* and applied it. This softened the boils, so she could lance them. This was a painful business as I often had several boils at once.

Eventually, to improve our overall health, Mum introduced detox Saturdays. It all started when Wasiu got infected with roundworm. Although a more modern house, the property's toilets were also housed at the back of the building. One evening while using the potty, Wasiu found a white, stringing worm dangling between his legs. His screams of terror nearly woke the neighbourhood. After that, Mum was taking no chances, so she bought a tincture named *Maku* (Don't die!) – an antidote for all childhood ailments.

Mum lined us up from the youngest to the eldest. I watched in consternation as one by one, my siblings fell victim to Mum's panacea. 'Open,' she said, while holding a teaspoonful of the lime-green concoction near my lips. I grimaced in anticipation. 'Funmi!' I opened my mouth, and she deposited the payload. I doubled over, gagging as the slimy, foul-tasting stuff coated my tongue. 'Swallow it, don't you dare bring it up,' she growled. I swallowed, then tried to retch. 'St–p, St–p.' Mum had a way of spitting out her commands like a sergeant major, and it worked. But by detox, Mum meant purge. For the rest of the day, no one moved. We all lay on a mat, grasping our stomachs, praying for the heaving and cramping to stop. By evening, dog-tired, all I wanted to do was sleep. The thought of food didn't even cross my mind. We spent Sunday recovering from the ordeal. As if to say sorry, Mum cooked Jollof rice, a Nigerian delicacy served at parties, to tempt our palate back to normalcy.

*

Mum announced that my maternal grandmother, Mama Iwaya, would pay us a visit. The last time I saw her was at Mum and Dad's traditional wedding. Named after my grandfather's village, Mama Iwaya was a petite woman, but her slight frame hid a formidable character. You could never have guessed by looking at her that she bore my grandfather eleven children, eight of whom survived to adulthood. She had a commanding presence, but underneath all that strength was a compassionate soul. She was just as quick to draw you into a hug as she was at telling you off.

My cousins knew Mama Iwaya was a superb storyteller, so in the evening they entreated her to tell us some tales by moonlight. At first, she refused, pleading tiredness, but soon relented. Bright-eyed, we gathered at her feet. 'Would you like me to tell you the story of why the tortoise's back looks like its shell has been broken into several pieces?' she asked.

Several heads nodded 'Yes!'

Mama began: '*Aalo o!*'

We chorused the timeworn story starter. '*Aalo!*'

We listened with rapt attention as she told us how the tortoise stole, lied and cheated his way into trouble before getting caught. Traditional stories always had a moral, and at the end of this one, Mama paused before saying, 'And this story teaches us not to be?'

'Greedy!' we all chorused.

*

In January 1970, I started school two months after my seventh birthday. I had been home-schooled for over a year. My parents considered sending me to a private establishment owned by the landlord's daughter. However, they couldn't afford to do the same for all the children living with them. Instead, I went to the local mission school, which was free and where Mum's second cousin was a teacher.

'This is my school?' I asked with rounded eyes as Mum led me through the site. St John's School, Shomolu, sat on a sprawling site on a slight hill. The school comprised several rectangular single-storey buildings with the blocks housing Primaries 1 to 3 uphill and Primaries 4 to 6 downhill, near the administration building. Between the buildings, a vast, somewhat grassy, playing field served as the playground. The school had no walled boundaries and strangers walked through the premises on their way to wherever.

I took a series of tests in the headmaster's office, so he could place me in the right class. 'Your English is excellent,' said the headmaster. 'I wanted to place you in Primary 6, but your arithmetic is nowhere near as strong.' He put me in Primary 3, a year ahead of my peers. As he led me to my class, I studied the buildings. Each rudimentary structure was covered with a tin roof and secured with wooden doors and windows. On the outside, what looked like the faint remains of green and yellow paint peeked through the cement walls.

In class, the headmaster introduced me to my teacher, Mrs Akindele. Young and tall, she wore a flowery English dress, which reminded me very much of Nan. Her dress only came down to her knee, which was unusual. Most of the women I met so far in Nigeria liked their dresses and skirts at least calf-length.

Unlike the administration block, the interior walls of the classroom lay bare and unpainted. With one exception, all the children sat in pairs at wooden desks and chairs, arranged in three columns facing the teacher. Mrs Akindele led me to the only empty seat and introduced me to my partner. My first day at school was uneventful, and I seemed to fit in just fine. However, reality intruded soon after.

During lessons the next day, Mrs Akindele walked up and down the two aisles separating the columns of benches and inspected our work with a frown on her face. We had no reading books, but we each had an English grammar and comprehension textbook, an arithmetic textbook and an exercise book for each subject. Outside, the dark grey clouds mirrored the storm about to let loose inside our class. Since the buildings lacked electricity, the class looked gloomy, the clouds having blocked out the sun, our only source of light.

Mrs Akindele walked back to the front of the class and asked a question no one seemed able to answer. At that moment, the heavens opened, and the rain beat steadily against the roof. With exposed rafters, the patter created its own staccato, drowning out the teacher's voice. Suddenly, Mrs Akindele threw her hands in the air and ordered everyone to the front. At first, I wasn't sure what was happening, but the agitated faces of my classmates soon made it clear. My teacher pulled out her cane. 'Please, ma,' some pleaded, rubbing their palms together in supplication. She ignored them. One at a time, each child held out their palm and received three strikes before going back to their seat. Some sobbed quietly, others wailed like the wind.

I didn't know why we were being punished, but whatever it was, we were all being held responsible for it. Each time I came forward, with my palm open, my teacher turned to someone else, until I was the only one standing. She ordered me back to my seat. I couldn't understand why she let me off. She didn't touch me for the rest of the year either, although there were plenty more beatings for everyone else. It turned out Mrs Akindele was a friend of Mum's cousin. She didn't know I was a seasoned cane-receiver. She thought I was still 'fresh' from England and not tough enough to survive the experience.

CHAPTER EIGHT

School Life

I travelled to school every morning with other children in the neighbourhood. I had outgrown all the shoes I brought from England, and although Dad bought me a new pair, they were reserved for special occasions and church. So, I walked everywhere barefoot, something I loathed with a passion. I wasn't used to the feel of feet scorched by the hot beaten tracks or of the tiny stones pricking my soles. But I detested walking on wet grass more. For a reason I still can't fathom, it made my skin crawl, and my toes would curl inward, even when wearing shoes.

No one warned me of the hazards of walking barefoot. The first time it happened, on my way home from school, I stepped on a nail which embedded itself in my heel. I couldn't walk on it, so I pulled the one-inch nail out and limped home with blood trailing all the way. Mama swung into action. The treatment was different this time but accompanied by the usual hallmark, pain. Mama lit the stove, then stuck our biggest kitchen knife on the open flame.

While the knife heated up, Mama washed out the wound with soapy water. Then she made me sit while she inspected it. Next, she took the now glowing knife off the fire, and for a second, I thought I was about to lose my foot. Instead, Mama put a small dollop of palm oil on the knife and immediately dropped the sizzling oil onto the wound. I screamed in agony and tried to yank my foot out of her hands, but Mama held on. As the knife cooled, she slapped it repeatedly against the wound for good measure. This was the traditional way of cauterising a wound and preventing deadly infection. She wrapped a white bandage around my foot and the next day I walked to school, barefoot, bandage and all. By the time I got home, I couldn't tell which was dirtier, the bandage or my foot.

*

There were two major routes to school, each with an obstacle in its path. The most straightforward one, and the shortest, required you to travel down the length of Morocco Road. At one end, it was a busy municipal street with houses on one side and a local hospital taking up most of the other. However, further down, Morocco Road transformed into a lonely tree-lined boulevard with a vast estate on one side and no houses at all on the other. The spidery shadows cast by the leaves of the *Dongoyaro* trees edging the road created an eerie pall that frightened even the bravest of children.

The estate belonged to a rich, old Moroccan, named, as you can guess, Baba Morocco. Rumour had it he ate little children for dinner, and we all believed it. Every morning on the way to school, several children, myself among them, would congregate at the start of Baba Morocco's estate. Having psyched each other up, we would sprint down the road as fast as our little legs would carry us. We figured that the more of us there were sprinting together, the less likely it was that he could catch any of us. If anyone was unfortunate enough to be late, that person would have to run alone or try route number two.

Route two was boring until the last hundred metres. At the end of the street, a narrow, six-foot-deep gully, with a stream flowing through it, separated us from school. During the dry season, when there was little rain, you could cross the gully by walking across a wooden plank, placed there by experienced locals. The first time I tried it, I hadn't realised how hard it would be. Other children had walked across. Some even ran, although I think more out of fear than bravado. On my turn, I put my right foot on the plank and pushed down. It held steady, but there wasn't enough room for both my feet side by side, and I realised I'd have to balance one foot in front of the other. I moved cautiously, then I hesitated. I was still close to the gully's edge. *Could I do this? If not, now would be the time to turn back.* I looked up. The children across the gully cheered me on. However, those behind me told me to hurry. They needed to cross too, and I was holding up the queue.

I took a steadying breath and dug deep. I stepped further onto the plank, arms held out sideways to counterbalance. Two more steps and suddenly the plank wobbled. My heart jumped into my mouth and I froze. I had travelled a third of the plank; there was no going back. With my heartbeat roaring in my ears, I continued, quickening my stride. I now understood those who had skated across. The quicker one got this over with, the better. Before I knew it, my schoolmates were cheering and celebrating my success. I had hated every terrifying minute of it, yet the threat of ending up in Baba Morocco's soup pot seemed worse.

Sometimes the planks were missing when we arrived. Urged by those who had crossed, we would climb into the gully and up the other side. There were plenty of willing hands to pull us out. If it was too muddy to get a foothold in the gully's walls, the stronger boys lifted us high until someone on the other side grabbed and levered us out. The experience was more dangerous during the rainy season when the gully filled with rushing water, and the planks were wet and slippery. Some days when the planks were missing, the most audacious children tried to cross via a long jump. Some even drowned doing this. Perhaps it was the excitement that came with danger, or we truly believed the risk of facing Baba Morocco was higher. As an adult looking back, I can only wonder.

*

At school, new experiences came my way. Mama gave me three pence each day for lunch. At lunch time, we trooped into the playground where a row of approved vendors set up their stalls. Each one sold a different dish. To avoid getting to the front of the queue before finding out what was on offer, I learned to spy what other children bought before picking a line. If the bell rang before I got my lunch, I had to go hungry, because going back to class late invited the cane.

The vendors served food in large banana leaves. No plates, no washing-up. On my first day at school, attracted by the aroma, I queued in front of the vendor selling rice and stew. She picked up a pre-wrapped parcel of rice, opened it and added a dollop of stew, before handing it to me. Handing over my money, I waited, expecting her to give me a spoon, but she moved on to the next customer. I looked around and noted no one had cutlery. I stood there befuddled. *How did one eat rice and stew with no cutlery?*

I waited until the girl behind me had her parcel and watched. She scooped some rice from the leaves with her fingers and moulded it into a ball as if it were *eba*. Then she dipped it into the sauce piled on top before lobbing it into her mouth. I followed suit. Mmm… I closed my eyes. The explosion of heat, combined with the smoky flavour of fried peppers and tomatoes, was to die for.

Once I had finished eating, I realised I had another problem. We had no access to water for drinking or hand washing. I watched my peers and saw how inventive they were. They fell into two camps. Some rubbed their oily hands along their legs, or if they were boys, through their hair. Others grabbed a fistful of dust off the ground and rubbed their hands together until the dust absorbed the oil. Pointing at the dust grabbers, I asked a child nearby, 'How will they get the dirt off their hands?'

'With the insides of their shirts or skirts,' she said.

'Why didn't they just rub the oil on their legs like the other children?'

'The dirt will absorb the oil better. If you get oil stains on your exercise book, your teacher will cane you.'

'Ah!' I wasn't keen on the dirt option, so I ran my hands over my legs. The oil made a nice moisturiser, turning my ashy skin into glistening brown. I wondered if the chillies would sting, but they didn't. Then I went one step further and did a final clean with the inside of my skirt. Feeling proud of my ingenuity, I returned to class.

Halfway through the week, after lunch, deep in concentration trying to work out some sums, I leaned my forehead against my clenched fist. The next thing I knew, my eyes were on fire. Then I did the worst thing possible. I rubbed them with my knuckles. The burning intensified several notches. I bolted out of my seat, eyes shut and whimpered.

'What's wrong with you?' my teacher bellowed.

'I've got pepper in my eye!'

The class burst into laughter. 'Wipe it with your skirt,' someone offered. I dared not, having cleaned my hands with my skirt.

'Here is a hankie,' said Mrs Akindele. 'Next time, keep your hands away from your eyes.'

I needed no telling. The hankie helped a little, but mostly I had to wait until the pain subsided by itself.

*

Another difficult change was using the school toilets. As much as possible, I avoided answering the call of nature at school. The latrines were the only option and for the first time, I got to see their inner workings. The corrugated iron shacks had wooden doors you could barely latch. Inside was a hole in the ground where you did your business. For the clean-up you had newspaper. Someone taught me how to make it soft by scrunching and kneading the surface. With no soap and water at school for hygiene, you used your left hand for sanitation and not much else. Therefore, handing someone something using your left hand was considered an abomination. As for left-handed people, there was no place for them in society. The urge was often beaten out of them before they reached school age.

*

If getting to school was hard, the return home each day was no less arduous because Mama would be waiting in her stall. Mama was a perfectionist and didn't believe in errors or mistakes. First, she would inspect the contents of my school box to ensure that my exercise books and pencil had returned. Lost items invoked her displeasure. Mama also inspected the insides of my exercise books. Or to be precise, since she couldn't read, she got the landlord's servants, who loitered in front of the house once their chores were over, to do so for her. Each sum or comprehension sentence marked wrong attracted a stroke of the cane. Mama was diligent in her caning. She believed it was an excellent motivator not only for good behaviour but for learning. Her favourite saying was 'The cane is a child's God.'

On the occasions when Mama couldn't be bothered to reach for her cane, she had several other forms of torture up her sleeve. The nicest one was to make you stand or kneel in a corner with both arms raised above your head until they grew tired and weary.

If you were ever tempted to lower them before Mama said so, she would reach for her cane. To be fair, Mama didn't have much use for this method. She considered it too easy and reserved it for the younger children.

A more popular punishment, and Dad's favourite on the few occasions he disciplined us, was the 'sewing machine', aptly named as it simulated a sewing machine needle's movement. You held your ears with your fingers and did rapid squats up and down. If Mama did not like your speed, she reached for the cane. Still, we all preferred the sewing machine. If you kept a close eye on Mama, whenever she was distracted, you could slow your squats right down and speed up again as soon as she looked your way.

We nicknamed Mama's go-to method for me and the older children 'stoop down'. This involved bending forward at the waist, head hanging down and balancing on your left foot and right forefinger. You lifted your right foot behind you while your left arm dangled uselessly by your side. If Mama felt kind, she might ignore you surreptitiously switching hands and legs. Most of the time, she left you there until your snot mingled with the tears running down your face.

But that wasn't the worst of Mama's disciplinary tactics. At the very top of the scale was the *Ijoko Idera*, a misnomer which translated into English meant 'sitting comfortably'. Mama would invite you to take a seat on the floor in front of her. Then you had to raise both feet and both arms, while balancing on your derriere. Again, on sentry duty, Mama would whack your legs if your feet touched the ground, or your arms, if they drooped. Given the nature of this form of punishment, I guess the elders had a sense of humour. Mama was never afraid to tell us off in front of my parents. But she reserved the more extreme forms of punishment for when they were at work or, since we shared a bedroom with her, the middle of the night.

*

As I had more people to interact with, my knowledge of Yoruba improved rapidly. I even knew how to insult people with minimal effort. The easiest way required you to point your right palm, with all five fingers spread wide open, towards someone's face. That meant 'Your mum', short for 'I curse your mum and all her ancestors'. It was also the quickest way to get into a fight, as mums were sacred and everyone was honour-bound to defend them. For maximum damage, you could add your left hand, which doubled the curse to include the other person's father and all his progenitors.

Another insult was 'kissing' your teeth. This involved bringing your teeth together, with your tongue pressed tightly against them on the inside. Then, with lips forming an 'O', you drew air in through the closed teeth to make a hissing sound. This action meant different things, depending on the context, none of them good, and was also guaranteed to provoke a response. If you planned to kiss your teeth at someone bigger, you needed to keep more than an arm's length away.

If you finished eating before the bell went, you could indulge in some games with other children. The boys had one game only, football. Girls didn't play football. Instead, we had hopscotch, locally known as *suwe*, which was easy to draw in the dirt and there was no shortage of stones to play with. At the end of the game, you had to wipe out all the etchings, or your mum would die! So said the other children. Another popular game, ten-ten, needed at least two people, but often we played it in two teams. You sang and stomped to a particular rhythm. On the last note of the song, you ended the game by pointing one of your feet towards your opponent. To win your turn, your opponent had to point the opposite foot towards you. If you and your opponent's feet matched, you lost the round.

One day, as I stood in the playground watching the others at play, a girl walked up to me. I had seen her before. She was in the class next to mine. We'd played ten-ten once, on opposite teams, and she was terrible at it. Her chubby frame made for jerky movements when she stomped, so her opponents always guessed which foot she would land on. Flashing pearly-white teeth, she said hello.

'Hi,' I returned.

She scrunched her tawny face. 'You sound funny. Are you the girl from London?'

I hadn't got rid of my English accent yet, although I was trying my hardest. Her accent was thick, much stronger than the typical Lagosian one. I nodded and resisted the urge to point out she didn't sound much better.

'What's your name?'

'Funmi.'

'Mine is Bosun. Do you want to be friends?'

I took in the person offering to be my friend. Her accent said she was not from around here and possibly an outsider, like me. It would be good having someone to share with. With an amicable smile, I proffered a hand. For a moment, she peered at it quizzically, then comprehension dawned. She grasped it and asked, 'What game do you like best, ten-ten or *suwe*?'

CHAPTER NINE

My Re-Education

It was almost two years since we left England. Nan's letters arrived sporadically, and in each, she complained that many of them were returned to her undelivered. I now understood why I had received no replies to some of my initial letters. Nan tucked in a few pictures she had of me with the letters, but one picture had me and Dad puzzled. Nan often scribbled notes such as 'You and Tom in the park' on the back of each picture. But this picture was different. The little Black girl wasn't me and on the back Nan had scribbled 'Nina'. Who was she? A child Nan fostered before or after me? We never did find out and I hoped whoever she was, she hadn't displaced me in Nan's affections.

Dad was promoted to the post of shipping manager at AC Christlieb, the Trebor sweet-making factory where he worked. I listened with envy as he and Mum discussed sending the twins to a private nursery school, with brand-new shoes and all. Dad could afford to with his increased earnings. However, he wasn't rich enough to send all the children in his care to private school. By keeping at least one of his own children in the mission school, no one could accuse him of treating his kids more favourably than the others. Dad could also afford more help at home, so another teenager, Auntie Abebi, came to live with us.

At the end of the previous academic year, the headmaster had stood in assembly and asked us to deliver a message to our parents. 'The war is finally over,' he said, and the assembly erupted into a loud cheer. The headmaster held up his hand. 'People are returning to the capital from all over the country. Those whose education was interrupted by the war will join us in January. We do not have enough space for everyone who wants to learn.' Silence descended as we all wondered what that meant. The headmaster continued. 'From January, we will shorten the school day and hold two sessions daily. Half of you will attend school in the morning and the other half in the afternoon.' An audible groan fluttered through the gathering as the import of the message registered.

So, here I was in Primary 4, attending school in the afternoon, and I hated it. The previous year, I got back from school a few hours before my parents did, and I wasn't alone with Mama for too long. Now, the afternoon sessions left me at Mama's mercy all morning, and she wasted no time capitalising on the opportunity this presented. Mama considered schooling as merely a means to employment. It didn't prepare you to be a good wife, so she set about my re-education with fervour. 'First,' she said, 'we Yorubas are the children of the land where you start the day by saying, "Good morning, did you sleep well?" As soon as you wake, you must kneel and greet your elders properly.' I gulped and nodded.

After greeting everyone, my next task was to take the twins to school, nearby. Lesson two was learning how to sweep the yard using a traditional broom. Mama picked up a broom and handed me one. 'Watch,' she said as she bent over and dragged the long strands over the bare floor. I did the same. 'No, not like that, use the sides of the broom, not the tips.' I leaned forward and applied a downward pressure, so the side of the broom touched the ground. 'Better,' she said. 'Now finish the yard.'

Traditional brooms were made of the central vein of palm leaves, plentiful in the tropical forests surrounding the cities. The leaves were de-veined and the central spine dried in the sun before hundreds of them were bunched together to make individual brooms. The base of each bunch was bound with colourful fabric or raffia to form an adult-sized handle, and I struggled to wrap my hand around its girth. This made the task uncomfortable and slow-going, and Mama didn't like slow. Every few minutes she barked, 'Have you finished?'

To my surprise, I enjoyed brushing the broom across the bare earth because its strands created a beautiful criss-cross pattern in the dust. I stood back and admired my handiwork until Mama's voice snapped me out of my musings. Luckily, over time, as each strand snapped from use, the broom became thinner and more flexible, making it easier to use. After each sweep, Mama would inspect the yard to make sure I had not missed any spots.

*

I already knew how to do the dishes, so next, Mama introduced me to doing the laundry, including her huge, velvet sleep covers, by hand, with soda balls. The laundry tired me out before the school day had even begun, and the soda balls irritated my palms, causing them to blister and peel.

On days when there was no laundry, I chopped *ewedu*, a dark-green vegetable and substitute for okra, my favourite vegetable. The task was more boring than onerous because Mama wanted it chopped to such a fine consistency that the slimy, forest-green blob glistened under the knife. Auntie Abebi and Auntie Kike did the bigger chores such as fetching water from a well, cooking for the family and doing Mum and Dad's laundry. Convinced Mama was deliberately making my life a misery, I resented the chores. A permanent pout took up residence on my face and when

I wasn't working, you could guarantee I was sulking somewhere in a corner. If Mama noticed my truculence, for now she ignored it.

Mostly, I kept my thoughts to myself, but sometimes the bitterness overtook my mouth and I blurted out my feelings, often to more censure. On one such evening, Mama, Auntie Kike and Auntie Abebi were chatting in the backyard. Next to them, I was busy washing an endless stream of dishes. Mum and Dad were entertaining, so just as it seemed the chore was finished, a fresh pile of dirty dishes arrived. Engrossed in conversation, Mama and the two maids appeared oblivious. Eventually, I could contain my frustration no more.

'Why am I the only one doing all this work? That's it, I'm not doing anymore dishes today.'

I stood up, folded my arms and struck a defiant pose. Mama and the girls stared at me with raised eyebrows. Mama spoke first. 'What are you complaining about now? The dishes? That will be the least of your chores when you marry. All women have to do dishes.'

'No, they don't. The Head of State's spouse doesn't. Anyway, by the time I'm grown up, a machine will do mine.'

The three heads snapped to attention. There was a moment of stunned silence, followed by raucous laughter.

'A machine that does dishes?' Mama sneered. 'Ehn, so you fancy yourself as *Iyawo* Gowon [Gowon's wife]?'

'Hahaha, *Iyawo* Gowon!' The girls chorused, before bursting into hysterics.

I had just earned myself a nickname. From then on, all three would call me Iyawo Gowon, always with a smirk on their faces. It infuriated me that they refused to use my name and I couldn't stop them. From then on, the housemaids and I no longer got along. While they never hit me, I would often catch them looking at me, followed by surreptitious whispers and giggles. Sometimes they used a different dialect of Yoruba so I wouldn't understand what they were saying. But their tone and the looks they gave me left me in no doubt that they were being rude.

*

At school, life wasn't much better, with chain-smoking, cane-happy Mr Adesanwo as my teacher. As soon as we got to class, Mr Adesanwo wrote some arithmetic or grammar and comprehension exercises on the board. Then, cigarette in hand, he disappeared to the class next door where he spent most of his time chatting to his colleague. In his absence, he nominated someone as monitor to control the class.

The monitor exercised his authority by creating a list of all those who talked, regardless of their loudness, and that was often people with whom he wasn't friends. As the noise levels in the class rose, a voice would ring out, 'Stop making noise!' The decibel would lower, then rise again. Once the monitor had a list he thought long enough, he strolled next door and invited Mr Adesanwo to come and sort out the class.

Mr Adesanwo's appearance at the door guaranteed dead silence. As dread filled the class, the monitor called out the names on his list. If you heard your name, you stood behind your desk and prepared yourself for what was to come. There were no appeals. Your name on the list meant you were guilty. Once the monitor finished, Mr Adesanwo proceeded with his caning procedure. He wasn't a friend of my Mum's cousin and didn't know or care about where I was born. So, he had no qualms about caning me along with the rest of the class. Not that it mattered. I was getting quite a thrashing from Mama, and half the time I didn't even know what for.

'*Oya*, who wants to go first?' Mr Adesanwo would ask. The first time this scene played out in front of my eyes, five or six pupils spurted forward and received two strokes of the cane each. Afterwards, they went back to their seats to watch the unfolding drama. Having caned the first lot, Mr Adesanwo looked around. 'Who's next?' he asked. Those remaining crouched backwards away from the teacher. 'No one? Right, it's four strokes now.' Another group surged forward, and I quickly joined them. We got our punishment amid loud wailings coming from those already beaten and those still expecting the pleasure.

Once the initial pain wore off, those of us sitting began to enjoy the spectacle and jeer at those yet to be caned. The cycle repeated itself twice more, each time with an increase to the number of strokes given. The remaining stragglers, girls, were trying to disappear into the wall at the back of the room. At Mr Adesanwo's command, the largest of the boys chased them around and carried them piggy-back style to the front of the class. There, Mr Adesanwo administered the punishment to their backs and bottoms to the continued jeers and laughter of the rest of the class.

The sad thing was, some of those girls in their mid or late teens, had had their education disrupted by the war. Some were even rumoured to be young mothers, but Mr Adesanwo didn't care. He caned them all. Once the caning was over, he wrote some more tasks on the board, before disappearing next door. Whenever a beating was due, I joined the first lot. Two strokes and I was done. If he ever taught us anything meaningful, I don't remember any of it.

*

By now, I hated most things about my life. My days were long, filled with labour, censure and threat, but my nights were even longer, filled with longing for my previous existence. I dreamt of the day I would return to England and often pictured myself running into Nan's arms, the terror of Mama and Mr Adesanwo a long-forgotten nightmare. The only shred of light piercing my misery was that Bosun was now in my class. She opened up my world to fun and friendship, two things I had missed since arriving.

Bosun's family had recently arrived in the city from the northernmost parts of Yoruba land, which explained her accent. Among the Yoruba, people with lighter skin tones were a minority and considered more beautiful. Bosun's colouring granted her favour with her peers and adults. In school, this meant an easier acceptance by the others, despite the accent, which would have left her open to ridicule.

Bosun introduced me to pleasures which until now were unbeknown to me. The first was the African star apple, locally called *agbalumo*. One afternoon, Bosun returned from the food vendors and offered me the fruit.

'What is it?' I asked.

'It's a fruit.'

I studied the dark-orange object. I had never seen fruit like it before. 'What does it taste like?'

'I don't know. Sweet?'

Intrigued, I held out my hand, and she plonked the oval fruit into it. I ran my fingers over its shiny, leathery skin. It was somewhat hard, not the sort of thing you felt compelled to bite into. 'So, what do I do with it?'

A mischievous grin lit Bosun's face. 'First, you suck it. Here, like this.' She plucked the fruit out of my hand and, using her forefinger, scooped out the stump left by the stalk, exposing its fleshy innards. 'Squeeze it between your palms to release the juice, then suck.'

I complied and my eyes widened when the milky juice hit my tongue. Extremely sticky, it was an intriguing combination of intense tang, mixed with a sweetness that lingered long after I had swallowed. I wanted more and slurped greedily until something stony entered my mouth. At once, I spat it out. Bosun chuckled. 'You are just getting started. That's the seed. You suck the flesh off each one until you are left with a smooth pebble. Then you can spit it out.'

It seemed that consuming a star apple was a protracted affair. One by one, I sucked each seed dry. With all the seeds gone, I slurped the juice at the bottom of the sack. The previously round fruit was now a misshapen flat shell, and I was just about to chuck it when she shouted, 'Stop!' Puzzled, I waved the empty shell at her. 'Open it,' she said. I peeled the skin apart and revealed the fibrous inner flesh. 'Gnaw that off with your teeth and chew. Don't swallow, just chew.' Once more, I obeyed my bossy friend, and a wonder occurred. The fibrous tissue in my mouth transformed itself into chewing gum. 'How much is this thing?' I asked.

'That's the best bit. *Apinny*.'

That was the Yoruba slang for half a penny. I beamed. Since leaving England, I hadn't been able to indulge my sweet tooth because Nigerian meals did not include desserts. There were other foods that could satisfy my cravings. In the right season, there were oranges, bananas, tangerines, mangoes and guavas, but none of these were cheap and my parents didn't buy them. The closest thing to a fruit crossing my lips since my arrival was the outer flesh of the fruit of the almond tree which grew in the front yard. The greenish-yellow pods often fell off the tree when ripe. If you could tolerate the acidity and sourness, and the birds hadn't pecked at them first, they were yours for the picking. I had derived a lot of satisfaction from consuming a star apple. Now I could save some of my lunch money and treat myself whenever I liked.

*

One day in school, as lessons began, I realised I couldn't find my pencil. I rummaged around the bottom of my satchel. No, it wasn't there. Fortunately, Bosun still had the butt end of her old pencil. It had just enough left for me to grip it between my thumb and forefinger and carry out the day's written tasks. I knew, once Mama went through my things, I would get into trouble for losing the pencil. At lunch time, I headed first to the vendor in the school grounds who peddled basic school supplies. I inspected the array of goods laid out on the table and my gaze fell on a pencil with silver and pink swirls delicately etched all along the barrel. I stroked the pencil longingly. 'How much is this one?'

'For that one, two pence,' the vendor replied.

If I skipped lunch, I had enough money for the pencil and some sweets. Moments later, pencil in hand, I savoured the sharp tang of the sherbet exploding all over my tongue. As I sucked, waiting for the bell to signal lunch was over, I marvelled at my own ingenuity. It was the first time I'd bought something for myself, and I had solved the problem of Mama too.

A few days later, Mama found the pencil in my school bag. I held my breath as she picked it up, my eyes following every movement as she twirled it around her fingers. Her gaze switched to mine, and her eyes bore into my soul. I recognised that look and my stomach churned. 'Whose is this?' Mama's tone held a menacing intent. Immediately, I remembered one of her other favourite sayings: 'If you lie, you will steal, if you steal, you will prostitute yourself.' I didn't know what prostitute meant, but I knew all about stealing and lying. I swallowed and opened my mouth to tell her it was mine, when another thought flitted through my mind. How would I explain that? I opted for a half-truth.

'It's mine Mama, I found it in the street on my way to school.'

Mama kept her steely eyes on me. 'Did it grow on the ground?' Her voice was deadly quiet.

'No, Mama,' I mumbled, starring at an invisible speck on the floor.

'So, you took something that belonged to someone else?'

Silence.

'Where is the one I gave you?'

'I lost it, Mama.'

'Ah. You lost your own, then stole somebody else's?'

Mama's question hung in the air. Two offences… I had already lost the battle. I lifted my head and our gazes met and held, hers questioning, mine somewhat defiant.

'You are looking me in the eye, ehn?' Her voice hitched. 'You think you are somebody, ehn? Okay, I will teach you to look me in the eye.' Mama reached for the cane. My eyes darted around the compound. *Perhaps there were other adults around who might plead my cause?* There weren't any, just the servants, and they enjoyed watching my humiliation. I knew the routine, and I proffered my hand. At the first stroke, I squeezed my eyes shut, bit my lip and swallowed my involuntary yelp. I would not give her or the servants the satisfaction. After the third stroke, Mama stopped. I sighed, eyes closed, rubbing my smarting palms together. It could have been far worse.

'Tomorrow you will return the pencil to the exact spot where you found it.'

My eyes flew open. Nooo! Not that, my eyes pleaded, but she looked resolute.

The following day, I gave the pencil to Bosun. At the shock on her face, I recounted the previous day's events. She promised to take good care of it. She even offered to let me use it during the day, then she could take it home after school. I declined. Mama had already given me another pencil from the stack she sold. I didn't want to risk the possibility of accidentally taking it home and incurring Mama's wrath for disobedience. Still, I had learned an important lesson. It seemed, whatever I did, Mama would always find a reason to cane me. It was far better to tell the truth, even if it resulted in a beating, than to lie and be caught in a web of my own making.

CHAPTER TEN

Life in the Slower Lane

Holidays brought blessed relief for several reasons. No school, no Baba Morocco, no gully, no Mr Adesanwo and better still, no Mama. Why? She often went back to her hometown, Ijebu-ode, to visit her brothers, which added no caning to the list. With Christmas approaching, I salivated at the thought of a blissful break, until Dad announced a real downer. We would spend the break in Ijebu-ode. The excitement of visiting Dad's hometown for the first time soon overshadowed my disappointment at not being able to get rid of Mama.

Mama came from Ijebu land, a Yoruba tribe northeast of Lagos comprising several major towns and numerous hamlets and villages. We travelled to Ijebu-ode, the capital of Ijebu land and often called Ijebu, via public transport. Weary from a four-hour trip, we stumbled out of the bus at the town's main bus depot, before chartering a run of taxis to our ultimate destination. A stream of relatives trooped out in welcome as soon as the taxi stopped in front of my great-uncle's house. Some I knew, some I'd never met. They enveloped us in embraces, before ushering us to dinner.

The following morning, after ablutions, all the women and children congregated around a large, open, wood fire in the backyard where breakfast and all subsequent meals were prepared. My great-uncle's family lived in a bungalow, within a sizeable compound, like most of the homes I'd seen as we journeyed the day before. I studied the courtyard with curious eyes. It was nothing more than a dusty clearing, with a boundary of wild bushes separating the holding from the neighbours. The furthest corners of the yard held the bathroom and pit latrine.

I stood back and watched the interactions between the surrounding strangers. The grown-ups chatted with an easy camaraderie as they sweated over the smoky wood fire. The compound teemed with cousins of all ages, clothed and unclothed, the latter mainly toddlers. With two wives and nine children, our host, Baba JCB ruled over a large household. He was Mama's youngest brother and drove JCB diggers on construction sites for a living. Still, all the children intermingled with each other like one happy family. I couldn't tell who was who, as the children called both wives 'mummy'.

Once breakfast was ready, the mothers ladled two bowls with *akamu*, a pap made of fermented corn, and placed them on two trays with a side dish of bean pudding. Two older youngsters took the trays to Dad and his uncle indoors. Then they served us children, and we all ate together in the backyard. Afterwards we shared the clean-up. There was a role for everyone. The youngest fetched the dirty plates from the adults, some collected the food scrapings for the neighbourhood dogs, some washed the dishes, some dried them, and some swept the yard. Communal living, it seemed, was all about sharing.

*

Ijebu provided a welcome contrast to life in Lagos. The family elders indulged us city dwellers, and the Ijebu air seemed to have a calming effect on everyone. Mum smiled more, and Dad drank more. Even Mama appeared more mellow. The things she would normally admonish me for went unnoticed. I broke a plate, and all she did was tut.

Many of the cousins were of a similar age to me and enjoyed more freedom than I was used to. Once we finished the morning chores, the adults allowed us to play outside, in the dusty streets. My cousins chose bike riding as the morning's entertainment. The last time I had ridden something that didn't have four wheels, it had been my trusty old tricycle in Pop's back garden. And I had depended heavily on that third wheel.

My cousins didn't own bikes. They just hired them for a penny per hour, from an ironmonger who traded second-hand bicycles up the street. There wasn't a single three-wheeler among the row of dilapidated bicycles outside the shop. Not even a two-wheeler with stabilisers. I swallowed and darted a nervous glance at my cousin, Jaiye. 'I don't know how to ride a bicycle,' I confessed.

'Don't worry, it's easy,' he said.

We walked the length of the rack, looking for something that would fit my height. 'This one is fine.' He pulled a green bike out of the row before handing it to me. He and his two older sisters, Bolanle and Tope, picked theirs. Jaiye leaned his bicycle against the wall and entered the shop to pay the ironmonger, emerging moments later.

Bolanle and Tope hopped on their bikes. 'We ride all the way down the road from here,' Jaiye said, as he held my bike so I could get on. Once I was on, he gave my bike a quick shove and let go. I turned the handlebar a sharp right, lost my balance and fell off. The girls, who were watching me take off, burst into giggles. Out of the corner of my eye, I spied Jaiye, doubled over in mirth, hysterically slapping his hands against his knees. I don't think he'd believed me when I said I couldn't ride.

I picked myself up and dusted down my skirt. 'Don't worry, try again,' Tope said, through the smirk on her lips. The second time around, I stayed on a little longer before the wheels crashed into a small boulder and I hit the ground. However, those extra seconds were all the incentive I needed. I hoped the third time, I'd be lucky.

With a death grip on the handlebars, I pushed the pedals and sailed forward. It was a very quiet road and, so far, we'd only seen the occasional taxi dropping off people from the town centre. A rush of joy filled my heart as I sailed down the dusty road, weaving left and right, trying hard to keep my balance. It was difficult, but I was getting the hang of it. I remembered how it had felt in England, racing round the old back garden, Dee in hot pursuit. I was still musing on my past and all the things that had happened since, when, to my dismay, a car appeared at the other end, heading in my direction.

My bravado disappeared in an instant. I wanted to stop until the vehicle had passed safely but didn't know how. I stopped pedalling, hoping that would slow my momentum. But my bicycle, having gained a mind of its own, sped up, uncaring, downhill. My muscles tightened, anticipating the impending disaster. The car heading in my direction showed no signs of slowing down. A few yards ahead, I glimpsed a thicket on the side of the road. It was that or the automobile. I aimed the handlebars and prayed they would do my bidding. Seconds later, I crashed into the shrub with a loud thud. Stunned, I lay there breathless and didn't even notice the car pass by.

Soon, I was surrounded by clamouring cousins, all trying to check that I was okay. Shaken, I dusted myself off once more and checked my smarting knee. Apart from an oozing scrape – nothing I hadn't seen before – and a few scratches where I had head-butted the shrub, I was relatively unscathed. Still, that had been scary, and I was ready to give up. 'No. You can't stop now,' my cousins chorused, 'you keep going until you learn.' Jaiye pointed to the handlebars. 'Here are the brakes. You squeeze them and they stop the tyres.' *I wished he'd pointed those out earlier.*

Back up the road we tramped, to start all over again. But, by the end of the morning, I was riding as confidently as all the other children, one more accomplishment behind me.

*

Halfway through our holiday, my cousins announced a trip to the public pumps two miles away from home, to fetch drinking water. Many houses, including theirs, had no wells, and where wells had been dug, they often ran dry. Most homes relied on rainwater for cleaning and laundry, and on municipal tankers who supplied drinking water weekly. When the tankers failed to show up, the adults sent the children to the pumps.

Before we headed out, my cousins each chose a container for the water. I eyed the round plastic bowls and tall metal buckets. The bowls looked larger, but my cousins all picked one, so I did the same. Since we had to carry the water on our heads, we left armed with a small piece of cloth to cushion the bowl. As other families saw us walk by, they sent their kids to join us. Soon our small group of four turned into a crowd of neighbourhood kids. No one hurried. The mid-day sun made us too sluggish. At the pump, we formed a queue with other children and amused each other with stories and songs while we waited. Hours later, bowls full, it was time for the trek home.

I rolled the cloth into a circular platform and placed it on my head, forming a sandwich between my skull and the bowl. With help from my cousins, I lifted the bowl of water, dipping my knees a little, so they could balance it on my head. As I straightened my legs, the water sloshed, and I shuddered as a trickle of cold water ran down my spine. I waited for my cousins and when everyone was ready, we started out. That's when my troubles began.

With each step I took, the water weaved back and forth, gathering momentum, before escaping over the rim of the bowl. I slowed my steps to reduce the motion, but soon realised I was trailing behind the group. Not keen on admitting the difficulties I was having, I sped up. But not only did the water splash crazily, I seemed to lose my balance, as the bowl and I swayed in tandem from side to side. It was a losing battle. If I slowed down, the group would leave me behind, and I didn't know my way home. If I didn't, I would lose most of my water. I chose to walk faster.

When we got home, Jaiye helped lift the bowl off my head and yelled, 'Hey everyone, look at Funmi's bowl!'

I covered my face with my palms and peeped at the water through the gap in my hands. *Silly! That won't make it appear any fuller.* As I stood there, dripping like a drowned hamster, the other children crowded round and stared in astonishment. I had barely half of the water left. Bolanle slapped me on the back in sympathy. 'Never mind, it was your first time.' The rest of the evening, I endured the light-hearted teasing from the elders who all found the story amusing.

The next time we headed for the pumps, I chose a tall bucket, looping its handle through my arm. Tope shot me a quizzical glance. 'What?' I asked. She shrugged and walked away, but not before I caught the wink passing between her and Bolanle. On our way back, with the filled bucket on my head, I realised I had an entirely different problem. My hands did not reach the top of the bucket, so I couldn't hold it securely and move. Bolanle lifted the bucket off my head, put it down and faced me with a questioning gaze. I looked at the others grinning at me. They had known all along this would happen. Even half-filled, the bucket was too heavy for me to carry with my hands. Exasperated, I poured my water into someone else's bowl and trekked back home with an empty bucket.

Once more, that evening, my water escapade provided all the dinner-time entertainment the family needed. As I lay on a mat that night, listening to my snoring relatives, I once again pondered my existence. Here I was, in a country full of people who looked just like me. I should be one of them, but I wasn't. I felt different; they knew I was different, and if I didn't fit in here, where exactly did I fit in? I went to bed thinking of Nan, Dee, Tom and Pop. I wondered what Dee was up to these days and imagined his expression had I been able to tell him some of my experiences.

CHAPTER ELEVEN

The Awakening

In January 1972, I moved up to Primary 5. It was a relief to see the last of Mr Adesanwo, and I was back to attending school in the mornings. I spoke Yoruba fluently and could even scribe Mama's letters to her brothers. Bosun and I were no longer in the same class. We made other friends, and our lunch-time hang-outs became less frequent.

I took an immediate liking to Mr Olowo, my new class teacher. In his late twenties or early thirties and newly married, he would remain my teacher for the next two years. With thick brows, high cheekbones and a square jaw, his was a well-sculpted face. A slight limp on his right leg, possibly the result of infantile polio, made him look shorter than his six-foot frame.

Mr Olowo never left the class except at break and lunch times. He took pains to explain things we didn't understand, encouraged us to ask questions and was disappointed when we didn't. Apart from Dad, I didn't know any adults who invited young minds to be inquisitive. All the ones I had met so far expected you to do as you were told and never ask why. Mr Olowo introduced us to social studies, where we learned that the Briton, Lord Lugard, created and named the country Nigeria. I found learning about

Nigeria's colonial past fascinating, and it explained how my parents ended up in London.

Like my previous teachers, Mr Olowo's cane rested daily on his desk, in front of the class, always on display. Mr Olowo didn't need his cane to control the class, since we were too busy enjoying learning and had no desire for making noise. But, like Mama, he had high expectations and his cane was our incentive to learn faster. In Yoruba culture, failure was derided and unacceptable, and I could recite nine different adjectives to describe the slow learners in my class.

As one of the brightest in the class, I faced competition from only one boy, Tomi, who was better at arithmetic. After our termly tests, Mr Olowo aggregated our scores and ranked every child from first to last. Tomi and I would come first and second, taking it in turns to bump the other off the coveted first position. Neither of us ever needed to fear Mr Olowo's cane.

*

As the Easter holiday approached, the adults talked about the government's proposed change to the driving rules. Nigerians had driven on the left since British rule began and continued to do so after the country's independence in 1960. In a conscious decision to break from its colonial past, the government now wanted people to drive on the right. Most countries in West Africa did, and the change would make transporting heavy goods across the region easier.

The country moved to right-hand driving on 2 April 1972, and a few months after that, the government announced another major reform. Nigeria would change its currency from the British pound in favour of a decimal system. The country I had inherited by virtue of descent was rapidly distancing itself from my country of birth. Yet, while I was adapting to my life as a

Nigerian, a large part of me still yearned for and looked forward to my return to England.

*

On 1 January 1973, the Central Bank of Nigeria released the new naira currency. A week later, I moved up to Primary 6. It gave a whole different meaning to our arithmetic lessons. Our teachers had taught us that twelve pennies made a shilling, twenty shillings made a pound, and twenty-one pounds made a guinea. There was no logic to it, just something we memorised. Now, under a decimal system, we had to count in tens. On the upside, our fingers and toes made it so much easier. The government introduced one more change. From the next academic year, the school calendar would run from September to June, instead of January to December. That gave every child six months of learning in the current year.

The change in currency gave Mr Olowo a new impetus to teach us how to manage money. He started a class collection to fund our valedictory party in June, and we all donated a portion of our lunch money to it. Mr Olowo appointed me as class treasurer and gave me the money in a tin box to keep at home. Now and then, he asked me to bring it in so he could check how much the class had saved.

All was well until Mama decided hunger would be my new sanction. Whenever she denied me lunch money, I borrowed a little from the class fund, the lure of the tin box too strong to resist. I told myself I would pay it back before the end of the year, from the cash gifts I got from Dad's incessant visitors. But my worst nightmare came true before I could. 'What is this?' Mama asked, holding up the tin box. She must have found it, rummaging through my stuff. I told her about the class fund. She leaned into my face, as if trying to sniff out the truth. 'You're lying. You think I am stupid? You have been stealing from me, haven't you?'

I held her gaze. 'No Mama, I haven't. It belongs to my class. You can ask my teacher.'

'Fine. If what you say is true, tell your teacher to come and collect it from me himself.' With that, she walked away.

At school the next day, my mind swirled as I considered various confessional scenarios. At lunch time, I approached Mr Olowo's desk. I wrung my hands together, but it did nothing to combat the churning sensation in my stomach. I didn't fear Mr Olowo's cane, but I couldn't bear seeing his eyes fill with disillusion. I coughed. 'Ahem, sir…'

Mr Olowo looked up from the exercise books he was marking. 'Yes, Funmi, what can I do for you?'

Did I tell him the whole truth or some of it? I sucked in a breath. 'Sir, my grandmother found the class collection. She didn't believe my explanation, and she says you have to collect it from her yourself.'

'Okay. Is that all?'

Now is the chance to come clean. 'Yes sir,' I said.

'Tell your grandmother, I will collect it today.'

That evening, Mama listened as Mr Olowo confirmed my story. 'Here is the box,' she said, 'please check that it's all there.'

It was time to confess. 'Sir, I borrowed a little from it.' I spluttered, then hung my head. A deadly pause followed my confession, and I could feel the laser eyes all trained on me.

'Why?'

My tears welled at Mr Olowo's softly spoken query. Mum swallowed a gasp when I told him Mama often withheld my lunch money. After expressing his disappointment in me, Mr Olowo turned to Mama.

'Mama, please forgive what I am about to say. I know it is important to discipline your child, but not through starvation. All it does is teach a child to steal.'

As my teacher defended me, the clenching in my stomach loosened and my admiration for him grew. A beating from Mama was inevitable, but for now, I felt vindicated.

The beating I expected did not come immediately. I had forgotten another favourite saying of Mama's: 'Don't beat the child after they spill expensive oil. Wait until they spill a glass of water.' You couldn't fault the wisdom behind the words. You were less likely to cause permanent injury if you beat them because they spilled water.

*

Kemi, the daughter of Mama's first cousin, came to spend her holidays with us. Kemi's mum had asked her to deliver a message to Mama Shomolu, another relative living nearby. Since Kemi didn't know her way around the neighbourhood, Mama told me to accompany her.

Neither of us had seen Mama Shomolu in a while. As we knelt to greet her, she pulled us into a hug, her wrinkled face beaming from ear to ear. 'Welcome, welcome my children.' Elders considered all children in the family as theirs. 'How are your parents and Mama?'

'They are fine, ma.'

'What about your siblings?'

'They too are fine, ma.'

Satisfied that all was well in our worlds, she gave us wooden stools to sit on, then hollered into the courtyard. 'Mama Alata, your children are here to see you o.'

Mama Alata, another family member, sold chillies at her local market. She was popular with children as she tended to fuss over them. Mama Alata emerged from her room. Before we could kneel, she threw her arms up in the air and screamed, 'Eh, my children! How you have grown! Ehn, look at you. You have both become *Sisi* [fine young girls].' We smiled at the compliment just before her hug engulfed us. Yoruba elders were effusive in their greetings when they hadn't seen you in a while.

After Kemi delivered her message, I stood up and said we needed to head back. A quick frown replaced Mama Alata's smile. 'But you only just arrived! You haven't eaten yet.'

'Mama Nurodu told us not to tarry,' I explained. Whenever she sent us on errands, Mama had a habit of spitting on the ground and saying, 'See that spit, it had better not be dry before you get back.' So far, I had never beaten the drying spit. Little did I know that Mama wiped it as soon as we left. It was a clever ruse to ensure that we ran errands quickly.

'We need to leave, Mama Alata, otherwise I will get into trouble.'

My entreaty fell on deaf ears. 'Not until you have eaten.' Then she paused and looked me in the eye. 'Did your mother tell you not to take food from me?'

With a half-suppressed sigh, I capitulated. It wasn't an argument I could win. Feuding extended families often cautioned children not to take food off their rivals for fear of poisoning. Mama Alata's question amounted to saying, 'Are they calling me a witch now? Is that why you won't stay and eat my food?'

I hoped the *amala* and okra stew she was planning to serve were worth it, as it may well be my last meal.

*

After our meal, we spent some more time with the mamas. It was considered impolite to leave immediately after eating a host's food. Soon enough, we left, but I did not hurry. There was no point. I approached our house with the usual knot in my stomach. Mama was not in the courtyard. I could hang around outside and delay the inevitable, but I wasn't made that way. I crept to the bedroom door, Kemi behind me and slowly pushed it open.

Mama sat facing the door, pottering in a corner near the back of the room. I hoped Kemi's presence might make her more amenable. Heart thumping, I knelt and offered the traditional greeting from someone returning home. '*Eku ile*, Mama.'

'What time do you call this? Where have you been?' the deadly, sinister tone signalled the coming dance.

'I only went where you sent us.' The churning in my stomach made me feel ill. My brow broke into a sweat, and it wasn't from the African heat.

'The spit dried up ages ago,' Mama said as she reached for her cane. The canes were fresh, having just arrived the day before with Kemi. As fast as I could spit the words out, I explained what happened.

'You are lying,' Mama said.

I smelt my own fear. 'No, I'm not, Mama. Ask Kemi. She was with me all the time.'

'It's true, Mama,' Kemi offered. 'Mama Alata insisted we stay and eat. We tried to tell her no, but she wouldn't let us leave.'

Mama ignored Kemi. 'I have told you not to lie to me.' Thwack! The first strike hit. Instinctively, I covered my face and ducked.

'Please Mama,' Kemi begged.

The next strike stung my shoulder. Mama's voice droned. 'If you lie, you will steal, if you steal, you will prostitute yourself.' Head bowed, I bobbed and dived, trying to avoid the raining assault. My arms, back, legs caught the worst of it. Still, the beating continued with Mama's litany ringing in my ears. 'I will mark you for life. You will tell your children's children stories about me.' Thwack!

The strikes were getting weaker and fewer. I sensed Mama was tiring. I lifted my head, saw the gleam in her eye and ducked, but it was too late. The cane's tip struck the side of my face. I felt the sting down to my toes as the pain radiated from eye to jaw. I clasped my face in my hands and hopped, waiting out the pain. Satisfied, Mama stopped and left the room, but I stayed doubled over, cowering.

I sank to the floor and curled up into a ball for an interminable length of time. I could feel my cheek and lip stretching as they filled with fluid. Slowly, I unfurled myself and moved to the mirror hanging on the wall. For a full minute, I peered at my face. Mama had outdone herself this time. A three-inch welt ran diagonally from the base of my left ear to the corner of my mouth. An open, bleeding wound ran right through the middle of it. I knew it would leave a scar, one that would take a long time to heal. *My secondary school application photograph won't be pretty.* I took a deep breath, exhaled and vowed. No matter what she did, Mama would not break me. I would fight and survive this place, and somehow, someday make it back to England alive.

I stayed in the bedroom all evening, and my face continued to swell. Mama left me well alone. She didn't even bother asking me to help with dinner. I heard Mum and Dad return from work but remained out of sight. They would notice my absence soon enough. Eventually, Dad called me. I left the bedroom and headed for the parlour. I watched in detachment as first shock, then horror, flitted across my parents' faces.

'What happened?' Mum whispered.

'Mama beat me.'

'What did you do?'

I shrugged. 'Nothing.'

They both stared at me as if I were crazy. Dad tried again.

'Why would Mama beat you for nothing? You must have done something. Tell me what happened from the beginning.'

So, I did. When I finished, Dad sent me back to the bedroom. Before I got to the door, an arresting hand on my shoulder halted my steps. Mum turned me around. Her hand reached under my chin and tilted my face up to hers. For seconds, she just looked without saying a word, her face thunderous. Finally, she broke the silence. 'Does it hurt a lot?'

I nodded.

'Wait here.'

She disappeared into her bedroom and came back moments later with some aspirin. She held them out. 'Have you had dinner?'

'No, Mum.'

'You need to take these with food. Come. I'll find you some.'

She led me through the courtyard, ignoring the hushed voices of the maids and other children, right past Mama, to the kitchen and dished up some *eba*. Under her watchful gaze, I ate a bit.

'I don't want any more, Mum.'

'Okay. Take the tablets and go to bed.'

We walked back inside, and Mum left me at the bedroom door. I entered the room, laid out the mats and settled down to sleep. As the painkillers took effect, Mum's yells rose in the background. She was telling Mama to leave her children alone. Dad's voice soon joined the affray. I'd never, ever heard my parents' voices raised in anger before. I listened intently as the argument continued, then oblivion descended.

*

I snuck another peak at the mirror. The swelling had all but gone down. But the raised welt on my face, a mixture of purple and black scabs, stood in proud testimony of what had occurred a week earlier. With a sigh, I set off for school. It would be a long day of explaining.

My classmates were curious, but since most of us were beaten at home at some point or other, they all took it in their stride. 'Tell me the truth,' Mr Olowo said, after I explained what happened. 'What did you really do?'

'Sir, I'm telling the truth.'

'You didn't steal or lie again?'

'Sir, I promise you I didn't.'

A disbelieving Mr Olowo turned up at my home that evening. Having asked Kemi her version of the event before she returned home, my parents confirmed my story. I wasn't party to the rest of the discussion between my parents and Mr Olowo. But from then on, Mama avoided hitting me. I presumed she concluded that any further caning might incur both my mother's and my teacher's wrath. While Mum rarely spoke up against her mother-in-law, it was clear she was quite capable of doing so.

And so, began our game of cat and mouse, with Mama and I tolerating each other in an unequal truce that didn't last long. In response to my increasing belligerence, Mama used one of her many other forms of punishment. But I no longer cared. I reckoned there wasn't a lot she could do that she hadn't already done. I might not be able to stop her from punishing me, but she couldn't stop me from telling her what I thought of her. If she told me off, I'd mutter under my breath, loud enough for her to know I said something, but not loud enough to hear what. If she challenged me, I'd wisely feign ignorance.

One evening after another skirmish, I announced with more than a hint of malice, 'There's someone in this room whose funeral I will not attend.' The shocked silence was palpable. Auntie Kike gagged and spluttered the liquid in her mouth into the cup in her hand. Auntie Abebi's mouth formed an O and would not close. If Mama felt anything at my pronouncement, she did not show it. Instead, she looked up and asked, 'Are you talking about your mother's mum?' I stared straight back at her and let my eyes do the talking. *You know I'm talking to you.*

*

As the advent of secondary education drew near, I sat the Common Entrance Examination and attended interviews at each of the three schools my parents chose. Top of the list was Girls' Secondary Grammar School, Bariga, the school the landlord's children attended. My parents reckoned that if it was good enough for the landlord's children, it was good enough for me. They also liked the idea that it was an all-girls' school.

At each school, the interviewers seemed more interested in the fact that I was born in London and that my Dad was a shipping manager, than in my person. I answered all their questions about England as best as I could and hoped I impressed them enough to secure a place. Only two of the schools on my parents' list had boarding houses, and I desperately needed to get into one of them. That was my only means of escape from Mama.

One day, Dad came home with the good news. The Girls' Secondary Grammar School had accepted me. Despite all the horror stories the landlord's daughters told about seniors who punished you at will, I thought nothing could be worse than Mama. Nothing could keep the spring out of my step. I would soon be free.

CHAPTER TWELVE

The Great Escape

It was 3 September 1973. I woke with a start and the thoughts crowded in. Today would be the first of the rest of my life. I was off to boarding school. I crept off the mat, careful not to wake anyone. The stillness outside told me it wasn't even dawn yet. No sound of cockerels heralding sunrise, no calls by the chief Imam inviting devotees to Salat at the nearby mosque. I padded to the bathroom, for once thankful I could get to it before the morning queues. I washed quickly, got dressed in my new day dress and school shoes and gathered my stuff together.

Since leaving England, I had never owned so much. The rolled-up mattress, pillow, coal iron and metal pail sitting in a corner were brand new. Beside them a suitcase bulged, stuffed with my school uniforms, two more day dresses, a party dress, bedding, mosquito net and 'provisions'. The school had provided a list of the kinds of food allowed and mine included powdered milk, cocoa powder, sugar and some *gari*, the grainy staple from which you made *eba*. Mum threw in a jar of Marmite last minute. She loved the stuff and never shared it with anyone. That was her way of telling me she loved me, and I didn't have the heart to tell her I loathed it.

The previous night, I overheard Mama, Auntie Kike and Auntie Abebi discussing my impending departure. 'Do you think she will cry at the thought of leaving?' Auntie Kike asked.

'I doubt it,' said Auntie Abebi, 'she's too hardened.'

'Who knows,' Mama added, 'she might.'

Soon others rose, and the world became a blur of activity. My parents had taken time off work to take me to school. After a quick breakfast, it was time to leave. I knelt and said goodbye to Mama, my face hard, my eyes unblinking. Even if I'd tried, I wouldn't have been able to fake any tears. I was way too happy.

'Goodbye,' Mama said, 'May God look after and protect you.'

I wasn't sure her prayers were genuine, but I chorused an Amen along with everyone else. Then I climbed into Dad's car and we were on our way.

*

A frisson of excitement coursed through my veins as we approached the school gates. Dozens of cars queued, all waiting to drop off girls who would be my new friends or foes for the next five years. After parking the car, my parents escorted me to the dormitory where we met an elderly lady who introduced herself as the Matron. We said a teary goodbye and my parents left. I was two months shy of my eleventh birthday and on my own for the first time.

I scrutinised the dormitory. With its entire front facade clad in burglar-proof iron railings, the imposing two-storey building looked more like a prison than a residence. The attempt to soften the look with the pastel pink, yellow and green painted exterior made no difference. A large metal gate welded into the railing provided access to the dormitory. Matron checked my name on a notepad she was holding. 'You are in Red house. Stand with those girls. Someone will see you to your dorm shortly.' She went back to checking in other girls.

I studied the other girls next to me. *Why was I so much shorter than everyone else?* An older girl approached. 'I am Senior Rose, your house prefect,' she said. 'Follow me. Take whatever you can carry now. You can come back for the rest later.' I picked up my suitcase and bucket and with the other girls followed her into the building. Senior Rose spoke as she moved. 'You must address everyone in the forms above you as "Senior". There are four halls in the building. Each represents Red, Yellow, Green and Blue houses. You will remain a member of Red house until you leave the school.'

We walked through the gates and found ourselves in a long, open corridor. She turned left, opened a door and led us into a large room filled with rows of bunk beds. 'This is your dorm. Find a lower bunk with your name tag on it. Then get the rest of your stuff. In twenty minutes, I will be back to show you how to lay your beds.' She left us alone, and we all scrambled to find our beds. I found mine at the back right corner, next to a window.

Senior Rose returned with a second group of girls. This time, she stayed to demonstrate how to string up the mosquito nets and lay our beds as crisply as you would find in any decent hospital. We spent the rest of the afternoon unpacking and storing our non-food belongings in the lockers lining one side of the hall. We each had a locker for food items in a separate storeroom elsewhere in the school compound.

By evening, the dorm teemed with hundreds of girls. After supper, Senior Rose allocated each girl a chore, which ranged from sweeping a section of the school premises to helping kitchen staff with school meals. Also, she showed us how to wear our uniform correctly, with our fabric belts tied in a double Windsor knot to the back and our berets centred on our heads. None of us could master the Windsor knot at first, but I managed a close approximation. Later, some of us would test the boundaries by attempting to get through the day with berets perched at a slanted angle or with belts trailing to the front or side.

Before bedtime, the bell rang for night prayers. As we gathered in the corridor, I noticed the large iron gates in the centre of the burglar-proof railings were padlocked. I suspected they were just as effective keeping girls in as they were keeping burglars out. The girls sang a familiar hymn and Matron said prayers before sending us to bed. Matron, who the older girls nicknamed Mama Saro because she was Sierra-Leonean, and her younger assistant were responsible for the hundreds of students living in the dormitory. They both lived in a mini-apartment within the enclosed block.

*

The wake-up bell at 5 a.m. had me scrambling out of bed and assembling in the corridor for morning devotion. When the gates opened, we flew out of the dorm towards the bathrooms as if our lives depended on it. Two hours later, the dusty quadrangle outside my classroom sparkled. My allocated chore was almost too easy given Mama's training over the years.

At 7 a.m., the clanging noise announced that the dining room, a large shed filled with long, wooden tables and benches, was open for breakfast. We filed in, found our allocated table and waited while the girls on kitchen duty, supervised by an older student, collected and dished out the food. 'Never arrive late, unless you want to miss breakfast,' the food prefect warned, before saying grace.

I wolfed down breakfast and made it to class just before the bell for assembly rang at 8 a.m. Boarders and day students alike trooped to the great lawn behind the principal's office for the second devotion of the day. The school had admitted 150 girls into Form 1, spread across five classes labelled A to E. Rumour had it that the brightest students were in Form 1A and the dullest in Form 1E. I guessed my presence in Form 1D spoke for itself.

At noon, we had lunch in class, since the dining room wasn't big enough to accommodate us all. Day students managed lunch-time duties, collecting the food from the kitchen, serving it and returning the dirty plates. When the school day ended at 2 p.m., boarders headed back to the dorm for a compulsory afternoon siesta. This was followed by 'prep' time when we completed homework, then free time before dinner. A shorter prep time followed, before bed at 9 p.m. Like all the other girls, I soon settled down into the highly regimented routine.

Sometime that week, a girl walked past me in class. 'Her shoes are nice, I said to the girl sitting next to me.' The milk-chocolate-coloured shoes moulded gently around her feet, unlike mine, which were loose around the edges and seemed to weigh my feet down every time I lifted them.

'Those are Clarks,' said my classmate. '*Ajebutter* girls wear those.' She glanced at my feet. 'Yours are Bata, for the *ajepako*.'

I baulked at the remark. True, I couldn't afford to eat butter, but I had a toothbrush rather than a chewing stick.

'I am not *ajepako*,' I said. 'My dad's a shipping manager and I was born in London.'

'Really? What kind of chocolate have you got in your locker? Ovaltine, Milo or Bournvita?'

'Pronto.'

'As I said, *ajepako*.'

I soon discovered why the distinction was important. Ajebutter girls banded together and although no one spoke about it, your circle of friends depended on your social influence, which was determined by wealth. I also found out that Clarks were made of super-soft leather and were both comfortable and durable. The upper part of Bata shoes had a nasty habit of separating from the soles, and we were forever searching for glue to stick them back together.

*

On our first weekend, the seniors called the first of many social gatherings. In our party dresses, we spilled into the open courtyard where wooden benches were arranged in a massive circle. The evening's proceedings began with a song, followed by introductions. Each girl came forward, said their name, their form and, if they had one, their nickname. The crowd cheered whenever a girl announced a nickname. I liked the idea, a lot, although all the girls with nicknames were in higher forms. As the introductions got closer to my section of the circle, I scrambled my brain, trying to think up a suitable moniker. As my turn approached, my heart thumped in anticipation and a prickly sensation fluttered over my skin.

The gathering fell silent as I stepped into the circle and braved the undivided attention of several hundred faces. I took a deep breath and puffed out my chest. 'My name is Funmi Ogun, alias Afro Girl, and I'm in Form 1D.' A stunned silence followed my announcement. That wasn't quite the reaction I was aiming for. I ran my tongue over dry lips, wondering what next.

Then someone started a slow clap in a corner, which soon grew into a deafening roar. I relaxed my hunched shoulders and hopped to my seat where my classmates met me with smiles and back thumps. I was an instant celebrity, but only for the evening. Like with Mama and the *Iyawo* Gowon saga, I had just forfeited the right to be called by my first name. From then on, the seniors would only ever call me Afro Girl, and because of the hint of a sneer I detected in their tone, it infuriated me.

*

I met Dunni, who became my best friend for the next eighteen months. We were neither in the same class nor house, yet our affinity to each other was instant. We were the smallest and youngest girls in the school and tiny compared to most of the others. Mama Saro, quick to notice our immaturity, took it upon herself to check up on us regularly. Being in different classes and houses limited our time together, but we made up for it at prep time. Soon we were inseparable and although we looked nothing alike, some thought we were twins.

'Have you chosen a school mother yet?' Dunni asked one evening. A school mother was someone in a higher form who looked after your interests for agreed favours, like doing their laundry or hair.

'No, I haven't, but I'm thinking about it.'

I had set my eyes on Tolani in Form 2, my sole criteria being the fact that she looked stunning. Her brown, oval eyes were fringed with long eyelashes and her lips had just the right amount of fullness. She was tall, willowy and fair skinned, and I had never met anyone so captivating.

I wrote her a delightful letter, asking if she would be my school mother. Too bashful to deliver it myself, I sent it through Dunni. Tolani wasted no time in accepting, but soon after, I found I'd made an error in judgement. By choosing someone only a year ahead, I had no protection from seniors in Forms 3 and above, which, come to think of it, was most of the school. I needed to fix the problem and it would take crafty manoeuvring.

The answer to my predicament was at the top of the school chain. Senior Evelyn, the head girl, was my school mother's school mother, which technically made her my school grandmother except no one had one of those. Still, I wasn't about to let such minutia deter me. I made my services available to Senior Evelyn and my attentiveness did not go unnoticed. When anyone asked why I was hanging around, I told them she was my school mother. The news of my defection reached Senior Tolani at bush-fire speed. One evening, she cornered me in the school yard, flanked by four of her friends. 'I hear you've been telling everyone Senior Evelyn is your school mother,' she said.

I nodded and swallowed the saliva tickling my throat.

'What about me?'

I could neither hold her gaze nor explain my defection without sounding like a conniving little brat. 'You can still be my school sister.' I offered the meaningless peace offering and hoped for forgiveness.

She glowered at me, and her friends kissed their teeth. For a moment, a sadness entered her eyes, then she spun on her heels and walked away. Her friends did the same, but not before giving me the 'evil eye', the one that said, 'watch out'. However, with the head girl's protection, I was safe, at least for the time being.

*

'Funmi, stop. Why have you got a damp patch on your bottom?' I stopped and sighed. The rest of my mates trotted back to class from assembly while I turned to answer or perhaps not answer Senior Evelyn's question.

I scanned her face and took in the faintly amused smile. *Yeah, she knew, but she would still make me say it.*

'I had to dry my panties underneath my mattress, and they were still damp this morning.'

Most nights they were dry by morning, but the previous night's thunderstorm had kept the air humid.

'And you are down to a single pair of panties because…?'

'I lost them.' I kept my eyes to the floor.

'How careless of you.'

I couldn't agree more, having lost almost everything I owned. All I had left of my clothing was a single uniform, one day dress and a pair of panties. My bedding hadn't fared much better. I only had one bed-sheet and pillowcase left. I assumed people stole them while they hung on the lines drying. Most girls sat in the baking sun and watched over their drying clothes. Not me. I was too busy playing. Even my bedspread was missing. I had survived the last few weeks of term with a faded one from a senior who had an old one to spare.

*

A week later, Dad pulled into the school car park. The year had drawn to a close. 'How well did you perform this year?' he asked, as we drove home. My report card showed I hadn't done too badly.

'I ranked 36th out of 135 students.'

'Hmm.'

I couldn't see the expression in his eyes, but his next words confirmed his disappointment. 'You used to be first or second. What happened?'

I hung my head. I didn't have a decent answer, although, to be fair, I ranked 1st and 2nd in my class of 40, not the whole Primary 6 cohort. Despite being ranked within the top third of the cohort, I was allocated to Form 2D. The rumour that we were grouped based on academic prowess must have been false.

The holidays turned out great, memorable for one thing only – no Mama. She had gone to Ijebu-ode. I couldn't imagine how many strokes of the cane she might have attempted to give me otherwise. Mum wasn't around much during the day and in Mama's absence, all the children in the family revelled in the lack of discipline. We did the barest minimum of chores and completely forgot to do our laundry.

Mama surprised us by returning a week before the break ended. My siblings and I tip-toed around, hoping to attract as little scrutiny as possible. Alas, it was not to be. After Mama finished distributing her gifts to the landlord and other neighbours, she turned her attention to the state of her bedroom.

'Mama wants all of you inside,' Auntie Abebi said. One by one, we assembled before her. She waved her hands at the jumble of clean and dirty clothes scattered all over the floor. 'Look at this mess. Ehn. Even pigs are cleaner!'

We had turned the room into a giant pigsty, and humiliation would be our reward.

'Each one of you, pick up a bundle and take it outside.'

We each grabbed an armful and dragged them into the courtyard where we built a mountain of clothes. The landlord's children gawked at the growing pile.

'Come and see their shame,' Mama said. 'This is the filth they have been living in since I've been gone.' She turned to us, 'Each one of you, sort out your own clothes from this mess and start washing them.'

For once, I was grateful that Mama refrained from christening the brand-new bundle of canes she brought from Ijebu. A week later, I headed back to start my second year of secondary education.

CHAPTER THIRTEEN

If You Lie, You Will Steal

I returned to boarding school with extra clothing and underwear. 'Mum, I need new bedding too,' I pleaded.

'Sorry. I can't afford to replace those,' she said. 'You'll learn to do without.'

After breakfast on the first Saturday back, I headed down to the dorm for the weekly inspection. Like the other girls, I stood to attention beside my neatly laid bed as Matron strolled by, notepad in hand, trailed by the four house prefects. Afterwards, Matron would rank the dorms, and the cleanest and neatest one got the highest points. The house with the greatest number of points won an annual award. As she drew alongside me, Matron paused. She looked at my bed, glanced at me, noted something down and moved on. My house prefect sent me a warning glare as she too walked past. I knew what she was saying. Everybody else's bed sported a royal blue cotton bedspread, whereas mine had a faded denim vibe going on.

An hour later, Matron announced the winner and Red House had come last. 'Oi, Afro Girl, come here.' The house prefect's tone spelt trouble. I wondered just how much.

'Kneel down,' she said.

I fell to my knees in obedience.

'You know we lost because of you, right? From now on, every time we lose, I will punish you.'

I stayed mute. Short of stealing someone else's bedspread, I couldn't change the status quo. Another incident a few weeks later sealed my fate. On the way to prep one evening, a senior called out, 'Hi, shortie.'

You've got a nerve, you're as leggy as a giraffe. I retaliated. 'Hi Senior Longus.' I reasoned that although she was a senior, she was repeating the year with my form and that gave me rights.

In no time, the entire school heard about my rudeness. It didn't help that quite a few people were aware of my school mother to school sister escapade of the previous year. Seniors began falling over themselves to give me an attitude adjustment, and since my school mother had graduated, I had no protection. I became their general dog's body and resigned myself to misery. 'Afro Girl, here, shine my shoes,' one said, as she lay on her bed during siesta.

'Afro Girl, here, wash these uniforms,' said another one Saturday morning. I took the uniforms, dipped them in water and hung them out to dry. Later that evening, I saw her re-washing them in the schoolyard. That taught her.

The school library became my means of escape. I spent as many hours as I could in there, hiding from seniors, and my love of reading blossomed. I discovered Enid Blyton and her Famous Five, and Mills and Boon romance stories. They reminded me of England, and in their pages, I lost myself in a world where children enjoyed similar rights to adults, and women equalled men, when they weren't swooning.

*

The year in Form 2 proved to be an eye-opening one. The secret to surviving boarding school, I discovered, was stealing. 'Lifting', is what the girls called it; this sounded much more civilised, and I needed to learn how, soon. I was forever turning up to assembly minus my beret or belt, offences which all attracted punishment.

I took a stroll through the clothesline one afternoon, my heart galloping at a hundred knots, thinking about my intentions. Beyond doubt, it was wrong, but as they say in the local slang, 'How for do?' Once I found an aisle with no people, I swiped a belt and tucked it into my bag. But I couldn't hold on to it, and soon I had to do it again. Thereafter, pinching a belt here and there became so much easier. They often belonged to the newcomers in Form 1 who were just as gullible as I had been. Berets were harder to come by. People didn't wash them often, but occasionally one would turn up.

In class, the one item that many girls stole at some point was the 'almighty pen'. We nicknamed it 'almighty', because without it, you couldn't learn or show what you'd learned. 'Who took my pen?' was a well-versed chorus, repeated many times a day. Often, it was me singing the song. Stealing pens required skill and prowess as everyone was on the lookout for the pen thief. We even gave it its own special name: 'tapping'.

So far, the only way I knew how to survive a pen loss was via pen-sharing. This was when you bargained away the best part of your lunch for sharing a friend's pen during note-taking. It wasn't for the dim-witted or those lacking dexterity, as it required you to hold copious amounts of information in your head while you waited your turn for the pen. Since you each only had a few minutes to write before handing over the pen, you wrote fast, really fast. And you had to ensure the teacher didn't notice the hand-overs, as that would attract a sanction.

I needed a far more efficient system, and tapping seemed the only way. Another girl in class took pity on me and showed me how. All I needed to try it out was a thin exercise book with a piece of chewing gum stuck to its centre. I bent the book into a C, gum facing inward and concealed, and looked around. My eyes landed on a classmate who had left her pen in full view on her desk. I walked up to my unsuspecting victim and started a simple conversation. Once I'd distracted her, I inched closer to the pen, frame by frame. My heartbeat ratcheted up a notch. It surprised me she couldn't hear it. A nervous tick throbbed at the base of my throat. If caught, I would be shamed as a pen thief, but the reward was worth it.

I held my nerve and continued the steady flow of conversation, all the while maintaining eye contact. With slow and deliberate hand movements, I turned the exercise book the other way round. Still chatting, I used the exposed gum to pick up her pen, before folding the book over to conceal it. Soon after, I brought the conversation to an end before sauntering back to my seat. I let out a whoosh of air and wondered how long it would take her to notice her pen was missing.

About half an hour later, above the din, someone yelled, 'Who stole my pen?' It had taken her far longer than I expected, and she did not connect it to my visit. I was home free. I wondered how I could apply the neat trick to stealing a bedspread. At least then, part of my woes would be over. However, although I had mastered the art of pilfering from others, it weighed heavy on my conscience. Now and then, Mama's voice rang in my head, '*If you lie, you will steal, if you steal…*' I was on a slippery road to prostitution, and I still didn't know what it was.

*

The rest of the term was uneventful until I grew out of my school shoes. Getting a message to my parents that I needed a new pair proved impossible. I approached a day student who lived near them. 'What do I get for giving up my time and energy for you?' she said. It was common practice to barter favours. But I was all out of things to trade except for Mum's love token. 'I've got a jar of Marmite,' I said, my voice hopeful.

'You are not serious!' she spat. 'God forbid. Who eats Marmite?' She clicked her fingers in a gesture that said 'Not on your life!' and flounced off. I tried again with someone else, with a similar result. Marmite just didn't cut it.

Meanwhile, every time I put my shoes on, the pain shooting through my big toes told me I needed to get creative. I borrowed a sharp razor blade from a friend and cut a small semi-circle out of the toe cap. I slipped my feet into my shoes and sighed in ecstasy. Now I too understood why necessity sparked invention. But my relief was short-lived.

Bata shoes were not designed for ingenuity. With each step, the stiff leather around the new arc rubbed incessantly against my skin. Within a day, the nasty blisters that appeared on each toe had me limping. I wished I could walk barefoot, which was ironic, since I hated the four years I had to do so in primary school. Now that I really could benefit from walking barefoot, it was against school rules and forbidden. With nothing to do except put up with the pain, I covered the blisters with plasters that Matron gave me. Eventually, the leather softened, the sores healed, and my converted sandals served me well, albeit with some discomfort, right up to the end of term.

CHAPTER FOURTEEN

No Longer a Girl

In the middle of the second term, Dunni and I fell out, something to do with Busola and Dayo, two other girls we sometimes spent time with. We were now sworn enemies, although I could no longer remember why. We ignored each other in passing and it would be years before we spoke again.

Busola and Dayo had been friends since Form 1, and with the demise of my friendship with Dunni, they enveloped me into an incongruous little trio. Leggy and slim, Dayo was tall for her age. Her chest was already beginning to show the budding signs of puberty. Busola was stocky, her short afro hair emphasising her boyishness. Although shorter than Dayo, she was still a full head taller than me. I had grown over the year, but next to Dunni, I remained the smallest in our form.

In the second week of the last term, I woke with a start in the middle of the night, rolled onto my stomach and stifled an involuntary groan. It felt like someone was wringing my intestines like a wet towel. I lay awake drawing deep breaths for a while, hoping whatever it was twisting my insides would let go, but the pain only worsened. Eventually, I rose, snuck out of my dorm and headed for Matron's quarters. With tousled hair and sleep in her eyes, Matron let me into her apartment. After giving me two aspirin tablets, she let me lie on her couch while they took effect, before sending me back to bed.

A week later, the same thing happened. The stomach cramps appeared without warning and disappeared after Matron handed me more painkillers. After the third occurrence in as many weeks, I became worried. I didn't know what was causing the pain. *What if I was dying from some unknown disease*? I met up with Busola and Dayo during free time.

Busola nodded in my direction. 'What's wrong? You are quieter than usual.'

'I keep getting stomach cramps in the middle of the night. Each time, I had to wake Matron. I don't think she likes that.'

'How many times has it happened?' asked Dayo.

I held up three fingers. Dayo and Busola exchanged a glance, the way they often did when communicating silently.

'What was that about?' I asked.

Dayo looked at Busola, who responded with an imperceptible nod.

'We think it's your periods,' Dayo said. 'They are coming.'

'What are they?'

'When you become a woman, you bleed between your legs,' Busola offered.

'Whaaaat! For how long? And what has that got to do with stomach cramps?'

'Calm down,' Dayo soothed. 'Just a few days each month. Four or five maybe.'

'Four or five every month? Forever?'

Both heads bobbed in unison.

'But why?'

'It's about being able to have babies.'

'That's it?'

The shoulder shrugs told me they knew no more.

'You still haven't explained the connection with stomach cramps.'

'We both had cramps before our periods started.'

My eyes widened. 'You mean you…?'

'Yeah,' said Dayo. Busola nodded in agreement.

'What happens when they arrive?' I asked.

'Let me show you.'

Dayo led us to her provisions locker. She opened a plastic pack, pulled out a long, rectangular pad of cotton wool covered in a herringbone weave netting. Each end of the pad had an extended piece of the netting which contracted and narrowed into a tube.

'What do you do with that?'

My eyes grew rounder as she explained how to tuck it between your legs before putting on your underwear.

'What are the tube extensions for?'

'You tie those into a loop and attach a special belt to them, so the pads stay in place.'

'Do you have a belt?' Her head wagged from side to side.

'How do you walk with it? Isn't it uncomfortable trying to keep it in place with just your legs and panties?'

Another shrug. I looked to Busola for confirmation. 'It is what it is,' she muttered.

I remembered spying similar towels in other people's lockers. Not knowing what they were, I asked a senior, but she'd laughed and said they were for women. I reckoned that if I were about to become a woman, I needed a pack. It was early in the term and I still had some pocket money to trade with, so I sent a message home through a day student. Mum responded by sending me several packs of sanitary wear. I didn't need them yet, but I displayed them in my locker, for whoever cared to look.

Two weeks later, halfway through the school day, a girl in class pulled me aside and pointed to the crimson patch on the back of my uniform. Heat flooded my face as I pondered how to hide my shame. I grabbed a fistful of my skirt, enough to hide the offending stain, and hauled myself back to the dorm. Despite my discomfiture, I was pleased. I was officially a woman and for a short period, pun intended, I wore my badge of honour with pride.

Soon, I wasn't sure the ability to brag about being a woman outweighed the negatives. I thought once my periods started, that would be the end of the cramps. Not so. They occurred monthly and were bad enough to lay me flat on Matron's couch. There were other inconveniences too. Sanitary wear came in a single size and was not suited to tiny bodies. When I moved, it bunched, making the simple task of walking a huge palaver. Then there were leakages, day and night, that required more clothing and bedding than I possessed.

*

I glanced at the wall clock in the classroom. It was the second period after lunch, on a Monday afternoon, half an hour before the end of the school day. A steady hum of conversation floated over the air. With our teacher off sick, the lesson had become a free period, leaving us to our own devices. Some girls read quietly at their desks. A group of four gathered in one corner of the room playing Uno, a card game. Others chatted with each other. I had just finished my English homework and that hadn't taken long. I tried talking to Remi, the girl at the desk next to mine, whose head was buried deep inside an Archie comic book. She ignored my overtures. I unfurled my legs in the aisle separating our two desks and stretched like a cat. I could sense my own restlessness, that feeling of needing something to do, but not knowing what. From out of nowhere, a memory flashed through my mind... my five-year-old self, on a clear sunny day, in the park with Tom.

Seated on a swing, I dared him to push me higher. I sighed. Although a lifetime ago, it seemed only yesterday.

Remi stood up and walked over to another girl. I rested a hand each on my desk and hers. If she'd been there, she would have swatted my hand away. Still locked in the past, supporting my weight on my hands, I lifted my legs and swung gently back and forth. With my eyes closed, I returned to Priory Park and a relaxed smile snaked across my face. I continued swinging back and forth, each time just a little higher. Suddenly my hand slipped, my foot caught, and I fell. It happened in seconds and although I tried, I couldn't break the fall.

Thwack! My chest and face hit the floor and a similar crack exploded in my head. Stunned, I lay there dazed as black fairy lights twinkled before my eyes. Then helpful hands grabbed my underarms and lifted me off the ground. 'Get some tissue,' someone yelled, 'she's bleeding!' Only then did I register the salty, metallic taste in my mouth. I clamped a hand over my mouth to stem the flow, while a dozen elephants trampled through my brain, and my lips grew longer before my very eyes. 'She needs to go to sick bay,' someone said.

'I'll take her,' several voices chorused at once. My classmates were falling over themselves to help.

Two girls led me to the sick bay. 'Open,' the school nurse said, as she bent to inspect my mouth. 'You have snapped one of your incisors in half, horizontally, right across the middle. You need to see a dentist, so I am sending you home.'

'We can take her,' the two volunteers who had bagged the role of seeing me to the sickbay offered. *That explained why they were so eager to help. They were angling for a day out.*

'Erm, I don't think so,' the nurse said. 'You are both too young to be in charge of her.' She gave me a sick note and found two seniors to escort me home.

*

Two bus rides after leaving school, my escorts and I arrived at our residence. 'I'm sorry, but your parents have moved home,' the landlord's wife said. 'I can give you the address. It's one of our properties in Bariga.' Armed with the new address and directions, we headed out once more. The elephants had stopped playing with my head and a hundred thundering bulls took their place. Two more bus rides later, I could barely see through my puffed-up eyes, as we walked up to the door of my new residence and knocked.

My sister, Taiwo, opened the door. For a moment, she stared, mouth wide open, then did the most stupid thing. She shut the door in my face and ran off. The door opened again and this time Mum stood on the threshold. 'Funmi, is that you?' she gasped. I nodded carefully, trying to avoid another ricochet of thumps through my brain. 'What happened?' she asked, as she led me to the couch. I tried to work my double-sized lips, but the words tumbled out sort of garbled. 'I was just walking in class when I tripped and fell.' *God forgive my lie.* I had told the school nurse the same story.

Mum looked at my escorts. They shrugged their shoulders. They were not classmates and didn't know how I came by my injuries. Mum refocused on me. I knew that look. She was trying to decipher whether to believe me. I held her gaze. She sighed and asked how I was feeling. *How did I express that in words?* Mum went into her bedroom to ferret out the usual analgesics. From the parlour, I heard her explain to someone that I was home from school with injuries. I tensed as Mama padded barefoot into the room. I didn't bother kneeling to greet her as I couldn't muster the effort it would take.

'*Pele o*!' Mama offered the universal Yoruba greeting that covered all eventualities, as she took in the state of my face. I started to nod but halted the movement. 'How did this happen?' Mama waved her open palm in question. I wished Mum would hurry so I wouldn't have to answer. No such luck. After a terse silence, I offered Mama the same story. Mama, whose default mode was suspicion, peered through my puffy eyes. Her expression said she didn't buy my tale, and on this occasion, she was dead right. She shook her head. 'We sent you to school to learn, not play.'

Mum arrived with the analgesics and saved me from the interrogation. She thanked my escorts and gave them enough money to cover the return fare to school, plus some extra. When Dad got home from work, an hour later, he took me to see a pharmacist friend of his. There would be no visit to a dentist. They were few and far between and cost a fortune. The pharmacist gave Dad a mouthwash and told me to gargle with it twice a day. That would be the extent of my medical treatment until adulthood, when the untreated, exposed nerves became infected, and the tooth had to be extracted. Both parents fussed over me, and even Mama left me alone. Within a few days, the swelling reduced sufficiently that my parents agreed I could return to school on Saturday.

*

On Thursday, Mum confirmed that my periods had started. The next day, she came back from the market with a live chicken, killed it and prepared a pepper stew. At dinner time, bowl in hand, my siblings and I queued for supper. But, instead of the usual tiny piece of meat, Mum put a whole thigh and a wing on my plate. My eyes rounded in wonder. *I ought to crack a few more teeth if this is the reward.* Mum read my expression and explained. 'I cooked the chicken in your honour. You are a woman now. This is to celebrate your womanhood.'

I didn't know what to make of that. My siblings eyed my plate enviously. My brother Kehinde asked if I would share. I gave him a baleful glare. '*Share ko, share ni.*' I muttered the sarcastic Yoruba retort that said 'Not on your life!'

After dinner, Dad called me for a chat. Unusually, he wouldn't meet my eye and I wondered why. He cleared his throat. 'Ahem,' he coughed again, fidgeting with his hands. 'Now that you are a woman,' he began. *Ah! It was all beginning to make sense.* 'You need to be careful around boys. You don't want to get pregnant.' I rolled my eyes silently. I didn't see how that could happen in an all-girls' boarding school. Dad continued. 'I have very little. When I die, you won't inherit anything. Your inheritance is your education. Pay good heed to it. Work hard, face your studies and remember this, when you finish secondary school, you can visit your Nan in England.'

My ears perked up. That carrot again. But I believed him. The message was loud and clear. We were living in poverty, and education was my only way out. I had to complete my secondary education successfully to earn a ticket back to England. I wondered if Mum planned to have a similar conversation with me before I left, but she didn't. The next day I headed back to school.

CHAPTER FIFTEEN

All Together Again

I settled back against the plush, brown fabric lining the front passenger seat of Dad's Peugeot 404, as he manoeuvred out of the school gates into the dense Lagos traffic. We eased into a comfortable silence as Dad concentrated on avoiding the throng of vehicles, motorcyclists and pedestrians all juggling for space on the dusty road. Shifting so his eyes connected with mine, Dad asked, 'So how did you do this year?' The peaceful feeling evaporated. I had expected the question, but I thought he would wait until we were home before asking.

Not knowing how he would receive my news, I fidgeted with my fingers before speaking. 'I was ranked 42nd out of 153.' The cohort had grown over the year. Within the top 30 per cent, my performance was similar to the previous year, but I had slipped five points on the previous term's results. 'I performed better than over a hundred students,' I added, as I awaited his response. I sneaked a peek at his face and realised I needn't have worried. Although he was not smiling, he didn't scowl either.

'You need to work harder. I am sure you could perform better if you put your mind to it.'

I nodded. My teachers had all said the same. We relaxed once more into a comfortable silence, and I wondered what the end-of-year break would bring.

As Dad parked the car in the driveway, my sisters and brother ran towards me, arms outstretched, squealing with excitement. A few moments later, I entered the parlour, and the tantalising aroma of spinach and stock fish stew teased my nostrils. I sniffed in appreciation. *It was good to be home.* I headed straight for the kitchen where I found Mum on a low stool, a large pot of half-mashed *eba* gripped tightly between both feet. With a traditional wooden spatula, she repeatedly pulled and smashed the *eba* against the side of the pot to smooth out any lumps. Auntie Abebi stood, watching beside her, a cup of hot water in her hands, ready to be added to the *eba* if Mum needed it. In a corner, the fish stew bubbled on the stove.

I knelt and offered the traditional greeting, 'Mummy, *Eku ile*.'

Mum looked up with a smile. 'Welcome home. How are you?' Her hands continued the pummelling.

'I'm fine, Mum.' Not used to having much conversation with her, I said no more.

'Did you have a good term?' Her hands stopped the mashing. She poked the *eba* in several places with her forefinger, checking to see if it was lump-free.

'I did, Mum.' I had nothing else to say. Auntie Abebi was listening, and I knew she would repeat anything I said to others.

Mum looked up and tried again. 'Did you do well?' She signalled to Auntie Abebi, to take over the *eba* and start dishing out the food. I nodded in the affirmative.

Her smile deepened, and she rose from the stool. 'Well done.' She reached out and gave me an awkward pat. 'Put your things away and come and help serve supper.'

'Where's Mama?' I asked Taiwo, as I made my way to the bedroom to deposit my stuff, wanting that greeting over.

'Didn't Dad tell you? Mama has gone to Ijebu to help Auntie Bunmi look after her newborn.' Auntie Bunmi was Mama's niece, whom she had raised from a baby.

'When is she coming back?'

'Not for a long, long time.'

My stomach somersaulted, anticipating what I hoped would be a brilliant summer if what my sister said was true.

*

With Auntie Kike married, the household shrunk to twelve people. Brother Segun and Brother Femi slept in the boys' quarters, a room in a separate annexe built for male servants behind the main block. The rest of us lived in the tiny two-bedroomed flat, my parents and siblings in one room, the rest of us in the other. Mama took her mattress with her to Ijebu, so I put mine on her bed, grateful that I no longer need sleep on the floor.

My siblings introduced me to the Adelekes who lived in the opposite house. We were distant relatives through the complicated extended family network on my maternal grandmother's side of the family. Age-wise, I slotted nicely in the middle of the seven siblings and Mum allowed us to play with them most days. As they had liberal parents, their home was a magnet for the neighbourhood's kids.

The holidays passed by in a blur, and as they drew to a close I contemplated my immediate future. On the last day of term, my house prefect told the Form 4 student taking over the role to watch out for me. 'Don't come back without a new bedspread in September,' the new prefect warned, but I couldn't see Mum replacing the bedspread. Boarding school had been my great escape from Mama, but with Mama gone, I had more enemies at school than at home. The answer seemed obvious if I could get my parents to agree. I approached Dad, the more rational of the two. Stretched out on the sofa, eyes closed, fingers laced behind his head, he hummed away happily to the radio. I hovered. 'Dad, can I talk to you for a moment?'

He opened his eyes, tilted his head and invited me to take a seat opposite. 'Yes, what's going on?'

I asked if I could become a day student, pointing out the proximity of home to school and the cheaper cost of transport compared to the boarding school fees.

'How would you get to school?' he asked.

I explained the bus routes, and Dad mulled over the information.

'Are you sure about this?'

My head bobbed up and down. 'Yes!'

'Have you discussed this with your mum?'

My enthusiasm waned. 'No.'

'Okay, I will discuss it with your mother.' He dismissed me with a wave.

For the next two days, I prayed Mum would agree. I overheard them discussing it. Mum didn't seem too keen, worried that without the structure and discipline of boarding school, I wouldn't work as hard at my studies. However, the financial logic won, and Dad agreed.

*

I started Form 3B brimming with excitement, empowered by the knowledge that I was no longer the runt of the herd. The 300 juniors in Forms 1 and 2 were mine to command if I so chose. Busola and Dayo, who were still boarders, were both in other classes, and I rarely saw them. Soon, I made new friends with Lolade, Ade and Dupe, fellow day-students.

Lolade was quiet, assertive and loyal. Her family lived in a townhouse, in Surulere, a middle-class Lagos suburb. Dupe, a genius from a similar background, couldn't see a thing without the round, thick-rimmed spectacles that obscured her eyes. Ade, the most complicated of the three, combined a timid personality with drive and a brilliant mind. She and Dupe were the brightest students in the class and scored the highest marks in tests and assignments. I had chosen my friends well. They made me want to work harder.

I was closest to Lolade. We just hit it off. She was the first person who believed I had been born in London. Everyone else laughed in my face and told me to prove it. When I brought in a photograph of me and Nan, they called me a 'pretender'. To be fair, I wouldn't have believed me either. Thin as a chewing stick, I no longer looked anything like the chubby six-year-old in those photographs. In addition, all the other girls in the school who had been born abroad were rich or bi-racial, and I was neither of those.

The school allowed Form 3 students to choose some subjects. I chose domestic science over art because I couldn't draw to save my life; and I chose history over geography because I didn't like the geography teacher. In a lesson, the previous year, she had asked who the governor of the Mid-West State of Nigeria was. I knew the answer and raised my hand. Noticing this, she pointed at me.

'Ogbemudia,' I said.

'What!' she rapped. 'You opened your big mouth and said Ogbemudia? How rude of you. That would be Lieutenant Colonel Samuel Ogbemudia to you, thank you very much. Remain standing!'

I bowed my head as my classmates sniggered. Months later, I was still smarting from the humiliation. Geography teacher aside, there was no contest between the two subjects, because I adored learning about the past and about different countries and cultures.

I also enjoyed domestic science, not so much for the cooking part but for the sewing, and it would become a lifelong hobby. By the end of term, I had hand-sewn my first garment, a beautiful, pink, gingham baby dress. I smocked the bodice in an intricate, herringbone pattern with red and white embroidery thread. It was a true labour of love and my effort earned me an A.

The new science subjects were interesting. I liked biology and enjoyed learning about the human body and the animal kingdom. Chemistry was a bit of an enigma. Our teacher insisted we memorise the Periodic Table, and no matter how hard I tried, I couldn't tell one atomic number from the other. I didn't fare much better in physics. In one test, the teacher asked, 'What is a couple?' I didn't remember ever being taught anything about this, so I wrote my answer. 'A man and woman in a relationship.' Needless to say, I flunked that test.

On the last day of the first term, we collected our report cards. Ranked 12th, in a class of 39, I was satisfied. I turned to my friends to find out how they had done. It was no surprise Dupe came first. We exchanged a hi-five. Lolade was somewhere in the middle, and philosophical about it. 'As long as I try my best, my dad is happy,' she said. The three of us looked across the classroom to Ade's desk and our jaws dropped. With her head on the table, her body heaved with suppressed tears.

Quickly, we surrounded her. Someone handed her some tissue paper. I put my arm around her shoulders. 'What's wrong, Ade?'

She sniffled. 'Nothing.'

The rest of us exchanged a puzzled look. *Maybe she came last?* I laughed silently at the idiocy of the thought. That wasn't even remotely possible. Of the four of us, she worked the hardest.

'No one cries like this for nothing. Tell us the problem. We might be able to help,' Dupe said.

'You can't help!' She burst into a fresh flood.

'Come on, at least tell us, so we know for sure,' I whispered.

'I came second,' was the muffled reply.

Another puzzled look flitted across our faces.

'Why would that make you cry?'

'I'm in trouble. I can't go home.'

'What do you mean?' Dupe asked.

'My dad expects me to be first. Every single time. He will say, "Somebody's daughter came first, why couldn't it be you?"'

When the rest of us mucked around during free periods, Ade read her textbooks. We could never convince her to take a break. Now we knew why.

'Is he going to beat you? Can your mum help?' Lolade said.

She shrugged.

At a loss of how to solve Ade's dilemma, we all crowded in and gave her a group hug. With a down-turned mouth and sad eyes, Ade picked up her bag while the rest of us followed, subdued, our earlier euphoria forgotten. At the school gates, we waved goodbye, each heading to a different bus route. All the way home I pondered Ade's situation, for once thankful for Dad, who encouraged me whatever my ranking.

CHAPTER SIXTEEN

Mamma Mia!

Until this point in my life, as the family matriarch, Mama had been the main force shaping my daily experiences. Meals, chores, rest, she dictated all of it. With Mama out of the picture and Mum in charge, I saw a different side to her. Mum no longer worked in an office. Mama and Dad's other relatives worried that she might attract too much male attention at work. So, she gave up her job at a textiles firm and opened a carpet and rug shop. Mum wasn't very demonstrative, but I soon realised she cared a lot more than I thought. It was in her indulgent smiles and the way she ensured we were all well fed and healthy. And when she used my pet name, Olu, it made me feel special and signalled something good was about to happen.

Mum was also a strict disciplinarian. Although not half as bad as Mama, she was a lot stricter than Dad. She hated procrastination and expected us to carry out instructions promptly. So far, the only people who had ever caned me were Mama and my primary school teachers. That was about to change. One morning, Mum asked me to do her laundry. Because of my experiences with laundry and Mama, I detested the chore. By early evening, the clothes still sat in a basket, unwashed. I was secretly hoping Mum would give them to someone else to do. Suddenly, in a tone that sent chills down my spine, Mum yelled, 'Funmi!' I didn't need anyone to interpret that. 'Yes, ma!' I replied, my pulse quickening as I crept indoors, following the sound of her voice. A quick peek in the kitchen and parlour signalled she wasn't there. That left only her bedroom.

I met Mum at the entrance to her bedroom, cane in hand. Mum preferred the fat end of the cane. I had seen her using it on occasion with my older cousins. Now it was my turn.

'Give me your hand.' Her voice brooked no dissent.

I extended my right palm. Thwack! the first stroke hit. I hadn't been beaten in a while and I had forgotten how much it stung. I hopped on the spot, shaking my wrist repeatedly, waiting for the sting to subside a little. With Mama, the blows would have rained all over. Not Mum.

'I'm waiting,' she announced patiently.

I offered my left hand, repeated the previous dance and rubbed my hands together vigorously. It still hurt.

'Two more to go, hurry up!'

Another key difference. With Mama, you never knew how many strokes to expect. Knowing I only had two left, encouraged me to proffer both hands in quick succession.

'Why did I cane you?' Mum asked.

'Uh?' I couldn't help the involuntary question, but she met my gaze with a hard stare.

'I said, "Why did I cane you?"'

'Because I didn't wash the clothing,' I mumbled through gritted teeth.

'Now you know better. When I ask you to do something, you do it straight away. Is that clear?'

'Yes, Mum.'

'Good. Now get it done.'

'Yes, ma.'

It became apparent that Mum used the same tone whenever she was mad at someone: a certain cadence in her voice, a definite giveaway. Taiwo, who hated being caned, exploited this. As soon as she heard that tone, she would bolt to the next-door neighbour and remain there, inconsolable, until they came home with her to placate Mum. The culture demanded that Mum listen to the entreaties of the neighbours and shelve the intended punishment. However, having pleaded on her behalf, the same culture gave the intervening neighbours a vested interest in my sister's behaviour. Therefore, many people monitored her actions. But I preferred my privacy and never once involved a neighbour. Also, since Mum was disciplined in her caning, it made it bearable. She gave you two, four or six strokes, depending on the severity of the offence (Mum liked even numbers), and always on your hands.

*

Family was paramount to Mum, and she was the centre of her siblings' universe. She had grown up in a polygamous home, her mother being the third of my maternal grandfather's three wives. Besides the seven surviving children my grandmother bore, Mum had five other half-sisters and one half-brother. Despite being the fifth of my grandmother's children, Mum held a lot of sway. At first, I thought it was because she had been to England, but watching her in action, I realised she was drawn to people and they to her. An attentive and impartial listener, she was never afraid to tell people they were wrong, even when they were older than her. The downside to Mum's skills was that various uncles and aunties were constant visitors in our home.

Most of Mum's full siblings lived in Lagos, and they all preferred living as close as possible to each other. After we left Morocco Road, one by one, they all moved until they lived within walking distance of our new flat. At first, I thought it was a coincidence, but future moves proved my theory. One of my uncles was polygamous like his father and had two wives. In polygamous families, regardless of age, wives were ranked in seniority based on who married into the family first. My uncle's two wives loathed each other, so he solved this problem by keeping the junior wife with his mother in the village. However, after a while, fed up with not seeing enough of him, the junior wife packed her bags and moved to Lagos. Within weeks of both wives staying in the same house, they were at each other's throats.

As always, the role of peacemaker fell to Mum. Evening after evening, both women turned up and tabled their disputes. As the weeks sailed by and the quarrels continued, Mum decided they needed to stay apart during the day. The junior wife would spend the daytime at our home and return to hers in the evening when my uncle could manage his wives himself.

Mum's decision became the backdrop to my next skirmish with Auntie Abebi. My relationship with her was still fraught and neither of us disguised our dislike of the other. One morning, during the half-term break, Auntie Abebi and I were both at home when my aunt arrived with her youngest child, a five-month-old baby. Around noon, she changed the baby's nappy and decided not to put a clean one on her. Then she placed the bare-bottomed baby on my bed for a nap. Worried that the baby would soil my mattress, I approached my aunt, confident that as she was a wife in my mother's family, culturally, I had seniority over her. Although I was only thirteen, she had to listen to me.

I found my aunt in the back courtyard chatting to Auntie Abebi. 'Auntie, can you put a nappy on the baby, please?'

'Why does she need to do that?' Auntie Abebi barked.

Keeping my focus on my aunt, I ignored the intrusion.

'I don't want to put a nappy on her. She has a nappy rash, and her bottom needs some air,' my aunt said.

'I understand that Auntie, but if she wees or poos, that would ruin my mattress.' *Surely, she could see my logic.* My aunt stayed quiet.

'If you don't want to put a nappy on her, can we put her on a mat instead?' I figured I could rinse the mat if necessary, and it would dry a lot quicker than my mattress. After a few moments, my aunt made a move, and I sighed in relief.

'You don't have to do anything she says,' Auntie Abebi declared.

My aunt paused, looked at me, looked at Auntie Abebi, then sat back down.

My nostrils flared. 'Auntie, please!'

'Ignore her,' quipped Auntie Abebi.

My aunt remained seated, and the rage that had been simmering inside my gut bubbled to the surface.

'Fine, if you won't remove her, I will.'

Teeth clenched, I stomped to the bedroom and pulled a mat onto the floor. Silently, I picked up the slumbering baby and gently laid her on the mat. Although I was mad, I didn't want to wake her. Auntie Abebi strolled into the bedroom, with my aunt in tow. As soon as she saw what I had done, Auntie Abebi picked the baby up and placed her on the bed. Less careful than I was before, I lifted the baby and put her back on the mat. The once sleeping child opened her eyes wide, saw the contorted faces of two angry teenagers standing over her and let out a loud wail. Her mother, only now realising that neither of us would give in, picked her up and went home.

*

At 8 p.m. that evening, there was a rapping knock on the front door. I opened it and came face to face with my uncle. I took one glimpse at the ice in his eyes and the twitching vein in his neck and stepped back. He pushed past me and demanded, 'Where is your mother?' Hearing her brother, Mum emerged from her bedroom. As I disappeared back into the bedroom, Mum asked him what was wrong. While my uncle ranted in the parlour, I prepared myself for what was coming. Soon Mum hollered, 'Funmi, Abebi, both of you, here, now!' We both entered the living room where Mum, Dad and a slightly calmer uncle awaited. 'What happened with your uncle's baby earlier today?' Dad asked.

Auntie Abebi fell to both knees, and with tears running down her face, she relayed the events of the afternoon. But the way she told it, she was just trying to prevent me from being unkind to the baby. Arms crossed over my torso, I directed a baleful glare at her tears and feigned contrition. It was all an act. My uncle and possibly Mum would believe her, yet I couldn't bring myself to adopt the same humble stance.

As she spoke, my uncle interjected, 'See, I told you this child of yours is *asa*. Too feisty, too cold. She has no respect. If you don't do something soon, she will bring shame and disgrace on you both, especially you,' he pointed to Mum. 'A good child belongs to its father, a bad one is all down to its mother.'

Dad stopped the tirade in its tracks. 'Can you at least wait and let each one of them tell their story first?'

My uncle stopped talking, and Auntie Abebi continued. Once she finished, Dad turned to me.

'So, what happened from your point of view?'

After I narrated my version of the events, Dad settled into judge mode. Turning to Auntie Abebi, he gave his verdict. 'You deliberately goaded her and ignored the point she made about the mattress. Given that you are older, that is disappointing.' Auntie Abebi had the grace to look chastised. He turned to me. 'It was unfair of you to turn the baby into a ping-pong ball.' With an encompassing look he ordered, 'Now both of you, apologise to your uncle at once.'

I swallowed the bile in my throat, knelt before my uncle and said sorry. He glowered at me before shaking his head in disgust. Dad dismissed us. 'You can both go now.' As we rose and headed back to the bedroom, I noticed the sneer on Auntie Abebi's face. From then on, the unspoken battle lines were drawn. As I settled on my bed with a book, I heard Dad tell my uncle that his wife, being the adult, should have known better. I smiled. I could always rely on Dad to be fair.

*

Living at home, I began getting to grips with the Lagos street life. Lagos was an overcrowded city, and everywhere you looked, it heaved. Houses, classrooms, streets, buses, all seemed to contain more people than they should. Every day, a cacophony of sounds filled the air. Bus drivers pressed their horns incessantly, to warn pedestrians and other cars to get out of their way and partly to ease boredom. Amid the blaring horns rose the shouts of bus conductors announcing their bus's next destination, and petty traders advertising their wares.

Above this din, music shops blasted the dulcet tones of King Sunny Ade from his latest album. Not to be outdone, born-again Christians armed with megaphones proclaimed the second coming of Christ, and doom and damnation for all those who failed to heed their warning. This was Lagos, an undecipherable mixture of organised chaos sprinkled with the grit and determination of people resolutely going about their daily business.

My journeys to school presented unexpected challenges. Lagosians did not queue for anything. Every morning, throngs of people milled around the bus stop looking to catch one of the scarce buses. No bus timetables, or idea of when the next bus would come along, left people desperate to board the one in front of their noses. When a bus rolled in, people clawed, punched and pushed their way onto it. This was more than my tiny frame could handle daily. I needed new skills to avoid getting to school every day bruised, battered and late.

Two kinds of vehicles plied Lagos streets, disguised as public transport. The first, called *molue*, large Mercedes Benz buses, ran the major roads and inter-city routes. Their smaller cousins, Volkswagen camper vans that Lagosians called *danfo*, operated in the suburbs. On my journeys, I noticed people boarding moving buses before they reached the bus stop. To beat the crowds, I tried it. I walked a hundred yards away from the bus stop, towards the oncoming traffic, and waited. *Molues* always had their doors open. Alert and ready, I prepared myself for the next one.

As the vehicle whizzed past me, I ran alongside it, picking up speed until I matched that of the slowing bus. Just before it got to the bus stop, I skipped, hopped and jumped onto the moving vehicle. I fist bumped the air, congratulating myself. It did not occur to me once that had I mis-stepped, I might have ended up underneath its wheels rather than inside the bus. Over time, I perfected the technique until it became second nature, even at faster speeds.

I learned the hard way to have the correct bus fare at all times. On one journey, I handed a one naira note to the conductor. Instead of giving me back my change, he asked me to wait. That wasn't unusual, as conductors often collected all the fares, before giving out change. However, this time, despite several reminders, the conductor ignored my request for my change. As my stop came into view, I became more agitated. Just as I was ready to alight, the conductor held out a note and pointed to the two people also getting off behind me. 'Here's the change for the three of you, thirty kobo each.' With that, he jumped back in the bus as it took off, leaving three bemused strangers in his wake. We ended up buying sweets to get change to share.

When Mum and Dad couldn't afford the bus fare, I walked to school. Municipal street planning was restricted to the posh parts of Lagos. In the back-end suburbs like Shomolu and Bariga, people built their homes wherever they could buy land. This made for interesting street layouts. There were no pavements for pedestrians. Wider roads had sufficient space for people to walk alongside the traffic. But on smaller roads, people, bicycles, motorcycles, cars and buses all jostled for the same space. Some major roads were tarred, most were not, which made for a constant swirl of suffocating dust. Open gutters often ran right along the major roads. The dust, the stench from the gutters, the exhaust from the passing traffic, combined with the sweltering heat and humid air, made for the most uncomfortable treks.

Although catching a bus was fraught, the daily sexual assaults when walking were far worse. Inside, *danfos* had three rows of benches and conductors crammed four or five people on each one. The conductors did not sit, instead preferring to hang precariously on the railings of the open sliding doors as the buses commuted up and down. This put them in a unique and advantageous position, as I found out one day, when to my horror, a conductor slapped my bottom as his bus went by.

From then on, I walked facing oncoming traffic. That way, I could at least try to pre-empt the bus conductors' intentions by ducking as they approached. Even so, I had to be careful. I once ducked too hard into other pedestrians, who pushed me back into the path of moving vehicles. Having to make the daily choice between getting touched or being in an accident was tiresome. In defence, I would hit out at the offending boys, and when my hands connected with my target, my elation knew no bounds.

CHAPTER SEVENTEEN

Mama Yaba

Dad decided it was time I met my great aunt, his mother's older sister. Mama Yaba (who lived in Yaba) was a legend, so everyone greeted the news with curiosity.

'I'm glad I'm not going,' my brother Kehinde said. Taiwo nodded her agreement.

'You won't enjoy the experience,' Auntie Abebi crowed, relishing the idea that I was about to face something unpleasant.

'Don't worry about it,' Mum said, 'you will be fine. Just do what your dad tells you.'

I wasn't sure how I felt about the whole thing, but I understood their reactions. At least half of the extended family, and that was a multitude of people, thought she was a raving lunatic. The other half considered her a cleanliness-obsessed eccentric.

Mama Yaba, a wealthy, childless widow, lived on her own, which was almost unheard of. With so many less fortunate extended family members to choose from, Mama Yaba need not lack companionship, but she wanted nothing to do with family. Rumour had it, she had disowned every member of the family in her will. That she even had a will was shocking, and to the superstitious Yoruba tantamount to sending a hand-written invitation to death himself. It petrified the elders that she might die, and nobody would know for months. There was no dignity in that, for her or the family.

A socialite in her youth, Mama Yaba had married a Ghanaian businessman. Her friends reflected her wealth and status and included the wife of the State Governor. As a teenager, Dad lived with her for a while. But that story ended with her denying knowledge of his identity, before handing him to the police for a minor infraction. Still, as her only family in Lagos, Dad felt obligated and duty bound to check on her welfare. That responsibility would become mine.

On the way to Mama Yaba, Dad warned me about the dos and don'ts: 'Stand behind me at all times, unless instructed otherwise. Do not touch the bannisters as you climb the stairs to her front door. Take your shoes off at the door. Do not sit down unless she offers you a seat.' Given the rumours circulating, I didn't need convincing. As we strolled up the street toward Mama Yaba's house, I realised she lived in a more affluent part of Lagos. Mama Yaba's neighbourhood, off Herbert Macaulay Way, contained tree-lined boulevards, with proper pavements for pedestrians.

Dad turned into Montgomery Road, stopped and pointed. There it sat, right on the corner: Mama Yaba's house, one of several she owned. Rather than the typical box shapes common in Lagos, the front facade of the house rounded gently, to follow the curvature of the plot. With the entire building enclosed behind a wall, I couldn't see a thing on the ground floor level. But the first floor towered, with three large louvred windows set into the curved section. On the flat side, four casement windows, each framed by an extruding, mint-green architrave, stood in sharp relief against the building's cream background. It made a striking pose, one I had never seen before.

Dad strolled up to the side gate and pressed the doorbell. While we waited, I studied the rest of the structure. Mama Yaba lived in the first-floor apartment, the ground floor having been converted into offices. A tiny walkway connected the building and the entrance to her doorway to an open, walled terrace on the right. Mama Yaba poked her head out of her window and asked who was calling. Dad identified himself and prostrated himself right there on the street. Mama Yaba threw down her keys so we could let ourselves in. As we walked through the compound, I noticed that the lower half of the terrace doubled as a carport. I put each foot in front of the other and followed Dad up the stairs, careful to avoid touching the bannisters. At the door, Dad slipped off his shoes, and I did likewise. Once inside, Dad introduced me as his eldest.

Given her reputation, Mama Yaba greeted us warmly, before allowing us to sit in her hallway. My first impressions were that Mama Yaba carried herself with poise reminiscent of an English lady, which was rather odd, as I was certain she had never left Nigeria. Unlike all the family elders who wore traditional clothing, Mama Yaba looked scandalous in a 1950's style midi frock. Sleeveless and gathered at the waist, it came down to just below her knees, showing off shapely ankles and feet tucked into dainty slippers. I swear I could see the outline of a bra underneath Mama's dress. *How could this woman be the sister of my barely clad, bosom-swinging grandmother?*

*

At five-foot six, Mama Yaba was much taller than both Dad and my grandmother. I peered intently, trying to find some connection between them. Except for her oval face and the three tribal marks on each cheek, I saw no similarities. In stark contrast to her sister, Mama Yaba's tanned skin tone made her, by far, the fairest member of the family. With high cheekbones, sparky eyes, and lips with just the right amount of fullness, she could easily have been a model in her youth. She was beautiful despite the lines marring her cheeks. I was still contemplating the puzzle when I remembered overhearing my cousins say that Mama Yaba was my grandmother's half-sister. *That must explain it.*

Mama placed a tray of biscuits and two cans of Coca-Cola on a stool next to us. My mouth salivated as the sweet aroma of caramel and malt wafted up my nostrils. I couldn't remember the last time I drank Coke or ate biscuits. Mama poured the drink into glasses before handing one first to Dad, then to me. I thanked her before taking a sip. The ice-cold liquid trickled down, easing my parched throat. Moments later, Dad caught me eyeing the biscuits. With an imperceptible nod, he gave his permission. I reached out and plucked one off the tray.

I had just bitten down when Mama said, 'So you were born in London? Do you still remember it?'

I nodded in quick succession, trying to swallow the biscuit before answering.

'Tell me, were the streets as clean as they say?'

Was she testing whether I could talk and eat at the same time? I gulped and swiped my mouth with the back of my hand.

'Yes ma, they were.'

'I bet they are much cleaner than in this filthy country. *Obun!* Full of muck! That's what they are around here,' she cackled, shaking with mirth.

I watched in awe as she bounced from one foot to the other, enjoying her own joke. I wasn't sure how to respond to her disparaging remarks about her fellow countrymen, so I kept silent. She leaned towards me, as if sharing a secret, 'I bet you can't wait to go back.' Her eyes twinkled, inviting me to comment.

I thought it prudent to agree with everything Mama said, so I nodded. I was desperate to return to London, and cleanliness had nothing to do with it. Still, while I didn't think London was immaculate, it beat dusty Lagos. Mama engaged me in more conversation about my studies. Her smiles suggested she liked me well enough, and Dad's shoulders relaxed. We took our leave soon after, with a promise from Dad that I would be back. From then on, I paid Mama quarterly visits, to check on her welfare on behalf of the rest of the family.

The rumours about Mama Yaba's obsessive cleanliness were not exaggerated. At my first visit following our introduction, she asked me to fetch a bag from her living room. When I entered the room, my steps faltered and came to an abrupt halt. The drawn curtains let in just a shard of light, but it was enough to see that every single item of furniture was shrouded under plastic dust sheets. Even the sofa was covered up. I doubted she used it much. Almost macabre, the room conjured images of an abandoned, haunted house, without the dust and cobwebs. The bag Mama wanted sat on a mantel near the window. I wanted to linger but knew better. I grabbed the bag and hurried back to the corridor.

On the way home, I wondered why she lived like that. When I told Dad what I saw, he shed some light on the topic. Mama Yaba was obsessive about dirt from childhood, a trait inherited from my great-grandmother. Her older sister, whom I hadn't met, was reputedly worse in her youth but had mellowed after bearing nine children. To some extent, my grandmother had similar tendencies, and it explained her constant haranguing about clean floors and clean laundry.

*

On my third visit, Mama Yaba asked me to help clean the terrace outside her apartment. Mama Yaba poured copious amounts of soapy water on the concrete floor while I scrubbed with a long-handled bristle brush. Sweat trickled down my brow as I baked under the high noon sun. Suddenly, Mama Yaba pointed and screeched, 'There! There's a cobweb in that corner, make sure you get it.' She threw the water in her hands at the offending cobweb and jumped backwards. I stopped and stared. Mama Yaba, it seemed, was scared witless of spiders. For the next hour and a half, she kept fetching more water as she urged me to scrub harder. But now she just handed the bucket over, refusing to step foot on the terrace.

'They are gone, Mama,' I whined, as she headed back for another run.

Mama Yaba paused mid-movement from the safety of the doorway. 'Are you sure?'

'Yes, Mama, they are all gone.' I sighed and massaged my temples. The hours of drudgery in the sun were getting to me.

'Let's add one more bucket.' She disappeared into the kitchen.

Nine buckets later, I just about convinced her that all the cobwebs and their architects were gone, and the concrete gleamed as if it had been freshly rendered. All that hard work made us both hungry, so Mama Yaba let me sit in the corridor as she boiled some yams for lunch.

Despite my tiredness, it felt more than a little uncomfortable watching Mama Yaba cook. I'd been told it was a terrible child that sat while the elders worked. I wondered why she wouldn't let me help. *Did she think there was a cobweb or two still lurking on my clothing?* I giggled. Mama sent me a quizzical glance which wiped the smile off my face. It wouldn't do for her to think I was laughing at her. I remembered the pristine state of her living room on my previous visit. With her aversion to cobwebs, I reckoned she cleaned and dusted it several times a day.

My gaze followed Mama as she pottered around her kitchen, which was as modern as her house, with built-in cupboards, a gas cooker and not one but two sinks. Again, I marvelled at the differences between her home and mine. Our kitchen was less than half the size of Mama's, its only furniture, shelves, a small kerosene stove and an even smaller wooden stool.

After lunch, Mama made me place my dirty plate on the floor, near the sink nearest to the kitchen door. After she finished eating, she washed my plate in the first sink, then transferred it to the second sink for a second wash along with hers. As she worked, she talked, mainly about all things dirty. I suspected she was lonely, and my visits gave her someone to talk to. After doing the dishes, Mama put them into different cupboards. It seemed she kept the dishes she used for guests away from those she used for herself. When it was time to leave, Mama drew a five naira note from her wallet and handed it to me as a gift. I beamed and thanked her profusely. Despite my tiredness, there was a spring in my step as I headed home, thinking of what I could buy with that much money.

For all her eccentricity, Mama Yaba was amusing company and generous. Unlike my grandmother, I never felt threatened or censured in her presence, and at the end of each visit I would depart laden with gifts of money, shoes or bags. The rest of the extended family soon got to hear about this, and jealous cousins started calling me *Omo Mama Yaba* (Mama Yaba's baby). While I disliked the moniker, interestingly, Mum liked it, I suspect, for what it stood for – the richest and one of the most important members of the family favoured her daughter.

CHAPTER EIGHTEEN

I'm All Woman

Without being fully aware of the fact, subtle physical changes signalled my budding womanhood. One morning, I stood in front of the mirror and soaked up my image. I'd grown an awful lot since leaving England. *Would Nan even recognise me if she saw me?* Moving my neck left then right, I scrutinised my reflection. Wide-set eyes and heavy lids, framed by gently arched brows, stared back at me. I fluttered my eyelashes and smiled at my own silliness. I liked my nose. The short bridge fanned out into a more rounded apex. I sighed at the full and plump lips dominating my face. I puckered and moved them in different directions, wishing they were a tad thinner. In my head, thinner lips looked better.

I scanned my body, below my neck, and the down-turned corners of my mouth lifted. My previously flat chest now sported two gentle mounds. I could just about cup each one with my hand. On closer inspection, the right one was smaller than the left one. *Was that even normal?* I would need a bra soon and wondered how to buy one. I continued the perusal, both intrigued and scared at the changes I saw. Lower down, my hips flared, revealing a sprinkling of soft downy hair at the apex of my legs. I had noticed hair in my armpits a few months back. I hadn't realised it would grow in more places. *Did everyone go through this? Were the other girls hiding the same changes underneath their uniforms?*

There were other changes. Every time I was near Sesan, one of the older Adeleke boys, my heart tried to escape my chest. I needed to discuss this with someone, but who? I wished for the days when I was friends with Dayo and Busola. I could have frank conversations with those two, but my new comrades were different. Ade was still flat-chested and thought girls who had periods were wicked. She would rather die than talk about such things, and Dupe wasn't much better. It would have to be Lolade, I decided. Her chest was bigger than mine, so she was probably going through similar changes.

At lunch time, I dragged Lolade into a corner outside the classroom. Careful to avoid anyone overhearing, I whispered into her ear. 'I've noticed hair growing down there. Is that the same with you?'

'Down where?' she asked with a smirk.

'Don't be silly, you know where.' I tilted my head and signalled with my eyes.

She smiled. 'Yeah.'

'Phew! I thought it was just me.'

She rolled her eyes.

'Guess what? Every time I'm near Sesan, my heart beats faster. Why do you think that is?'

She gave me a knowing look. 'You're the Mills and Boon expert. You tell me.'

'I like him.'

'You don't say!' Lolade planted both hands on her hips and pulled her chin down to her neck in mock surprise.

'But why him?' I continued. 'His brother looks similar, and I don't feel a thing when he's around.'

'How should I know?' she shrugged. The bell rang, signalling the end of lunch time and our conversation.

As we walked to the bus stop after school, I asked Lolade where she bought her bras from. 'Yaba market,' she replied. That was splendid news. It was near Mama Yaba's house.

When I asked Dad if I could visit Mama Yaba the following Saturday, he raised an eyebrow. Usually, he had to remind me to go. I decided I'd make my purchase on the way home, so I wouldn't have to explain any packages to Mama Yaba. The visit passed in a blur, my thoughts fixated on my impending purchase. After a few hours, I said goodbye and armed with the cash she had given me on this and my previous visit, I headed for the market.

*

Lolade told me I needed the second-hand clothes section of the market, which was dominated by Igbo traders. They were in a spill-over area, next to the nearly defunct railway tracks. When I got off the bus at the Yaba depot, the bustling bodies heading in all directions made it hard to see more than a few footsteps ahead. I walked a hundred yards, pushing through the throngs until I reached my destination. Vendors lined both sides of the tracks, far into the horizon, each stall, if you could call it that, comprising a plastic sheet on the ground and the occasional table. On top of the sheets, clothing lay strewn in a jumbled mass, overflowing onto the train tracks. Trains still plied the route but were so rare that the vendors disregarded the danger. Behind each batch of clothes, the traders stood sentry as they watched prospective customers with eagle eyes. In the background, the sound of bus conductors announcing their destination mingled with the hum of hundreds of haggling voices.

I skipped in excitement and made my way to the first vendor that caught my attention. Seeing my approach, the vendor's apprentice eyed me up and down and whistled. My scowl only encouraged him. 'Come on Sisi, you dey fine kampe.' He reached out a hand to touch my chest. I slapped it away and dodged out of reach. Undeterred, he tried again. I was just a plaything, lightening up the dullness of his day. 'No be like that now, fine Sisi,' he sneered. A few of his fellow traders tittered in amusement. He clearly had no intention of leaving me alone. I hissed through my teeth, turned my back and searched for a different vendor.

I continued along the railway line until I reached a section with a thinner crowd and another stall caught my eye. From the array of bras, panties, camisoles, I homed in on a white broderie anglaise bra, edged with pink, eyelet lace. The pale-blue ribbon threaded through the eyelet ended in a dainty bow right at the centre. I picked it up and ran a finger over the front, before turning it over. The gently padded underside of the bra was just what I needed to give the semblance of a fuller cup. I found and checked the label. St Michaels: 28A, it said. It was a UK brand and considered better than local merchandise.

For a moment, my thoughts wandered back to England, to the occasional trip to the market with Mum before we left London. Both markets bore similar hallmarks: the noise, traders and customers, except in London, goods were laid on tables or carts, and I didn't remember wandering hands trying to touch me. A jolt from a passer-by brought me back to the present. I didn't know what size I needed, but the bra in my hands looked small enough. I slanted a glance at the other women surrounding me. Some were cupping the bras over their bosoms and checking the fit there and then. *Could I?* I cast another surreptitious gaze around and zoomed in on a pair of male eyes watching me with a knowing gleam. I turned my back on the voyeur and quickly lifted the bra to my chest. It looked like a good fit.

I called out to the vendor. 'Madam, how much?'

'Two naira.'

'One naira,' I countered. She hissed. I had gone too low.

I upped the offer. 'One naira, twenty.' She ignored me.

'One naira, fifty!' That got her attention. She looked at me, trying to decipher how serious I was.

'One naira, eighty,' she returned.

Although I wanted that bra, I had observed Mum haggling before and I knew that for a good buy, I should knock at least a quarter off the price.

'One naira, fifty, final offer.'

She shook her head before attending to another customer. I called her bluff and walked away.

'Sisi, *Oya*, come.'

Triumphant, I turned back, pulled my wallet out and extracted the cash, careful not to let anyone see how much I had. Yaba market was notorious for thievery. I handed over the payment for my purchase, which she stuffed in a plastic bag.

*

It was hard to describe the feelings coursing through my veins as I made my way home, all because I had bought a bra. I guess it was that sense of triumph at navigating another first. I could have asked Mum to buy me one, since she still purchased the rest of my clothing and underwear. But there were two problems with that. I imagined broaching the topic with her and cringed, and to be honest, I'd rather avoid the risk she might say no. Dad was the other option, but I remembered the embarrassing puberty talk. The big question was, would anyone realise the difference, and if they did, what would their reaction be?

Mum was the first to notice. 'Are you wearing a bra?' she asked right in front of Dad.

My cheeks warmed. 'Yes, ma.'

A puzzled look replaced the curiosity in her eyes. 'Where did you get it from?'

'I bought it at Yaba market.'

She and Dad exchanged glances, one of those silent messages I could never decipher. Mum let the topic drop, but the next day she asked me what size I had bought. A week later, she surprised me with an additional bra. I received the gift happily but realised that if I had asked Mum in the first place, I wouldn't have had to spend my money. I revised the advice to self: *Ask first, then if the answer is no, do it anyway.*

*

The Adelekes were boarders, so during term time, I spent my evenings at home. However, once the school breaks arrived, I passed time hanging out in their front yard with other kids. A waist-high brick fence shielded the large courtyard from the street. In its centre, a huge Mimosa tree cast its shadow, providing much-needed relief from the sweltering heat. Even at sundown, temperatures rarely dropped below 23°C. So, this was our favourite spot to hang, as we discussed crazy teachers, science projects and disco parties, something I was yet to experience.

One evening, as I made my way across the street, Sesan came out of his house. Our eyes met and held for a second and my heart skipped a beat. Hands in both pockets, he sauntered through the yard, meeting me at the fence. 'Hey,' he smiled the welcome. I returned the greeting, then sneaked a peek at everyone else, but no one paid us any heed. 'You look nice,' he whispered. He, too, cast a furtive glance around before turning back to me. I beamed at my first genuine compliment from the opposite sex. 'Thank you,' I said, refusing to meet his eye. I felt his gaze on me, then he leaned against the brickwork, his long legs stretched in front of him and stared into the horizon.

We settled into companionable silence for a moment, the Mimosa tree's fern-like leaves providing a cooling breeze, as they swayed in tune with the wind. I stared at my admirer. At sixteen, his five-foot nine frame towered above mine. I was thirteen and under five foot. He looked smart. Green polo shirt, beige khaki trousers, short hair, almost crew cut, and nails neatly trimmed, he clearly took pains over his appearance. With the prominent brow ridge dominating his oval face, he wasn't handsome in the classic sense, yet I admired what I saw.

Sensing my perusal, he glanced at me, flashing perfectly aligned, white teeth. As his smiled widened, two tiny dimples winked at me. He took my hand, and I let him. As we both gazed at our conjoined hands, I couldn't control the delight, the tremors or my racing heart, and I liked it. That week, we spent every evening together, away from prying eyes, under the cover of the Mimosa tree, talking and stealing kisses we hoped no one would see. My first visceral and emotional connection to someone else was heady stuff. But half-term breaks only lasted so long, and soon my new boyfriend headed back to school.

CHAPTER NINETEEN

Here She Comes Again

I watched through the louvred windows of the parlour as the rain beat a steady rhythm on the cement front yard. Fat rivulets of water fell from the sky, the thunderstorm typical for June. At the height of the rainy season, they came, suddenly and often. I didn't mind the rain, but hated thunder and its twin, lightning. The latter could kill, and I had an abiding fear of death. Sesan once said the thunder was God rearranging his furniture. That made me laugh and reduced my fear.

Not much moved outside, pedestrians having taken shelter in empty doorways or under the few trees gracing people's front yards. It was a week into the school holidays following the end of my year in Form 3. Hence, for once, there was nothing much to do. A slight commotion drew me from my reverie. *What could possibly be happening out there in this weather?* I stretched my neck through the window to get a better view. 'Eh! Mama! *E kaabo!*' Our next-door neighbour squealed the welcome. My faced tightened and I squeezed my eyes shut, savouring the last few moments of freedom. She was back. My grandmother, Mama Nurodu, blown in, just like the storm raging outside. I got up to let her in.

Over the next two days, the household came alive with neighbours and relatives popping over to smile their greetings. In return, Mama gave out gifts she had brought with her: a bottle of palm oil for some, snacks for others and, of course, her canes for the children. Mama claimed her bed, and I went back to sleeping on the floor. Older and more confident, I no longer feared Mama as much, having built up a picture of her past and what made her tick by listening surreptitiously to adult conversations. I also understood a lot more about the extended family.

The fourth of six siblings, Mama had two older half-sisters from her mother's first marriage, and contrary to what I had heard, she shared both parents with Mama Yaba and two younger brothers. Unlike her siblings, Mama dropped out of school and never learned to read or write, which might explain why she tried to beat the learning into me. I wondered whether she suffered the same fate as a child.

All Mama's siblings were more affluent than her. Mama Yaba moved in the upper echelons of Lagos society, and Mama Ijebu, another of her sisters, married into royalty. One brother worked in construction and the other in a bank. The family had royal connections. Proud of their status, they weren't afraid to brag about it. In contrast, my paternal grandfather's family history was shrouded in mystery. I once asked Dad why we didn't bear his name. He was silent for aeons before replying. 'My dad died while I was still young, and I grew up in Mama's family.'

'What about the rest of your dad's family?'

'Remember Mama Ita-ale? She is my dad's sister.'

'The family has only two members?'

'The family is a lot larger than that, but they are actually not Ijebu. My dad came from Modakeke, a town near Ife. The rest of the family are back there.'

'Why don't we ever visit or see them?'

Dad stared into the distance. I wasn't sure if he was just concentrating on his driving or thinking about my question.

Then he sighed. 'Something bad happened in the family, so bad that my dad made me swear on his deathbed, never to go back there. I have an older half-sister somewhere, but we lost touch after my dad died.'

'Wow,' I breathed. I hadn't imagined anything that tragic in the family, but it answered a lot of my questions.

Older and less agile, Mama's arms no longer reached the centre of her back. So, once a week, I helped her scrub it before leaving her to her ablutions. I had paid little attention to the etchings on Mama's back before. Now I did. The black tattoos stood in sharp relief against Mama's brown skin, starting from just below her nape down to her hips. Each row depicted a delicate pattern of tiny diagonal strokes, with alternating left or right slants, followed by a row of stars. It was a beautiful work of art.

I knew that in Mama's time, only the most daring of young ladies used such tattoos to adorn their bodies and attract a mate. I couldn't imagine having that done to my entire back. Mama must have been quite the girl in her youth, I mused. Her tattoos showed she possessed a high tolerance for pain, and I wondered if that made her less sensitive to the pain she inflicted on us.

*

Four weeks after Mama arrived, a seismic shift in the country's political fabric occurred. A bloodless coup displaced General Yakubu Gowon in his absence, while he was on an international summit in Uganda, and replaced him with Brigadier Murtala Mohammed. I barely registered the immediate changes brought by the coup. Its significance only unfolded later.

Meanwhile, Mama launched into the next phase of my re-education with renewed fervour, hoping I'd make a suitable bride someday. One afternoon she sauntered into the kitchen. Mum hovered over Auntie Abebi, who was cooking, while I sat in the dining area next to the kitchen. 'Mama Funmi,' Mama said.

'Ma?' Mum replied.

'Why are you training someone else's daughter at the expense of your own?'

A terse silence followed. 'Funmi, come and take over,' Mum said.

'Yes, ma.' I moved to the kitchen, took the stool vacated by Auntie Abebi and smashed the *amala* against the side of the pot.

The next day, Mama lined my siblings up in front of her. 'From now on,' she said, 'you will not call your big sister by her first name. Is that clear?' Their little heads bobbed up and down, while I stared in shocked silence. Afterwards, it was strange hearing my siblings call me Sister Funmi, although I soon got used to it. Next, on the curriculum, came a lesson in poultry cooking. But before that, I had to catch, kill, clean and cut up the chicken. Although I'd watched many times, this was a job done only by Auntie Abebi or Mum.

The easiest bit was catching the chicken. Mum brought live chickens home from the market with a piece of string attached to both legs. The string was long enough to allow the chickens to move about, but not so fast that you couldn't catch them. To fatten them up, we fed the chickens dried corn kernels once a day. I picked up the tin of corn and rattled it. The chickens, conditioned to the sound, came running, and in less than a minute, half a dozen squawking birds surrounded my feet. While the birds were busy pecking at the corn, I swooped and grabbed the wings of the one I wanted.

The captured bird screeched, attempting to flap its wings and escape, but I held on. I had seen the next bit done several times, and it required precision. I moved the bird to the edge of a small gutter within the courtyard and trapped its feet and wings under each of my feet.

Grasping the chicken's neck with my left hand, I picked up a knife with my right one, pausing as the enormity of what I was about to do sank in. My siblings and Mama had all congregated to watch my first kill. My heart thumped as I scanned my audience. I looked at Mama and she nodded, telling me to go ahead. I gulped a deep breath and lowered the knife.

Three to four see-saw motions later, the animal's blood spurted into the gutter. Its body jerked violently, the movement vibrating into my feet. I jumped. 'Don't let it get up!' Mama shouted the instruction. For a second, I froze, horrified, as I imagined myself chasing a headless chicken around the courtyard. I jolted myself back to reality and held it down. Soon after, the jerks slowed to intermittent twitches before stopping altogether.

While I was dispatching the bird, Auntie Abebi lit a wood fire under a large cauldron of water. Wisps of steam, dancing on the surface of the water, signalled its readiness. I tucked the bird's dangling head underneath a wing, lifted it up and took it over to the cauldron. Holding it by a wing, I dipped it in the simmering water, swishing it back and forth so the water soaked through the feathers. I pulled it out and immediately started plucking the feathers.

'Ow!' I yelped and blew hard on my fingers, trying to cool them down. The scalding water had softened the feathers, making them easy to pluck, but it also burned my fingers.

'Give it a few seconds first,' Mama said. Moments later, everyone, including my siblings, joined in the task, pulling feathers from every angle. No one spoke. The grown-ups had taught us that if we did, the feathers would grow back. Although I knew this wasn't true, the silence made the kids pluck faster. I dipped the bird again, repeating the process several times, until its naked skin gleamed.

Almost every part of the chicken was edible, including the neck, liver and gizzard. Mama hovered, a slight smile on her lips as I chopped and divided the chicken in a tray. Satisfied that I had everything under control, she left. I slit the gizzard along its seam, scraped out the contents, peeled off the top layer of skin before adding it to the pile of meat. Almost done, I picked up the liver and considered the most difficult task of all: separating it from the bile sac and its contaminates.

Back on the cutting block, I made the first tentative cut, then checked it. I needed to keep the sac intact, while saving as much liver as possible. I put it back down, made another nick in the fleshy mound and watched in horror as the sac's green contents spewed out. 'Mama! Mama!' I screamed, my insides a quivering mess. I needed to save the chicken before the slimy gunk touched it. Mama arrived, took one look at the tray and yelled, '*Ororo!* [bile] Somebody get the salt and a bowl.' Kehinde dashed indoors for the salt while Brother Femi produced a bowl. Auntie Abebi, Mama and I frantically scooped the chicken into the bowl.

I groaned as the green sludge skirted and enveloped the last few pieces of chicken still in the tray. *Now what?* Sweat broke on my brow. I couldn't imagine the chicken pieces being thrown away. We couldn't afford that kind of luxury. As it was, two or three children often shared a single piece of chicken. Mama snatched the tray out of my hands and scooped the liver into the bin. I stepped back as she moved to the edge of the gutter with the soiled chicken, the salt, which had now appeared and some water. After washing her hands, she rinsed the chicken pieces before rubbing the salt all over them. She repeated this a couple more times and then handed the chicken over to Auntie Abebi.

I paced the courtyard while Auntie Abebi cooked dinner. Until someone tasted the chicken, it was hard to know how big a disaster I had created. To my relief, Mama had salvaged the chicken. The salt, an antidote to the bitterness infused by the bile, saved the day. And to my surprise, instead of the scolding I expected from the grown-ups, besides the small piece of chicken that was my due, I got the chicken's entire neck. This was a Yoruba tradition. Whoever spilled an animal's blood got its neck. As I gnawed on the bony piece, I reflected on the day's events. I couldn't help but wonder what Nan would think when I told her in my next letter I had killed and dismembered a whole chicken.

*

September saw the start of a new academic year. Mama commuted more frequently between Lagos and Ijebu, spending weeks with us at a time. To avoid censure when she was around, I stayed out of her way as much as possible. When she left, life became pleasant again.

I ended the previous academic year much better than in previous years, having been placed 28th out of 154. I was in Form 4B and enjoying the status that came with being a senior. Except for those in Form 5, there was nobody left to punish me. In the first week back at school, I chose eight subjects to study for the West African School Certificate (WASC). The school offered no counselling for future career prospects, so I consulted Mum and Dad for advice. Like all good Yoruba parents, mine were ambitious for me and wanted me in the top-paying and most prestigious professions. I quite liked the idea of becoming a teacher. I still thought about Mr Olowo, my primary school teacher and the way he had inspired me. However, Mum often said no child of hers would be a teacher. They weren't paid or regarded well enough. She even held nurses in higher regard.

'What do you want to be when you finish schooling?' Dad asked when I broached the subject. Before I responded, he continued, 'You could be a doctor, dentist, pharmacist, mmm… or an accountant.'

'For those, I would need to study physics, chemistry and biology.'

Raised eyebrows met mine. 'Is that a problem?'

'They are not my strongest subjects.'

'I guess you will have to work harder.'

His eyes returned to the newspaper in his hands, the conversation at an end. I consoled myself knowing that he had given me four choices of profession. Some of my friends had only one. Ade's dad told her she would study medicine. The fact that she was squeamish and hated the sight of blood did not deter him.

Besides the three sciences, mathematics and English, I also studied Yoruba, English literature and religious studies, all compulsory subjects. However, taking the three sciences meant I had to drop history, a subject I loved. While I did well in most of my subjects, I struggled with chemistry and physics. The latter, I am convinced, was at least partly because of the ineptitude of our physics teacher. Many of us held him in utter contempt, and I had a habit of paying no attention to people I didn't respect.

*

Next to English and English literature, I liked Yoruba the most. We nicknamed our elderly and charming teacher Baba Yoruba. He loved teaching so much, he came back out of retirement, and we loved him right back. Since we were all fluent in Yoruba, Baba Yoruba taught us about the culture, regaling us with stories about glory days gone by, long before the white man came along. I showed a particular interest in learning about marriage customs since, according to Mama, that would be my undoing.

In one lesson, I learned it wasn't unusual, in pre-colonial days, for girls to be betrothed to much older men, sometimes while still in their mother's womb. The man's family secured the bride by paying a hefty dowry while the child grew up. Scandalised, I raised a hand to ask a question. 'Sir, what happened when a girl grew up and decided she didn't like or want to marry the man?'

'She couldn't do that,' he said, 'not unless her parents agreed and returned the dowry.'

'But what if she insisted, they wouldn't force her, would they?'

'Yes, they would.'

'But how, sir?'

'The husband would kidnap her on the way to an errand arranged by her own parents.'

I didn't take my teacher seriously until I got home, and Mum confirmed that one of her classmates was kidnapped on the way home from school.

In another lesson, Baba Yoruba taught us how important it was for a bride to be pure on her wedding night. In the old days, a bride who wasn't a virgin spent the rest of the year followed by a male child. This served a dual purpose of keeping tabs on her and telling the world she couldn't be trusted out on her own.

'Sir, how would they know she wasn't a virgin?' I did not expect the answer he gave.

'She had to provide proof of purity on the wedding night. While the guests celebrated outside, the husband consummated the marriage. If he came out with blood-stained sheets, the guests cheered.'

Horrified that they made something that private so public and glad to be a product of the twentieth century, I stopped asking questions.

Proverbs, I found, were the key to understanding Yoruba culture. Every proverb he taught us underlined a particular way of thinking and behaving, and I understood now why my life in Nigeria was so different from my early childhood. Yoruba culture valued kinship, community and conformity, and one person's mistakes brought shame to the rest of the clan. In Britain, you could be whoever or whatever you wanted, and people took personal responsibility for their actions. Britain had a government-sponsored welfare system for people who fell on hard times. In Nigeria, your family was your only source of help, hence the need to maintain good relations and listen to your kin.

One proverb grated on my nerves more than any other. Translated into English it said 'Let's continue to do things the way they have always been done, so things can remain the way they've always been.' Every time someone said it, I gnashed my teeth. While I understood the cultural differences, I didn't want to be like everybody else, or accept things the way they were. At home, I still got into trouble with my extended family. I wasn't humble enough, I talked back and I interjected during conversations when adults spoke. My uncles showed their disdain by calling me *asa* (too feisty), and their wives whispered behind my back. The culture wanted children to be invisible. I wanted to be heard. I was coming to the stark realisation that no matter how hard I tried, I would never fit in.

CHAPTER TWENTY

Win the Battle, Lose the War

In the six months since taking power in the July 1975 coup, Brigadier Murtala Mohammed, the Head of State, had impressed the nation, or so said all the adults around. He forced swathes of civil servants into early retirement, making more jobs available to younger people. Then he created a new national development plan to tackle corruption and, on 3 February 1976, announced the creation of a new capital for Nigeria. He chose its location, Abuja, in the centre of the country, as a unifying force, since it didn't fall into the territory of the three main ethnic groups. An area of low population density, it would be the first planned city in the country.

The same day, he created seven additional states, one of which joined the Ijebu and Egba Yoruba tribes together in a single state. Ecstatic, Dad put his plans to buy a new car on hold, just so he could have the Ogun State number plates. It seemed that everyone agreed Murtala Mohammed was doing a splendid job changing the country for the better. Charismatic and popular, he was hailed as the country's saviour.

Ten days later, dressed and ready for school, I emerged into the parlour to find Mum, Mama and Auntie Abebi crowded around our faithful old radiogram. I stopped, puzzled, since the only sound coming out of it was a military-style marching tune. Mum looked up and waved me over. 'What happened?' I whispered.

'There's been another coup. We know nothing more.'

'Wow!' *That was worrying. Coups signalled a major change and not always for the better.* 'Should I still go to school?'

'No, it's safer if you stay home today.'

I returned my bag to the bedroom and re-joined the family in the parlour. A voice with a northern accent came over the radio. The speaker identified himself as Lieutenant Colonel Dimka, confirmed the coup and imposed a 6 a.m. to 6 p.m. curfew. He told us to wait for further information and ended the statement with, 'Thank you. We are all together.' I looked at Mum with raised eyebrows. *What on earth did that mean?* She shrugged in reply. The radio resumed playing military music.

Dad walked in fifteen minutes later, having aborted his journey to work, a sombre expression on his face. 'Murtala Mohammed is dead,' he said.

'How do you know?' Mum asked.

'BBC Radio World News in the car.'

We all sank back onto the sofa in contemplative silence. Dad twiddled the controls of the radiogram and tuned into the BBC station. The announcer confirmed the rumours of the Head of State's demise, but said the situation was still developing.

'What does that mean?' Mum asked.

'It's possible they are still fighting,' Dad replied.

The family set about mundane daily tasks as the morning morphed into early evening. I was sweeping the courtyard when noises in the parlour alerted me to new developments. I dropped the broom and raced indoors. The radio had sprung to life. This time someone else came on air and identified himself as Lieutenant General Obasanjo. He announced that the coup d'état had failed, and the plotters had been captured or were in hiding.

However, he confirmed the Head of State's death. The latter news overshadowed our elation at the failure of the coup. We went to bed wondering what the immediate future held for the country.

Early the following morning, General Obasanjo, now declared as Head of State, announced seven days of national mourning for the fallen hero. Soldiers flooded the route to school. Bus drivers tooted their horns at them, acknowledging their presence as they drove past. Even school had a distinct buzz as I headed to class.

'Have you heard?' Dupe whispered as I swung my bag over the back of my chair.

'What? The coup? Everyone's heard about it.'

'No silly. About Sope's dad.'

Sope was another girl in my year group. She wasn't a friend, but I remembered her from my boarding days.

'What happened to her dad?'

'He was Murtala Mohammed's aide-de-camp.'

Realisation struck. 'No!'

'Yes.'

I winced. The news said the aide-de-camp died along with the Head of State. *Poor girl.*

'Is she still in school?'

'No, the principal sent her home yesterday.'

Our form tutor walked in and we settled down for the roll call, but my mind stayed with Sope's family. I imagined her desolation. I'd hate it if something happened to my dad. He was my anchor.

Until the events of the previous day, I had been ignorant of national politics. Now I found myself caught up in the intense sense of loss and nationalism. Over the following days, the disparate tribes in the country, who rarely agreed on anything, all came together in an outpouring of grief. Still, there were some divided opinions. While newspapers claimed Murtala Mohammed was the best leader we'd ever had, dissidents whispered that he bore all the hallmarks of a would-be dictator. Sadly, we would never know.

*

To meet up with my beau during school breaks, I became quite inventive with saving time on chores, and that led to frequent skirmishes with Mum. I was forever in trouble for not doing things right: dishes not washed on time, laundry not cleaned well enough. Dad, my only ally, was gone most of the day.

One evening, during the Easter break, my uncle, whose baby I'd played ping-pong with, turned up and asked to speak with Mum. His hostile glare left no doubt as to the subject of his discussion, so I retreated to the bedroom. Less than ten minutes later, Mum called me out of hiding. I found her in the courtyard, next to my uncle. She was in full battle mode, her left hand rested on her hip while her right foot tapped the floor impatiently. I gulped, squared my shoulders and waited.

'I hear you've been sleeping around,' Mum said.

I stiffened, my skin tingling from a sudden rush of adrenalin. 'Says who?' I lifted my chin, my eyes meeting hers head on.

Mum shared a glance with her brother. He spoke up. 'You've been cavorting with Sesan next door.' His eyes dared me to deny it.

I scowled. I presumed my aunt was feeding him stories since she was at ours all the time. 'That doesn't mean I'm sleeping around.'

'So, you don't deny being with him?' Mum said.

'I deny sleeping around.'

A terse silence followed, before Mum launched into a litany about silly girls who ruined their lives by getting pregnant. She ran out of breath, stopped and looked at me. The quizzical glare suggested she expected a response, remorse maybe? I wasn't sure, but I didn't feel the least bit remorseful. Shrugging my shoulders, I reiterated my previous stance.

'I'm not sleeping around and if you don't believe me, I am happy to submit to a physical examination by a doctor.'

Mum's jaw dropped, and my uncle lifted both his bushy eyebrows. Not sure what to say next, Mum threw her hands in the air and stalked off. My uncle stayed back, sizing me up. I glowered back at him. He too walked away. I relaxed my rigid body. *Phew!* Pleased at how I'd managed the confrontation, I headed for the bedroom thinking I'd won.

The following week, I snuck next door every evening, but somehow found it impossible to get close to Sesan. He was present, yet he wasn't. He flitted around the group's periphery, but never still enough for me to get near. *Was he avoiding me on purpose?* He was leaving for boarding school on Saturday morning, so on Friday I left home earlier, determined to catch him before the yard filled with teenagers.

I found him packing his suitcase in the bedroom he shared with a brother. 'Hi,' I said.

He glanced my way. 'Hi.'

I took in the stiff shoulders as he continued packing. Something wasn't right. 'What's going on? You've been avoiding me all week. Did I offend you?' Silence. *Would he make me ask again?*

Finally, he lifted his head. 'We shouldn't see each other anymore.' His tone was bland, but his Adam's apple throbbed.

I tried to search his face, but he wouldn't meet my eye. 'Why?' I took a step forward, but he held out a hand to stop me. I paused. 'Why?' I repeated.

A heartfelt sigh followed my question. 'There's no reason. I just think we shouldn't.'

'You are not making sense. Last week we were holding hands. Now you want to end it?'

He shrugged. 'I'm too old for you.'

'You've got to be kidding! You're three years older than me. My dad is seven years older than my mum. What on earth are you talking about?'

'Shush…keep your voice down. Everyone will hear you.'

I snapped my mouth shut, straightened my spine and took a step backwards. I took deep breaths, willing my shot nerves to calm down. Sesan continued packing, throwing clothes into his suitcase with angry jerks. With my voice decibels lower, I tried again. 'Can we at least talk about this?'

He looked up then. 'There really is nothing to discuss.'

The sadness in his eyes hurt, as did his reluctance to talk. My head throbbed with the effort of holding back the tears that were threatening. After one longing look, I turned around and left. I just about made it home before the first tear squeezed past my eyelid. I choked it back. There were too many prying eyes. My sorrow would have to wait until the cover of darkness when I could cry to my heart's content.

*

I woke up on a Saturday morning with a throb in both ears. By 11 a.m., I couldn't bear the drilling pain in each eardrum, or the burning in my throat when I swallowed. Mama hollered from the courtyard. 'Funmi, it's time to prepare lunch.' I clamped a hand over each ear and paced the bedroom, wondering what to do. Mum and Dad were out of town for a family function, leaving Mama in charge. I was in no state to prepare lunch for anyone. In despair, I slapped each ear repeatedly as the pain cranked up a notch.

My head in both hands, I headed for the courtyard. 'Mama, I'm not well.'

'What's the matter?'

'My ears and throat, they hurt.'

Mama knew I wouldn't come to her unless it was serious. 'Okay, sit down.'

She went indoors while I perched on a stool, still holding my head. Moments later, she returned and offered two aspirin tablets, which I swallowed with some water.

'Go and lie down until you are better.'

I picked myself up and retreated to the bedroom. After half an hour, the pain dulled to a throb, and I fell into an uneasy sleep.

Hours later, I woke with a start. The pain was back, worse than before. I lay on the mat, writhing and miserable, the tears rolling down my cheeks. I had to do something, so I dragged myself to the courtyard. It was still daylight, the early evening sun still visible in the sky. One look at my face and Mama knew it was bad. Even when she used to beat me, I didn't cry.

'It's still there,' she said, stating the obvious.

'It's worse,' I moaned.

Mama paced for a moment. 'Let's send for your uncle next door.'

Mum's youngest brother had just moved into the Adeleke's compound where he rented a room. He arrived within three minutes, took one look at me and announced, 'I think we'd better send for Mama Bola.'

Mama Bola, a midwife, was Mum's other younger brother's wife and lived a scant ten minutes away. By the time she arrived, still in her nurse's uniform, my throat was on fire. 'Where does it hurt?' she asked. I swallowed painfully, before pointing to my throat and ears. 'Okay, open your mouth and let me see.' I did as she asked. 'Say aaah.'

'Aaah,' I whimpered.

She peered down my throat for a few seconds, then straightened her back before turning to Mama and her brother-in-law. 'She's got *Belubelu.*'

Mama nodded as if that meant something. 'What should we do?' she asked.

'She must have it removed,' my aunt replied.

'I haven't got the money to send her to hospital and her parents are out of town.'

'She doesn't need a hospital. Mallams are very skilled at doing it. There's one on my street. Shall I send for him?'

Mallam was the generic Yoruba name for someone from the north, although the term officially described a Muslim scribe. My aunt looked at Mama for confirmation. I followed the conversation with my eyes, glad that someone knew what was wrong with me and had a potential solution. Mama gave her consent, and my aunt sent for the Mallam.

The Mallam found us all congregated in the back courtyard. Dressed in a flowing white gown and skullcap, he arrived with a satchel slung over his shoulder. After examining my throat, he confirmed my aunt's diagnosis.

'Ask him if he can remove it,' Mama said to my aunt in Yoruba.

'You fit remove am?' My aunt translated in pidgin English.

'Yes, no problem,' the Mallam said, 'five minutes, I don finish.'

I sagged in relief, thinking the nightmarish pain would soon be over. Mama, her interpreter and the Mallam continued the conversation, haggling over the cost. Not for a moment did I consider the ramifications of removing a body part.

Discussion over, at the Mallam's request, someone brought me a chair. The Mallam dived into his satchel and removed a lollipop stick and an object akin to a tiny sickle. He asked me to sit still and without me noticing, signalled to my uncle who moved behind me. Next thing I knew, my uncle grabbed both my arms and held them behind the back of my chair. Alarmed, I tried to wrench them back, but the adults yelled at me to stop. Like a frightened doe, I stopped and gawked at the Mallam. Once again, the Mallam asked me to open my mouth and this time, he depressed my tongue with the lollipop stick. He inserted the sickle into my mouth and in one deft stroke, scraped the back of my throat and pulled something straight out.

I jerked, my body rigid, before yelping in pain. My uncle let go of my arms. 'Spit it out!' my aunt instructed. I obliged and spat blood on the floor, oodles of it. My throat hurt like hell. I opened my mouth to say so and found I couldn't make any sounds, no matter how hard I tried. The other younger children in the compound peered at me while the adults yelled incomprehensible instructions. Weak, in shock and in agony, I rocked forwards and backwards on my chair, eyes shut, as the pain washed over me in waves. I continued to spit intermittently until the flow of blood slowed to a trickle. Mama led me indoors and my aunt produced a clean rag for me to dribble on. I collapsed on the living room couch, the pain now a burning throb. Mama paid the Mallam for his work. Before leaving, he left instructions that I gargle several times a day with a disinfectant made from a mixture of *ogogoro*, the local gin and ground black peppercorns.

*

On Sunday evening, my parents found me splayed out on the sofa, still unable to speak. Although I didn't know about it then, Mum went to war with Mama. My parents didn't take me to a hospital either, probably for financial reasons. Instead, Dad took me to his chemist friend, who told him I may have had inflamed tonsils. He prescribed antibiotics and assured him I would recover in due course. I set up camp in the parlour. The sofa was far more comfortable than the bedroom floor, and Dad indulged me. I continued taking the painkillers accompanied by frequent gargles with the gin.

After the first few days of intense pain, things improved, but I found it impossible to make intelligible sounds without significant pain, so I stopped trying. Besides nodding, I resorted to baby-like grunts in response to questions. A week later, I was well enough to resume minor household chores, but I still couldn't speak, so I stayed off school.

'What's with the babbling?' Mama asked, but I ignored her, memories of the pain still too raw for me to even want to try. By the end of the second week, Dad became impatient with my slow rehabilitation. 'You've got to at least try to speak properly,' he scolded.

'Buh it urs!' I spluttered in my new baby speech. *Unbelievable! Did he think I was faking the pain?*

'Yes, it hurts, but you need to push through the pain, unless you want to speak like this for the rest of your life?' I pondered that for a moment and realised it was fear holding me back and I had to get past it.

'O—ay, I w— try.' Dad nodded his encouragement.

From then on, I put more effort into my speech. It was tough, and I struggled with particular vowels, but day by day, I got better. As my speech improved, I noticed a distinct change. Every so often, I'd sense an uncomfortable pressure building in my neck, almost as if someone were pumping it with air. The only relief came from cranking my neck violently from side to side until it popped audibly. Then the pressure would dissipate, before building up again, hours later. The other problem was that I tended to choke, often, on my own saliva.

Years later, I found out that instead of removing my tonsils, the Mallam had amputated my uvular. This was a common practice in Northern Nigeria, which had a long-held traditional belief that the uvular caused all throat problems. Botched amputations often led to serious injury and even death. As the organ that produces saliva to keep the throat lubricated and closes off the nasal cavity to prevent food entering while swallowing, its amputation left me with permanent complications. Still, I was grateful to be alive. My convalescence eased into the Easter break, giving me extra weeks off. I returned to school, at the beginning of the third term, ready to catch up on missed work and double down on my studies.

*

The end of my friendship with Sesan hit hard, but I didn't confide in any of my friends. I couldn't bear the thought of being the object of their pity. At home, once I finished my chores, I avoided company, retreating into the bedroom, often with a Mills and Boon romance in tow. Not that the books were particularly helpful. The heroines' pain only seemed to amplify mine, plus there would be no happy ending for me. If Mum noticed my moroseness, she said nothing. I was positive she and my uncle had somehow got to Sesan, through his parents perhaps, but it was out of my hands.

The Adeleke's homestead remained the hangout for the kids in the neighbourhood over the six-week summer break. I had made my peace with the end of my romance with Sesan, but we hadn't spoken since the day we broke up. On the first day of the holidays, feigning nonchalance, I strolled over. Seeing my approach, Sesan met me at the fence where it all began. I crossed my arms over my torso before sneaking a peak at him. He swallowed and smiled.

'Hi,' he said.

'Hi,' I returned. *Déjà vu.*

'I'm sorry about the way things ended.' He had the grace to look sheepish.

'Yeah, me too.' I sighed. An interminable pause followed.

'Friends?' he asked. I nodded in agreement. It was time to move on.

CHAPTER TWENTY-ONE

The Beginning of the End

I strode into school on 5 September 1977 with a jaunty step. In Form 5, I was at the top of the pecking order, in my last year of school and, I hoped, my last in Nigeria. Nan and I still exchanged letters full of family news. Some of her grandsons were grown up. She had retired and the doctors had warned Pop to stop smoking. Tom still lived at home, and now that Nan no longer fostered children, the local Council had moved the family into a compact maisonette near the old Victorian house. Sometimes the letters made me feel as if I was right there with her, and I couldn't wait to see her again.

At assembly, the principal delivered unsettling news to my cohort. 'Due to your abysmal performance in the sciences, I am barring some of you from taking chemistry, physics and biology in the West African School Certificate examinations next June.' I cringed. My scores had contributed to those woeful results. 'If you don't spot your name on the list on the lab doors, find a substitute subject to study, or limit yourself to six.'

I headed first to the physics lab, where I searched the list twice, hoping my name would magically appear. I fared no better at the chemistry lab but found myself on the biology list. On one level, I felt relief at no longer having to study those subjects, and I could just focus my energy on the remaining six. But that left me no safety net. The West African School Certificate examination board aggregated the grades of each student's best six subjects, to award an overall grade. Should I fail one of the six, it would depress my overall grade and I needed to achieve Grade 1 or Grade 2 to proceed to tertiary education.

After lunch, I explained my dilemma to Dupe and Ade, who had both aced the three sciences. 'I heard Mrs Gbadero is accepting students for history,' Dupe said.

My eyes lit up. I still loved history, although I hadn't studied it for a year. 'Thanks, I'll go register for it straight away.'

At home, I waited until after dinner to tell Dad his plans for a doctor or dentist in the family were over. I found him sprawled in his favourite spot. Eyes closed, he lay on the parlour couch, listening to music, an abandoned newspaper spread across his bare torso. He often took his top off to get some relief from the balmy heat. I coughed. 'Ahem, Dad?'

He opened one eye and squinted at me.

'I need to tell you something.'

Both eyes opened, but he stayed prone. 'Okay, go on.'

'School won't let me study physics and chemistry anymore.' I infused just enough dejection in my voice to let him think the news upset me.

He bolted straight up, all signs of relaxation gone. 'What do you mean?'

'I didn't get good enough grades last year. The principal is worried girls like me might depress the school's grades in the final exams.'

He scratched his head. 'But you need eight subjects.'

'I don't. The principal confirmed I could study six, but to be safe, I've also registered for history.'

An obstinate look came over Dad's face. 'You've got to do eight.'

'Dad! I can't. The only subject options left are domestic science, art and geography. I can't do the first two because most of it is project based and the course work for the exams started in Form 4. And I hate geography!'

Dad ignored the outburst. 'We'll see,' was all he said. 'Fine,' I muttered, as I headed back to the bedroom.

A week later, Dad said, 'See Mr Adams at your school tomorrow. He will register you for art.'

My eyebrows flicked north. Curious, I asked, 'How do you know Mr Adams and how did you get him to agree to that?'

'Just go and see him.'

It turned out Dad and Mr Adams were drinking buddies. Although I had no course work at all from Form 4, I joined the art class. It was a nightmare, trying to make up for two years of work, when I couldn't master the simplest of techniques. If my life had depended on my ability to draw, I would have ended up beneath a six-foot mound. To catch up on the previous year's history classes, a benevolent classmate gave me all her notes to copy. My interest in the subject bloomed as I learned about the ancient West African Kingdoms of Oyo, Benin, Kanem-Bornu, Sokoto, Asante and Fante. I read about the Transatlantic slave trade, the misery it inflicted on millions, its abolition, the partition of Africa, Lord Lugard and good old Mungo Park, who discovered the river Niger. *Ha! That was funny. Surely, the locals bathing in the river since the dawn of time discovered it first.*

My history lessons turned to the colonisation of Africa and how Nigeria among other countries became a subject of the British empire. My reflections on African history left me outraged at the continent's suffering at the hands of European imperialists, but none of it changed my desire to return to England. Instead, I was confused. *Did my disassociation with Yoruba culture mean I was a traitor to my African heritage?*

*

Another era was ending at home with Auntie Abebi's marriage. As she had spent most of her teens with us, it was Mum's duty to prepare her wedding trousseau. I watched enviously as Mum tackled the task with vigour and generosity, buying her cooking utensils, crockery, clothing and jewellery. *Would I get the same treatment when my turn came?*

One Friday evening during the Christmas break, Dad called a family meeting. Everyone was home, including the twins, who were back from boarding school, having started secondary school in September. Once we had assembled in the parlour, Dad pulled out an oblong cardboard tube, popped the lid off and extracted a roll of paper. He unfurled it and laid it out on the coffee table. We all leaned in to catch a glimpse.

'These,' Dad began, 'are the floor plans for the new house I am going to build.'

The room burst into chatter, 'What? A new house? Where?'

Dad held up his palm. 'All right, all right, let me finish. I'll show you the plans first, then if you still have questions, you can ask.' The room quietened.

'This is the living room…' We gaped as Dad pointed out each room. Mum, Dad and Mama would each have their own bedroom. It wasn't unusual for Yoruba couples to have separate rooms if they could afford to. There were two additional rooms, one each for boys and girls, and a tiny storeroom. The house, a bungalow, included a dining room separate from the kitchen and boys' quarters at the back of the building.

'The location is in Ifako, a little further away from Funmi's school,' Dad continued. 'Any questions?'

I raised my hand. 'How long will it take to build?'

'I can't say. It depends on how fast the labourers work. We can build it faster if you all help.'

'When do the works start?' Kehinde asked.

'The ground-breaking and dedication ceremony is this Saturday.'

It was only Monday, and we buzzed all week, barely able to contain our excitement. Every Yoruba man dreamt of building his own house and after several promotions at work and saving for years, Dad was ready to fulfil his dream. On Saturday morning, Dad chartered a taxi and together with his car, ferried the entire family to the new building site. We drove through Bariga, past my school into the Ifako area. Soon, the tarred road merged into a bumpy dirt track down a steep incline. We turned a corner and all the houses disappeared. Instead, tall shrubs and bushes lined the road. The cars travelled a little further before hitting a pothole filled with water almost deep enough to swim in. Dad stopped his car, came out and spoke to the taxi driver. 'You need to keep to the left edge of the crater and drive through it slowly. It's less deep there.' He got back in his car and motioned the taxi to follow.

We held on tight as the taxi navigated through the pothole. But when the car tyres rolled over boulders deep in the muddy water, we couldn't stop ourselves jiggling up and down. My siblings giggled as their heads bumped against the car's roof. My excitement dimmed a little. *Where on earth had Dad bought his land? In the bush?* Once out of the pothole, the car made a left turn, cruising downhill before stopping in front of a flat plain. Dad stopped his car, and the taxi driver parked behind him. Dad stepped out of his car, beaming from ear to ear. 'This is it!' he waved.

Alighting from the cars, we stared. 'Nobody else lives here!' I quipped.

'Can you see up the hill?' Dad pointed into the distance.

I followed his finger and scanned two roof lines. 'That's only two houses, Dad.'

'Yes, but people have bought all this land.' He waved his arms in the expanse. 'It won't be long before it's full of houses.'

'But it doesn't even have a street name.'

Dad grinned. 'True, and that's why it will bear mine. I'll be the first to build and we will call it Ladipo street.' I smiled. Dad looked very chuffed at the idea, and so was I.

On the way home, Dad explained what came next. 'First, they will pour the foundations of the building. Once the foundation sets, we can start building the walls. That's when you'll be able to help.'

'When will that be?' Taiwo asked.

'In about six to eight weeks.'

Lost in thought, I reflected on the day. Another beginning. The year was turning out to be full of them.

*

Six weeks later, my siblings, home for the half-term break, and I turned up at the site with Dad. Where bare earth once stood, a square outline of the perimeter of the building greeted us. The building's footprint looked much smaller than I thought it would be. Within the foundation, the builders had carved out the layout of each room with a single layer of breeze blocks. It looked much like the floor plan Dad had shown us earlier. A giant petrol engine cement mixer stood in a corner of the plot. Next to it were two wheelbarrows, several bags of Portland cement, a mound of sand and shovels.

'How can we help?' I asked.

'Well, let's see,' Dad replied as he headed over to consult the builders. He came back after a few minutes.

'We will split into groups. Girls, you will fetch water from the well over there.' Dad pointed to the well I hadn't realised was there. 'Boys, you will work with the builders to mix the cement and make blocks.' Dad, as the building's owner, did not engage in any labour. The builders would never have let him. Instead, he supervised and encouraged us as we laboured.

Under the full glare of the sun, it was back-breaking work. My siblings and I soon found our rhythm, pausing only for sips of water or to wipe the sweat off our brows. When Dad said it was time to leave, fifty blocks lay in neat little rows before us. Dirty and exhausted, I climbed into Dad's car with a pervading sense of euphoria, pleased beyond measure that I was helping Dad and contributing to the building of our new home.

Halfway home, a thought occurred to me. 'Dad, won't someone steal the bricks before morning breaks?' I imagined all that hard work gone to waste.

'No, they won't.'

'How can you be so sure?'

Dad gave a deep-throated chuckle. 'Remember the boundary wall alongside the plot?'

I nodded.

'Army barracks lie on the other side. I've paid the commandant to station some of his men over the bricks and guard them at night.' I rolled my eyes. *Nigeria! For the right price, you could buy anything.*

For the next five months, after school, at weekends and during school breaks, I helped at the site. My siblings and the other children contributed too, when they were around. The building was taking shape, with walls and gaps for doors and windows. Our focus shifted to ferrying dried bricks to the builders. We were so proud of our contribution, boasting about how many bricks we carried on our heads. Each time, before we left, I walked through the building and imagined the completed rooms with beds and furniture. Dad had promised to buy enough bunk beds so that none of us need ever sleep on the floor again.

One afternoon, the roofing materials arrived. They looked different from the shiny corrugated iron sheets doming houses everywhere. These were thick sheets in a grey, matte-textured material. 'Why do these look different to normal roofing?' I asked.

'That's asbestos, the new rage,' Dad said. 'It is fireproof and better at resisting moisture than corrugated iron.' Admiring the roofing material, I rubbed a finger all along its length.

When the roof rafters and asbestos sheets went up, our excitement became palpable. The builders started pouring concrete into the floors. They plumbed a water cistern into the bathroom and bolted burglar-proof railings into each window frame. The only other jobs left were installing the wiring, ceilings, louvred windowpanes and doors. We were nearing completion. I imagined the finished floors and ceilings; where I would place my bed. I couldn't wait to move in. That's when calamity struck, back at the flat.

CHAPTER TWENTY-TWO

Last of the Summers

'Ole! Ole! Ole!'

I rolled over in bed, the incessant echo drawing me, unwilling, from my slumber. I stilled my body and listened. Someone was screaming thief, but those weren't the only sounds. Thwack! Thwack! The sound of a heavy object pounding something solid. I bolted upright and scanned the room. It was empty. *Where are Mama and Sola?* Then I remembered they had gone to Ijebu. I dashed into the parlour, disoriented. In disbelief, I stared at the front door. The thwacks were the sounds of someone hacking it down. For a few seconds I froze in terror, then shook myself out of it. I moved to the open back door, peered into the pitch-black courtyard and saw eerie shadows dancing far beyond. *Did I imagine that, or was my fear of the dark playing tricks on my mind?* My footsteps halted. *Did I want to go out there?*

I headed back towards the bedroom and nearly jumped out of my skin when another whack hit the door. *Where were Mum and Dad?* I turned their door handle and peeped. They weren't there. I needed to hide from whoever was trying to get in, and under the bed seemed a sensible option. On my knees, I tried crawling underneath it, but as I inched in, I met resistance. I paused, moved backwards and peered beneath the bed. Four pairs of owlish eyes stared at me. I sighed as realisation struck. My siblings and my cousin Dami, who had just joined the family, were hiding there, and by the looks of it there was no room for me.

Heart pumping, I stood. The space under the beds in my room was full of household stuff. I ignored the front door and headed back to the courtyard. Braving the dark, I crept to the boys' quarters, hoping to find Brother Femi, who lived there alone since Brother Segun had returned to his family. I turned the handle to his door and peered in. *Empty.* I returned to the flat and stood in the rear doorway, shivering. The front door had stopped heaving, although muffled voices echoed in the distance. I looked in the courtyard again. A shadow paced up and down the end of the compound. *Was that Brother Femi?* I couldn't tell from this far. The cries grew louder, a blend of shouts and chants. I hovered, undecided, in the door frame, for what seemed like an eternity.

A squeak behind me broke me out of the trance. I turned and watched in horror as the front doorknob rotated in slow motion. With one hand around my throat and the other over my mouth, I muffled my scream. The door thrust open and Dad stepped in, Mum right behind him. My shoulders flopped in relief, and I flew into their arms. Suddenly, there were people everywhere. Brother Femi arrived through the back door. The other children came out of hiding and joined us. We all spoke at once, crying and hugging each other. Other neighbours joined us and congregated in our front yard. 'What happened?' the voices clamoured.

When we all calmed down, Mum filled in the gaps. 'Dad and I woke from the noise. Dad crept into the parlour and came back almost immediately. "My dear," he said, "I think we have armed robbers at the door." Quickly, I pushed the children under the bed, and we headed back to the parlour.'

Dad took over. 'We screamed "*Ole!*" but the robbers said, "Shut up and open the door!" We ignored them and kept screaming.

Then they threatened to cut our tongues off when they got in. So, we ran into the courtyard, scaled the rear fence into the next street and hollered for help. The neighbours there came to our help with sticks and clubs.'

I stared open-mouthed at my parents. 'How did you climb over a six-foot fence?'

'Dad clambered over first, then Femi helped me over,' said Mum. *That explained the ghostly shadows!* I looked at my parents with a new-found respect. Who would have thought it?

*

The robbers never entered our flat. They retreated when they heard the neighbours coming, but not before raiding our next-door neighbour. The Adelekes and others on the same street hadn't been able to help because the robbers threw empty bottles at them as a deterrent. The tenants living above us were also spared, the iron gate leading to their floor proving too difficult to break.

Once the adrenalin-induced chatter died down and people left for their homes, we went back indoors. Dad bent down and picked up something shiny. It was half of the front door key. He gave the door a gentle push, and it collapsed, dangling on a single hinge. Sleep seemed pointless, so we spent the rest of the early hours talking about who hid under which bed. Nobody considered reporting the incident to the police. The adults thought they were less than useless in preventing or solving crime, and more often than not were the brains behind it.

Mid-morning the same day, my cousin Dami burst through the open door, back from an errand. 'We have trouble o!' he wailed, as the family gathered around.

'What's the matter?' Mum said.

'They are coming back.'

Dad leaned forward. 'I didn't catch that. Who's coming back?'

'The robbers! They sent a message to Number 57 and asked them to deliver it to us. They said they didn't complete their mission, so they will return and finish the job.'

Panic set in. We all turned to Dad, the same unspoken question hovering on our lips. *What are we going to do?*

Dad sank onto the couch, his brow furrowed, a fist underneath his chin as he contemplated his next move. Suddenly, in a moment of clarity, he snapped his finger, then stood up.

'Everyone, gather round.' He made eye contact with each one of us before announcing.

'We are moving to the Ifako house today.' A collective gasp echoed in the quiet.

'But it's not finished,' Mum said. 'It doesn't even have doors or windows.'

'That doesn't matter. If that message is true, we'll be safer there than here.'

'But we don't know it's true,' I said, but no one listened.

We began packing in earnest and by sundown were ensconced in the Ifako house. I wondered how we would be safe in a home without doors, but as always, Dad had a plan. He and the commandant in charge of the army barracks were now firm drinking buddies. Several crates of alcohol later, soldiers surrounded our home and remained on guard throughout the night, all week until Dad made the house secure.

That first night in Ifako, I lay awake, haunted by the sounds of the robbers hacking through the door. What would have happened had they entered and found just me inside the flat? I shuddered to think of it and fell asleep with that question ringing in my head.

*

The building work sped up after we moved in, the whirr of the cement mixer a constant buzz in the background. For the first few weeks we slept on mats on the bare earth, moving from room to room so that the floors could be done. Soon after, the builders installed the ceiling, doors and windows. Electricity would be installed last, as that required a significant bribe for NEPA officials.

If I thought life would be more comfortable in a bigger house, I was wrong. Sola stayed in Ijebu with her parents, but Mama came back with two of Sola's older siblings and a third child whose relationship to the family was obscure. Dad didn't seem to be able to say no to his mother. In their mid-teens, Sola's siblings, Tope and Bolanle, shared my room. Dad bought two bunk beds, so we each had a bed.

With Auntie Abebi gone, most of the household's cooking fell to me. The next time Mum asked me to cook beans for supper, I asked Mama for help with the accompanying chilli sauce. Mama hated using machine-ground chillies, always preferring to grind them by hand with traditional stones. 'Erm, I think it's time you learned how to do it,' she said.

I scowled. 'But Mama, I won't have enough time.'

'Oh yes you will, while the beans are cooking.'

I cringed. I had an inkling of what was coming, but I didn't realise how bad it would be.

Half an hour later, with the beans bubbling away on a wood fire, I positioned myself on a low stool in front of the granite stones. The grinders came in two parts, a large flatbed and a smaller oblong-shaped stone, held between both hands and used to crush the chillies against the flat stone. I scooped a handful of bird's-eye chillies into a bowl of water and rinsed them before placing them on the flat stone. Mama jumped up from the stool she perched on. 'No! You need to grind them in small portions. Scoop some back into the bowl.' I followed her instruction, leaving a third of the chillies on the flatbed. I picked up the smaller stone, placed it on the chillies and moved it forward. The chillies scattered in all directions.

Mama hissed. 'Don't slosh them around. Keep the chillies pressed between the stones.' She knelt behind me, grabbed my hands and demonstrated the kneading motion. With more understanding, I resumed the task.

Grinding chillies was much harder than I expected. In minutes, muscles I didn't know I had were screaming stop, but the chillies still looked semi-intact. When Mama did it, it looked so effortless. Now I knew better. Ten minutes into the grinding, my hands started tingling, the effect of the chillies burning my skin. Thirty minutes later, I was still grinding and on fire. 'I can't stand it anymore!' I yelled and jumped off the stool in frustration. Tears rolled down my face, but I dared not wipe them away with my hands. I dashed to a keg of water nearby, poured some water into a bowl and plunged my hands in it. *Ah, bliss!* But not for long. The heat resumed as soon as I took them out. In despair, I shook my hands in the air to cool them down.

Mama watched my antics, the shadow of an amused smile on her upturned lips. 'It will get better each time you do it, until you don't feel the heat anymore,' she said.

'I'm never doing that again.' I murmured, hoping she wouldn't hear, but of course she did. Mama raised her eyebrows and shook her head, before taking over and finishing the task while I watched with equal doses of admiration and disgust.

*

I sat through the Joint Admissions and Matriculation Board (JAMB) examinations, the new central clearing house system for all tertiary education establishments. I needed to pass this and the school certificate exam to gain admission to a college or university. I still wanted to teach, but my parents hadn't given up on me having a medical career. I offered a compromise and applied to nursing schools and teacher training colleges.

As my final examinations loomed, Mama sabotaged all my attempts to study in the evenings. While Mum eased up on giving me chores, Mama picked up the slack, dreaming up more tasks than I could imagine. Tope and Bolanle, the two new cousins living with us, worked, having ended their education early. They avoided chores by arriving home as late as possible. With the amount of cleaning and cooking to do daily, I had no time to revise. So, I started waking in the middle of the night to study.

While the household snored, I swotted, with a hurricane lamp as my devoted companion. Despite all his bribes, Dad was still waiting on NEPA officials to connect the house to the grid. When the hurricane lamp failed, I used a tin lamp, fashioned from an empty milk can and a cotton wick. Unlike the hurricane lamp, whose brightness and intensity I controlled by turning the wick up or down, a tin lamp had no controls. It didn't even have a glass shade to protect the flame from the wind. At the slightest movement, the flame would flicker and threaten extinction. Matches were a premium commodity, so I'd cup the flame and gently coax it back to life. The repugnant fumes from the burning kerosene mixed with its by-product, carbon monoxide, permeated the air nightly. I disliked the smell. Yet, none of that mattered. I had to pass those exams because my ticket to England depended on it.

The lack of sleep and tiredness were taking their toll. At school I was sharp with my friends. Dupe and Ade kept mute, but Lolade challenged me. 'What's the matter with you lately?' she asked at the end of another argument. We were loitering in the corridor outside our classrooms during the lunch break. 'You are always ready to snap someone's head off.' I sighed. She was right.

'I'm sorry. Just tired.'

'Why?'

'Working hard all day, then waking at three to study. I'm only getting about five hours' sleep each night.'

'Can't you revise in the evenings?'

'Mama won't let me.'

'Have you told your dad?'

'Nah.'

'Maybe you should. I am sure he'll understand.'

'You're probably right. I might.'

That night, before Dad retired to bed, I told him about my difficulties with Mama. Whatever he said, it worked. Mama backed off and stopped trying to fill my every moment with chores.

*

I had always suspected the relationship between Mama and Mum was fraught; now I had proof. Public arguments, previously rare, were now commonplace, with Mum becoming more vocal in her dissent. One day, she called me to her bedroom. 'If Mama gives you anything to eat or keep, you must not accept it from her.' Her tone brooked no argument. I wasn't sure how to refuse something from Mama, but arguing with Mum about it wouldn't help. I was even more worried about Mama's relegation to the category of 'people not to be trusted'.

A fortnight after Mum's edict, tucked into the lower bunk in my room, I was trying to revise when Mama approached late one evening.

'Keji,' she said.

'Yes, ma?' I looked up, my eyes narrowing. *What is this? Mama calling me by the name she gave me at birth?*

Her eyes probed mine. 'When do your examinations start?'

I didn't know why she was asking, but given our history and Mum's recent warning, I was smart enough to proffer as little as possible. 'In a few weeks.'

She hesitated, then cleared her throat. 'Here.' She offered a bundle wrapped in large banana leaves. 'It's special black soap. Use some to bathe each day. It will help you with your studies.'

'Thank you, Mama.' I accepted the soap and she left.

I sat on the edge of my bed in a fit of suppressed hysterical mirth. *First, she does everything to prevent me from studying, then she offers special soap to make me cleverer*. Mama's actions sounded dubious. I knew Mama's family were steeped in the occult, but just how deep did it go? Whatever I did, I couldn't tell Mum or Dad about it because I didn't have the energy to deal with the fall-out. I considered throwing it away, *but what if Mama really were a witch, wouldn't she realise what I'd done?* I pushed the offending soap underneath the bed and left it there. Five days later Mama asked if I was using the soap. I lied and said yes. However, when I looked under the bed, the soap had disappeared. *Now what? Had Mama retrieved it? If yes, what was her next move?*

Two days later, I woke in the middle of the night feeling suffocated. Although alert, my brain communicated no instructions to the rest of my body, my limbs and head immovable. I tried screaming but couldn't. I broke into a sweat. *What was happening? Was I dead and in hell?* With a heightened sense of dread, I fixed my eyes on the shadows on the wall. They crowded towards me, mocking my fear. *'God help me!'* I screamed silently. Then the dam burst, I jerked free and sat upright. I pulled in deep breaths to calm the drum beating in my chest. Slowly, my pulse returned to normal, and I lay back down. *What was that? A nightmare? My grandmother's handiwork?* With so many questions swirling in my head, it took ages before sleep claimed me.

The episodes, which I later learned were sleep paralysis, occurred several times a week. Not understanding and too afraid to tell anyone, I suffered silently. My instincts told me Mum would attribute it to someone's evil doing, possibly Mama. To be fair,

I half thought the same. If I told Mum, the ensuing war could destroy my family. I hated going to sleep in the dark, knowing that whatever happened was beyond my control. With the broken sleep and the worry, I moved through my days in a constant haze of unease and tiredness.

*

June arrived, and I sat through my examinations, glad to get them out of the way. The school held a valedictory service for those leaving. To my surprise, Dad and Mum both came. It was the first and last school function they attended in my five years at the school. I preened, my chest puffed out in my uniform, seated on the special benches reserved for fifth formers.

Later that evening, I approached my father. 'Dad, can we talk about England?'

He signalled with his hand. 'Take a seat.'

I sat on the adjacent sofa, my hands clasped in my lap, trying to still the quaking in my abdomen. I had waited so long for this moment. Taking in the expression on Dad's face, I tensed. He looked like someone ready for battle. *Was he going to refuse?*

'You know you can't go this year,' he said.

My stomach flipped. 'Dad! You promised!'

He lifted a palm. 'Yes, I did, but hear me out. You need to be in the country in August to collect your results and accept any college offers.'

I had to concede Dad's reasoning was sound, and I could hardly tell him the college offers didn't matter because I wasn't planning to come back. That would scupper my plan.

Dad continued. 'What's the point in travelling just for a couple of weeks when you can wait until next year and spend the entire summer with your nan.'

'Two weeks is better than nothing!' I replied.

'But eight weeks is even better. If I have to spend that much money sending you abroad, you might as well get the most from it.'

He was unshakable. My eyes watered. I closed them, willing the tears not to fall, my fists clenched tightly beside me. Once I had my emotions in check, I nodded. I swallowed my bitter disappointment and slunk back to my room. On my bed, I lay wondering. It was a return to the waiting game. *Would that day ever come?*

A week later, an enlightening conversation with Brother Femi revealed my uncle had been at work again. He'd pointed out the possibility that I might not come back. Dad had delayed my journey, realising there was a higher chance I'd return if I were already halfway through a course. He knew one thing about me; I always finished what I started. Armed with the new information, I worried that Dad might shift the goal posts again. I hoped he would eventually fulfil his promise, but just in case he didn't, I needed a Plan B.

CHAPTER TWENTY-THREE

Sweet Freedom

The saying that money doesn't bring happiness rang true for my family. As old relationships changed, different ones emerged in their place. With the luxury of having her own room in Lagos, Mama's visits to Ijebu became infrequent and shorter. This created more opportunities for wrangling with Mum, who was no longer content to stay in Mama's shadow. Dad, who had always liked his beer and could now afford to feed his habit, stayed out late. Often, he came home drunk, and when he didn't, he invited his friends round and drank for hours.

Even when drunk, Dad remained affable, if a little more amorous. Often, he'd burst into song and serenade an embarrassed Mum with Dele Ojo's 'Christiana'. Whenever he sent one of us to buy him more beer, a worried Mum counteracted the order. Then Mama would step in, defending her son's right, as head of the family, to do whatever he wished. Rumour also had it that Mama wanted Dad to take a second wife who might bear him more sons. Ours was not a happy household.

Dad finished building his boys' quarters at the back of the building, comprising a U-shaped single-story structure with several rooms, and more family arrived. Mum's younger brother, Baba Bola, whose wife oversaw my uvulectomy, rented a couple of rooms for his family. Brother Femi's older brother, Brother Lekan, whom I grew to like, also rented a room. Gentle and easy-going in a way that reminded me of Dad, he would become an ally. He was easy to talk to and a wonderful listener, and I found myself sharing my plans and aspirations with him. He'd sometimes offer advice without telling me what to do. As my respect for him grew, I confided in him even more. His trust in me would pay dividends later.

Meanwhile, Bolanle and Tope got busy carving out their own territory. Both had left a vocational college aged fifteen with secretarial skills, and Dad had helped them secure jobs in a typing pool in a Lagos firm. Tope was as fair as her sister was chocolate, her medium tan second only to Mama Yaba's complexion. This earned her the nickname *Oyinbo* as a compliment on the fairness of her skin, not the derogatory moniker that alluded to my 'white-man' behaviours. The Yoruba favoured fair-skinned people, a hangover from the colonial mentality perhaps, when Europeans were considered superior. With her lips and nails painted red, permed hair and high heels, Tope exuded the confidence of someone who thought themselves beautiful.

Bolanle, as outgoing as her sister, insisted I call her auntie because she was two years older. At first, I refused, but gave in under pressure from Mama. The girls, not content with bumping me down the pecking order, took great delight in excluding me from their feminine conversations, claiming I was too young to understand. So, although I shared my bedroom with them, I remained as lonely as ever.

From snippets of their conversation, I gathered that they both dated and wanted to marry men older and wealthy enough to provide for them and their future children. To achieve this goal, they had no qualms about being a second or third wife. In contrast, I knew I would never settle for a polygamous marriage or marry anyone for anything but love. As the girls' lifestyle became more apparent to Mum, she censured them, fearing their potential influence on me.

One evening Mum called me to her bedroom. 'I don't want you hanging out with those girls,' she said. 'That path will only lead to ruin.'

I snorted silently.

'If you fall pregnant, it will be all on your head.'

As her voice droned on, I held my tongue to avoid saying anything I might regret. It was so hard not to get frustrated with Mum. She didn't seem to understand who I was, what I would or wouldn't do.

'I don't hang out with them anyway,' I said to pacify her. 'So, you have nothing to worry about.'

As she was caught in her imaginary nightmare, I wasn't sure she even heard me, but I waited until she finished her warnings before excusing myself. The irony wasn't lost on me. The girls gave me grief because I wasn't sleeping around, and Mum did likewise because she thought I might be.

*

The day the term ended, I bounced into school energised. A tangible fizz bubbled over the Form 5 block. As we filed into our final assembly, we were a lot quieter than usual, the poignancy not lost on us. Principal Morgan spoke about entering the world as the school's ambassadors. As the girls sang the hymn 'Till We Meet Again', I realised I might never see some of them again. We spent the afternoon visiting each other's classes, saying our goodbyes. Lolade and I exited the gates as students for the last time and turned to each other. My throat tightened with the emotion threatening to overflow. I choked back the tears. 'Promise me you'll keep in touch,' I said.

'I will.'

She drew me into a tight hug, and we clung to each other before parting ways.

I headed straight to the hairdresser's salon half a mile from home. For so long, I had dreamed of having Caucasian-style, sleek hair. By the time I clocked twelve, it had become fashionable. But I couldn't because school forbade it, and Mum and the rest of society thought it denoted promiscuity. For me, it wasn't just about the looks. I grew out my short afro in Form 3, when I became a day student. After each wash, my natural, thick, coily hair tangled into an unruly mess and, besides the pain combing it inflicted, my hair broke more wooden combs than I could count. Mum said my hair took after Mama Yaba's, as if in some way that strengthened our family bond. But that was no consolation, and as I became older, on my list of things to do when I left school, a perm was right at the top.

For the last twelve months, I'd saved all my cash gifts for this purpose. I knew Mum would be livid, but I could handle that. She had few options besides shaving off my hair, and even she wouldn't do that. The hairdresser, another distant relative, had offered me a family discount. So, I sauntered into the salon in my school uniform and took a seat, waiting for a stylist to become free.

Half an hour later, an apprentice led me to a plastic chair and draped a black cape around my shoulders. She produced a tub of Vaseline and, following my cousin's instructions, applied it to my hairline and behind my ears. 'Apply it everywhere on her scalp,' her boss instructed from across the room. Prepped and ready, I hummed in anticipation of the next step. A junior stylist took over.

'How difficult do you find combing your hair?' she asked.

'Very.'

'In that case, we should use super.'

I didn't have a clue what she was on about. She must have read the puzzlement on my face. 'The relaxer comes in three strengths: mild, medium and super.'

'Ah, okay.'

She picked up a tail-comb, parted my hair from crown to nape and from ear to ear. Working from the back-left quadrant, she made smaller partings and applied the relaxer. I cringed as the unpleasant, tangy smell of lye and ammonia assailed my nostrils and stung my eyes, making them water. It took the stylist over five minutes to cover the first quadrant of my long, virgin hair with the chemical, and the skin around that section of my nape started tingling almost at once. As she completed two more quadrants, the smarting worsened.

I tapped her arm. 'My scalp is burning.'

'Yes. That's normal. It's the product in the relaxer, and how you know it's working.'

My face sagged. I had no idea the process involved pain, and by the end of the afternoon, I would question the wisdom of my choice.

*

Two-and-a-half hours later I left the salon with my hair coiffed into an 'off-the-face' style, reminiscent of the Queen of England's hairdo. I tried bouncing the finger waves cascading down the back of my head, but they remained immovable, lacquered by a final spritz of holding spray. If Mum were home, she'd be in the living room. To avoid the risk of running into her, I snuck down the side of the house and accessed my bedroom via the back door, but I hadn't counted on Mama Bola seeing me.

When the doorknob to my sanctuary twisted open without a knock, I braced myself. Mum entered, stopped and gaped. Eventually she found her voice. 'What have you done to your hair?'

My instinctive response was belligerent, but it wasn't in my interest to antagonise her any further. So, I answered. 'I had it permed.'

She stared again, then shook her head and left.

When Dad came home from work, I listened behind the door as Mum told him about my latest escapade. 'You should see what your daughter did today.'

I was his whenever I misbehaved. I smirked, waiting for his response.

'Ah well. She is growing up.'

I fist bumped the air. I knew it wouldn't bother him. With feigned innocence, I entered the parlour to say hello to Dad. He scrutinised my hair, his face deadpan. Although he wasn't cross, he didn't want to condone what I had done in front of Mum. He had a question for me.

'How are you going to maintain your new hairstyle?'

I hadn't considered that. Thinking on my feet, I responded.

'It won't cost much; I just have to buy the relaxer. I can do the rest myself.'

He shrugged and settled into conversation with Mum.

The following morning, I woke with a splitting headache and with parts of my scalp smarting. An exploratory finger-search revealed sections of my hair matted to my skull, the result of lye burns, which oozed a sticky fluid. I dared not share my concerns with Mum or Dad. I knew exactly what they would say. Instead, I smothered my injuries in Vaseline and left them to heal. *What a price to pay in the name of beauty!* Over the ensuing weeks, I considered my next move. Would I perm my regrowth? Definitely. Most girls in the city did, and I didn't want to be any different. But this time I resolved to do more research and use a reputable salon.

*

As June morphed into a slow July and August, I spent most of my days helping Mum at her shop. I made friends with teenagers in the neighbourhood and Mum allowed me to visit them or invite them over. One morning in the third week of August, I yawned, awakening from a fitful night. My sleep had been punctuated with dreams I couldn't recall, but which left me with a feeling of dread. Then I remembered. *Today was results day!* I pulled the covers off my body, sprung out of bed and started for the bathroom.

Over an hour later, my steps slowed as I approached the school gates. That long-awaited moment was finally here, and my entire future rested on it. My feet felt heavy, while my heart thundered in a surreal mix of dread and anticipation. I dragged myself over the school's threshold, all my senses attuned to my surroundings. The soft whimpers of people crying floated from the dining room on my left. In the field to my right, two girls twirled in jubilation, while a boisterous group high-fived one another. I wondered how my day would end, jubilant or despondent.

I joined the cluster of girls surrounding the notice boards outside the principal's office. No one spoke, except for the occasional whoops of joy. The school had ranked everyone from 1st to 155th, based on the overall aggregate of their best six subjects. I ignored the top of the list, my eyes zoning in on the middle. I scanned down the sheet, across to the next page and the one after that, finding Lolade's name on the sheet, but not mine. My stomach churned. *Surely, I wasn't at the bottom?*

I got to the end of the list and sighed my relief at not finding my name there. My eyes travelled back to the top, and I scanned more slowly. I found Ade and Dupe's names under the Grade 1 list. My heart leapt, glad at their success. To my surprise and delight, I topped the Grade 2 group. I bristled for a moment, cross that I'd missed out on Grade 1 by just one point. Then my perspective righted itself. Elated, I danced out of the queue and searched for my friends, but none were on the premises. Dying to share the news with someone, I left for home.

I spied Mama first, cooking over the wood logs in the back courtyard. My excitement toppled over. 'Mama! Mama! I passed!'

She looked up. 'Oh.' She nodded and resumed her task.

I stopped dead. The air in my tiny bubble of happiness burst and frittered away. *Really! That's it? Fine, I don't care what you think, anyway.* I swivelled around and left to find others to share the wonderful news with. Thrilled beyond measure and effusive in their joy, Mum and Dad both enveloped me in a massive hug when they heard the news. 'I'm so proud of you,' Dad said.

'Me too,' Mum chimed, wiping a tear out of the corner of her eye. For the first time, I stood tall before my parents, delighted at their pride in me.

*

I spent the next two weeks in a flurry of activity, following up applications to colleges and universities. The administration of the JAMB results, the first in its history, was a fiasco. Thousands of students had missing exam results, which meant institutions could not offer places. Once the bureaucracy collapsed, it became a case of who you knew and where, with families relying on their network of contacts.

Dad knew someone who had a contact at the University of Lagos. So, armed with my WASC results and accompanied by Dad's contact, Mum and I headed to the university. The admissions officer said most courses were full, but there were spaces left on the National Certificate in Education course. It involved three years of undergraduate study that qualified you to teach at secondary school level. It wasn't a degree, but I could study for a degree afterwards.

'Are you happy with that?' Mum asked.

Pleased, I nodded. My only other option was to study for A-levels, but I wanted to avoid staying at home for two more years.

'Have you got your results on you?' the admissions officer asked.

'Yes, sir.'

'Okay read them out, and I'll record them.'

I pulled out my results notification slip and reeled off the subjects and grades: 'English – A1; English literature – B3; history – C4; religious education – C5; mathematics – C6; biology…'

'Wait, what's that F9 on the list?'

The paper was translucent, and he could see the mirrored results through the paper's back.

'That's art, sir.'

'Art?' he barked.

'Yes, sir.'

He kissed his teeth, dismissing the subject without a second thought. I smiled. Most Yoruba adults thought studying art was a waste of time. Next, he needed my birth certificate. Mum handed it over. He started scribbling, then stopped, a deep scowl on his face. He put his pen down and looked at Mum. 'I'm sorry, I can't enrol her.'

My jawed dropped. Mum's face mirrored my confusion. 'Why not?' We both spoke at once.

'The university does not take students younger than sixteen.'

'She'll be sixteen in less than three months,' Mum offered.

'I'm sorry, I don't make the rules.'

He gave Mum an apologetic smile and handed the documents back, signalling the end of our meeting.

Mum rose from her seat, thanked him and made for the door. Numb, I dragged my feet behind her, hope diminishing with each step. Just before we walked out, the admissions officer asked Dad's contact to wait for a moment. We left the room and waited outside for him. A few minutes later, Dad's contact came out beaming. 'You need to get her a new birth certificate with an older date of birth.'

'Exactly how do we do that?' Mum asked.

'Get her dad to find a notary public and swear an affidavit that he's lost her birth certificate. Then provide a new date of birth. Once you've got the sworn declaration, bring it back to the registrar's office.'

Mum and I returned to the registrar's office a week later with a document that certified I was two years older. And with that, the university enrolled me. I returned home ecstatic. I wasn't sixteen yet, but I was finally leaving home to start a fresh life. Four weeks later, with an updated wardrobe of four dresses and two pairs of shoes, Mum and Dad dropped me off at the hall of residence. My journey to London was on hold, but someday, somehow, I would get there.

CHAPTER TWENTY-FOUR

The Flower Blooms

Dad's car made a left turn into the short driveway leading to the University of Lagos. A yellow and red structure with the university's emblem positioned in the middle towered over the front entrance. I hadn't noticed it on my first two visits. The stress of the registration process must have dulled my powers of perception. As we approached the gates, I took in the sight, my senses attuned to every nuance. A security guard waved us to a stop.

'Good afternoon,' Dad said.

The guard didn't reply, but he peeped inside the car before shifting his focus back to Dad. '*Oga*, what is your official business here?' he asked.

'I am dropping my daughter off to her hostel. She is a new student.'

'Which hall?'

'Queen Amina.'

'Past the gates, turn right and follow the road all the way down.' He waved us through.

The dual carriageway to the main campus stretched into the distance, its central reservation adorned with tropical plants. Dumb canes, cordylines, crotons, ixoras and hibiscus elbowed each other, jostling for space. Dad turned right, and more manicured gardens in fresh bloom greeted us. A spate of single- and two-storey buildings, presumably offices and classrooms, dotted either side of the road, the entire picture, one of tranquil modernity. We wound our way round a tree-lined avenue before arriving in front of the hall of residence. I stepped out of Dad's car and perused the modern-looking block before me. My stomach fluttered, tapping a light-hearted beat. This hostel would be my home for the next year. Dad opened the boot of his car and hoisted out my suitcase. The movement caught my eye and took me back to five years earlier when I had gone to boarding school. My emotions felt familiar – a feeling of standing on the precipice of something new, something big.

'Come on, Funmi, stop daydreaming.' Mum's voice jolted me into action, and I helped my parents carry my luggage to the building's vestibule. The sign above the entrance read 'Porter's Lodge'. The half-covered porch hardly qualified, since it looked more like a tiny cabin with a veranda. A chest-high reception desk created a barrier, behind which stood a middle-aged, balding gentleman who I presumed was the porter.

After looking at my papers, he pulled a key off the key cabinet hanging on the wall beside him and handed it over. 'We have allocated you to room 45 in the Old Block A. Your family can help you carry your luggage in.' I raised an eyebrow. *Isn't that what porters did?* The gentleman continued with his instructions. 'Every time you leave the halls of residence you must hand your key in here. The dining room is over there.' He pointed to the other side of the avenue, the part obscured by trees and shrubs. I thanked him for his help, picked up a suitcase and led my family into the compound.

Finding the old block was easy. It lived up to its name and was nothing like the section I'd admired near the entrance. I turned left into a narrow corridor and found my room on the ground floor.

I put the key in the lock, opened the door and stepped inside. *Gosh! It was smaller than I expected.* Mum and Dad crowded in behind me, leaving barely enough room to close the door. The bunk bed on my right took up the entire length of the wall. At the far end of the room, a single window provided much-needed light. Underneath it sat a simple desk and chair. Opposite the bed, built into an alcove, was a wardrobe and storage space. The bunk bed suggested I would have a roommate at some point. Meanwhile, with no one to vie for it, I chose the top bunk.

*

Mum fussed as she helped me put my stuff away. 'Where do you want your slippers?' she said.

'Mum, leave them, I've got plenty of time to sort my things later.'

'Okay,' she said, pushing the suitcase under the lower bunk.

Dad sat on the chair, trying to avoid getting in the way. 'I think it's time we left,' he said. He opened his arms, and I moved into them. Moments later his arms slackened, and I turned to Mum. She squeezed me tight and in a rare moment of emotion, dropped a kiss on my forehead. I held back the sob clogging my throat and leaned into the hug.

Once they had left, I headed for the dining room. During registration, I had bought a month's worth of meal tickets, to exchange for meals in the dining hall. Each enormous meal, including dessert, only cost fifty kobo, which at the time was equivalent to fifty pence. And yes, we had desserts – cake, ice-cream and jelly! I was in food heaven. After my meals, I returned to my room and climbed into bed with a Barbara Cartland romance. For the next three days, I repeated the same routine: meals in the dining room and an occasional stroll down the avenue before returning to my room. On the fourth day, it occurred to me that so far I had done a lot of eating and not much learning, and something drastic needed to change. Subconsciously, I was waiting for someone to round me up and corral me into a classroom. My face crinkled at my own idiocy. I donned some shoes and went in search of the buildings I'd seen the day I arrived.

I soon ran into another student. 'How do I sign up for classes?' I asked.

If she thought my question funny, she gave no hint of it. 'Were you not here for orientation week?'

'Nope, I missed it.'

She directed me to the administrative block where fellow students showed me the schedule of classes for first-year students on my course and how to register for each class. Besides the compulsory classes, I chose English and history as my subject options. Relieved that I was on my way to learning something new, I returned to my room and found a stranger sitting on the lower bunk. My roommate had arrived. Slim, with a bright smile and a smattering of grey around her temple, any hopes of us becoming buddies were dashed at first sight. She introduced herself as Mrs Sofola. She was studying for the Associate Diploma in Education, a one-year further education course for practising primary school teachers. 'I'm glad you chose the top bunk,' she said, 'there's no way I can get up there.'

I climbed up to my bed, to give her room to put her things away and considered my fate. While Mrs Sofola appeared nice, she was old enough to be my mother. I understood Yoruba culture well enough to know that I had just bagged myself a chaperone for the year. *How bloody unfortunate!*

*

My first semester got off to a rollicking start. I'm not sure how it happened, but I moved around with a new group of friends,

Bisola, Sayo and Funbi, who I met in the English class. At five-foot one and a dress size eight, I was the smallest and youngest student in the faculty and, except for a girl in Moremi Hall, the entire university. Bisola was the first to discover my age and couldn't wait to tell the others I was the runt of the group. 'Guess how old Funmi is,' she said one evening. The group had gathered in her room.

'Eighteen,' said Funbi.

'Seventeen,' Sayo suggested.

'You are so wrong, she's not even sixteen yet! I have two younger sisters who are older than her.'

The girls stared at me as if I had two heads. 'How old are you all?' I asked. *Was the age difference that huge?* They told me their ages with gusto. Funbi and Bisola were twenty years old, and Sayo was already twenty-one. I had an inkling of what was coming next.

'Under normal circumstances you and I wouldn't even move in the same circles. I should be "auntie" to you,' Bisola said.

'You know! If not for education...' Sayo slapped her hand against her thigh and left the rest of her sentence unsaid. But I got the essence of it. Education, a necessity, had brought us all together. I was mixing with my elders, and I needed to show some respect.

My head spun with the dilemma. Although I wanted to be their friend, everything inside me rebelled against calling them 'auntie'. I just wouldn't do it, so I opted for passive resistance. Hoping they would let it go, I offered a platitude. 'I hear you. Sometimes life sucks.' They all did, except Bisola. 'This is my roommate, Mrs Sofola.' I introduced the two when Bisola came knocking. Bisola dipped her knees, making a grand show of respect for the older woman. 'Good evening, Ma.'

A few minutes later, as we both left the room, she topped it with a saccharine-tipped, 'Goodbye mummy, it was nice meeting you.'

'So, your roommate is a "Mama Asoso",' Bisola said, as we made our way down the corridor. 'Do you call her by her first name too?'

Mama Asoso was the nickname students gave to the older women on the Associate Diploma course.

My nose flared. 'Of course, I don't!' I wasn't that mannerless. Torn between calling her auntie or mummy, I'd avoided calling my roommate anything, while still maintaining the deference expected by society.

'I was just wondering, seeing as you call me by name and all.'

I ignored the bait, determined not to discuss the issue. Eventually, she'd have to move on. However, since she had already called my roommate 'mummy', I decided I might as well.

*

Bisola's model looks, fair skin and social graces made her the class' star attraction. The archetypal social butterfly, she introduced me to her wider circle of friends and parties. Friday nights became a joy to look forward to. Bisola was never short of an invitation and she made sure they included her friends. My new-found freedom was as heady as the free alcohol flowing at the weekends. The parties, usually twenty-first birthday celebrations, were almost always arranged by boys from other halls of residence. The Yoruba elite celebrated twenty-first birthdays as a rite of passage into adulthood, and the university had plenty of students waiting for the honour. Often, the boys would task one of their number to collect carloads of girls from the female hostels. Most party nights, we left at eight in the evening and returned at six o'clock in the morning, sometimes on both Fridays and Saturdays. While I didn't overdo the alcohol, I loved the dancing and the exhilaration that came with being free.

For the first few weeks, my roommate ignored my nocturnal activities, but the Nigerian mother in her couldn't keep silent for long. 'Are you going out again tonight?' she said one Saturday evening as I balanced a bottle of nail varnish in my left hand while painting my toes.

'Uh-huh.' I didn't bother to deny it.

'Can I talk to you for a minute?'

I appreciated the fact that she asked permission. 'Yes, of course ma.'

'I understand that I'm not your mother and you youth want to have fun, but don't forget to study while you are here. You don't want to end up like me, studying at forty-five.'

'Thanks mummy, I will bear that in mind.' She seemed satisfied at my response and left me to it.

On the way to the party, I mulled over the conversation, impressed that she hadn't tried to lord her age over me. Although I was partying a lot, I decided then that I would put just as much energy into my studies. That weekend, I set up a work schedule that supported my lifestyle. I blocked out all the weekends leading to assignments and tests; no partying on those. I planned to cease all social life four weeks prior to any examinations and schedule every waking hour for studying. I had as much fun as I could with the time left.

'Didn't you wear that two weeks ago?' Bisola said when I turned up to her room ready for our next party. The four dresses I had weren't sufficient for my burgeoning social life. Bisola's family were affluent, and she had an older brother on campus who gave her money when she needed more. Funbi, the enterprising one, came from a large polygamous family but somehow managed on what she had. I asked her how she did it.

'Two things,' she said. 'You buy your clothes at a second-hand shop and you skip at least one meal a day. That way, your monthly meal tickets will last six weeks and leave you with spare cash.' I did the math. Dad paid for my meals and basic toiletries, but that was it. I had no allowance or funds for miscellaneous items. If I did what Funbi suggested, every three months, I'd have forty-five naira to spend as I wished. From then on, I adopted the poor man's eating schedule, dubbed 101 by students. The two ones represented your meals for the day and the zero symbolised the skipped meal.

Two months later, Funbi and I snuck into the second-hand shop on Davies Street, a mere ten-minute walk from campus. We'd missed a lecture to go in the middle of the afternoon and avoid meeting other girls from campus. The shop carried a wide range of styles imported from Europe and Asia. I rooted around the circular clothes racks until I found what I liked. Two girls from Moremi Hall walked in and pretended they didn't recognise us. We did likewise. An hour later, we jaunted back to campus laden with bags containing several items of clothing. It was amazing what you could do when you knew how.

CHAPTER TWENTY-FIVE

Life of the Party

I returned home for Christmas, and during the break I visited Lolade, who had opted to study for A-levels. While we were frolicking in her living room, her half-Ghanaian cousin, Kojo, walked in. I recognised him as someone I had seen on campus. He was in his second year of a law degree and we soon started chatting about campus life.

'It's my twenty-first birthday next week. I'd like you to come.' He winked at me with a lopsided grin. *Was he flirting with me?*

'I'd love to, but I am back at home for the Christmas break and my parents are not the most liberal. I also live miles away. It will be a difficult and unsafe journey home at night.'

'It's a luncheon party, from two to six in the evening, and I'll borrow my Dad's car and take you home myself.'

'You'd leave your own party to take a guest home?'

His grin grew wider. 'Why not? We'll have an hour to get you home and as the birthday boy, I can do what I want.'

'If you are sure. I can't promise to be there, because my parents might not let me, but I'll try.'

His face lit up like a firecracker.

*

Mum surprised me by giving her consent, but on the condition that I returned home by 7 p.m. I popped into the living room at noon to say goodbye to her. 'Hang on,' she said, pointing through the parlour window at Bolanle and Tope, who left two minutes earlier. 'Are you going with those two?'

'No, Mum. I told you I was going to Lolade's cousin's birthday party.'

Mum shook her head in disbelief.

'I honestly don't know where they are going, Mum.'

'Fine, just be back by seven.' I made a quick get-away before she changed her mind.

I arrived at Kojo's house at 2.30 in the afternoon and found I was one of only two guests there, if I didn't count Lolade. I hadn't banked on 'African Time,' the notion that made Nigerians arrive at parties at least two hours later than the published time. Kojo's party started late but as he promised, at 6 p.m., he tucked me into his father's car and, accompanied by a friend, drove me home.

*

I stopped wondering why Kojo left his party for me when halfway through the journey he asked if I would date him. Not sure of how much his friend could hear in the back seat, I hesitated, wanting to let him down gently. 'I don't think it's a bright idea. I like you, but not that way.'

'We'll be good together. Give it a chance.'

I shook my head. 'It won't work and there are others to consider. Lolade is my best friend. If we dated and it fell apart, it would affect both our relationships with her.'

An awkward silence descended. I squirmed, realising that by dashing his hopes of a relationship with me, he was getting nothing out of this trip, plus I'd taken him away from his party. I broke the impasse a mile to my home, as we approached a deep pothole filled with rainwater and treacherous in the dark. I pointed out the notorious hot spot, 'You need to slow to a crawl through the water. Keep as far right as possible.' In response, he slowed down and followed my instructions. As the car waded through the deepest part of the water, it coughed and spluttered. The water was almost as high as the top of the car's front grille. Kojo revved the engine to keep it going. The car shuddered twice and stopped dead. *Oh no! Not now.* I glanced at my wristwatch. Quarter to seven. I couldn't in all good conscience abandon him in a strange neighbourhood with a dead car. Mum would have to wait. I stood by the roadside for the next hour as local boys pushed the car out of its watery grave for a fee and Kojo tried to coax the engine back to life.

'What are you doing here?' The familiar voice behind me made me jump. It was Tope. She and Bolanle were heading home from wherever they'd been. While I was in the middle of explaining Kojo's predicament, the engine sprung to life. Kojo floored the accelerator, driving a few yards before bringing the car to a stop. He did a U-turn, drove back in my direction before drawing alongside me and the girls. 'My cousins,' I explained at his quizzical look. 'You head on home. I'll be fine walking with them, and thanks for the ride.' He nodded and, with a wry smile, set off.

'Didn't your mum say you had to be home by seven?' Tope asked.

'Yup.' I looked at my watch. The dial read quarter to eight.

'We'd better get a move on then,' said Bolanle.

*

Over the short walk home, I wondered how best to handle Mum. My leaving and returning with the girls looked mighty suspicious, and I was dead certain she would think I'd lied. Instead of the front door, I used the sidewalk to the boys' quarters and knocked on Brother Lekan's door. He opened it, invited me in, before locking it behind us. 'Your mother's furious with you.'

I groaned. 'I know.'

The doorknob rattled, just as I finished explaining what had happened. 'Lekan, open this door!' *Oh-oh. She was mad, all right.* 'Funmi, come out here, right now!'

I cringed. I couldn't remember her ever being this angry. Brother Lekan put a finger to his mouth, signalling I should stay silent.

He opened the door and planted himself, arms outstretched, across the threshold. 'Move aside, Lekan,' Mum said, in a deadly tone.

'Auntie, you need to calm down first.'

'I told her not to go with those girls. Today I will show her who's boss. I will show her pepper!'

I peeped through the gap underneath the arms blocking the doorway and glimpsed Mum waving a cane. She tried to push past him, but he held firm. 'Auntie, she didn't go with them. At least give her a chance to explain.'

'So, you are defending her now? Ehn? Okay. She will come and meet me inside the house. We'll see where she sleeps tonight.' With that, she stalked off.

I sighed. She was too far gone to see reason. Brother Lekan came back inside and locked the door again. He trained his eyes on me. 'Promise me you didn't go with Bolanle and Tope.'

'Brother Lekan, I wouldn't lie to you. I swear I told you the truth.'

'Let's give her time to calm down, then I'll try talking to her again.'

Agitated, I paced the floor, and in a moment of clarity, stumbled on the solution provided by Mum herself. 'Whatever happens, she's not beating me today. If I have to, I'll go back to the university tonight.'

He took one look at the mulish expression on my face. 'Don't you start! Sit down.'

I took the seat he offered and crossed my arms, fed up with my mother. If I turned up at the university with cane marks all over my arms, I'd be the eternal butt of endless jokes. *No, the caning stops here! Today!*

Having decided on a plan of action, the anger ebbed. In its place, sorrow wedged in my throat; sadness that my mother didn't trust me or my judgement and wouldn't give me the benefit of doubt. After thirty minutes had lapsed, Brother Lekan went in search of Mum and I locked the door behind him. He came back almost an hour later. 'You can go back in. She won't touch you,' he said.

'Are you sure? If she tries, I'm leaving.'

'She promised she won't.'

'What did you say to her?'

'I told her the truth and that you are too old for caning.'

Bless him! I gave him a hug, unable to put my thanks into words.

I crept back into the main house and to my bedroom. Bolanle and Tope thought the whole thing amusing. 'What has she got against us, anyway?' Tope asked. I shrugged and climbed into bed. I lay on my back, fingers laced behind my head, and contemplated my future. If I didn't want to be a virtual prisoner, I had to figure a way to avoid spending the next summer break at home.

*

Before I returned to campus, Dad introduced me to his newest tenant, a World War II veteran who fought for the British Empire in India. Baba Ibo was from the Igbo tribe and worked as a security guard at the university's main gates. 'She must have high morals,' he said to Dad, 'I haven't seen her sneaking out to parties at all hours.' His tone revealed his disgust at the latter behaviour. I smirked. *That's how much you know!* But his intent was clear; the campus had only one exit point, and he would watch for me and report to Dad. It seemed fate kept conspiring to keep me in check. On my way back to campus, I contemplated the two challenges before me: avoiding living at home during the summer break and getting out of campus unseen by Dad's watchdog.

When I shared my problems with Bisola, she rocked with so much merriment I regretted the impulse. Noticing my discomfiture, she let up a little. 'Baba Ibo won't be a problem,' she said, her eyes dancing.

'Why do you say that?' I asked.

'Here's what we'll do. On days we have a party to attend, we'll scope out the gates in the evening. The guards work in two shifts and the second starts at 6 p.m. If he's on duty, we'll know to prepare.'

'How will that get me out unnoticed?'

'If he's there, we'll hide you in the back of the car.'

'I can't see how. I'm not travelling in the car's boot and the guards routinely shine their torches into the cars.'

'You could crouch and pretend you are sorting a shoe buckle or something, or we could throw a scarf over you.'

I pursed my lips, unconvinced her solution would work. A hidden head might draw more attention.

'Do you want to attend parties or not? I promise it will be fine.'

I sighed, taking her word for it.

'As for your other problem, try getting a summer job on campus. My brother did last year, and he lived on campus the entire summer.'

My eyes lit up at that piece of news. 'Thanks, I'll explore it.'

'While you do that, have you thought about where you will live during your second year? The university only provides on-site accommodation to first and third-year students. You'll have to travel from home or rent somewhere local.'

I gulped. I hadn't known that. It made the summer problem appear minuscule in comparison.

'What if neither of those are options?'

'You could always become a squatter.' At my clueless expression she added, 'You find someone willing to let you sleep on the floor in their room. That's what most girls do.'

Whoa! There I was, thinking my days of sleeping on the floor were over.

Three Saturdays later, a chance to test Bisola's solution to the Baba Ibo problem presented itself. Sandwiched between my friends in the back seat of the car ferrying us to the party, I chewed the lipstick off my lower lip as the car approached the campus gates. When Baba Ibo bent to speak to the driver, I doubled over into the footwell, searching for an imaginary item. The second guard aimed his torch at the rear window. Bisola, who sat closest to the kerb rolled down the window a smidgen and flashed the brightest smile she could muster.

'Good evening, *oga*. How you dey today?' She didn't disguise the mischief in her voice. Shocked at her audacity, the guard grunted before giving Baba Ibo a nod. The barrier lifted, and the car glided forward. Amused giggles burst from my friends' lips as I stretched my torso. I shook my head in mock disapproval and relaxed back into the seat. *God knew how many times I'd have to do that before the year ended.*

CHAPTER TWENTY-SIX

Star of the Show

A poster on the hall's notice board promoted the university's annual sports day and invited students to take part in a range of track and field events. When we were gathered in Funbi's room, I asked my friends if they were interested. Bisola looked scandalised. Her fingers made a sweeping gesture over her chest and hips. 'Does it seem like God formed this body for sports?'

I sniggered and turned to Funbi.

She held up her hands. 'Don't eye me up, I'm not sporty.'

'How about you, Sayo,' I asked.

'Nope, not me either.'

Funbi fixed me with a contemplative stare. 'Maybe you should try it. I heard that if you represent the hall in sports, you can live in for your second year.'

'Interesting. I haven't taken part in sports since Form 2, but if that's true, it might solve one of my problems.'

In problem-solving mode, Funbi had more to say. 'The staff club hires students as waitresses over the summer. A contact has guaranteed me work, and I am happy to drop in a kind word on your behalf.'

'Yes, please, and thanks.'

Staying on campus through to my third-year final examinations now looked feasible.

*

I turned up to the sports field on a humid Saturday morning. As I trudged through the field, a vista of silver horizontal lines shimmered and flickered in the distance. A product of the warm air rising from the earth, the mirage was a sure sign of the impending scorcher. The previous night's thunderstorm had reduced the dust but did nothing to improve the heat. Instead, it fuelled the mugginess, leaving an earthy, mushroomy aroma in the atmosphere. I was glad they had scheduled the try-outs before noon and not later in the day.

I surveyed the smattering of students ahead as I approached the grandstand. In one corner, a group of lads larked about. A few girls loitered on the opposite end. I eyed the competition and counted the number of heads. A female student blew a whistle and drew the girls into a group. She produced a sheet of paper. 'Please write your name against the events you are interested in on this.' She handed the paper to a girl while the rest of us waited our turn. I spied another girl on the bottom rung of the grandstand's tiered steps. Nonchalant, she observed the proceedings with an air of familiarity, as if she'd done this before. Like the others, she looked older than me. She fluttered her fingers, and I waved back. I strolled over and sat next to her. 'Hi, I am Funmi.'

'Felicia. I have seen you around.'

'Yeah. I'm hard to miss.' I wasn't bragging. Everyone knew of my existence. Someone had even written about me in the campus magazine. The irritating article hadn't said much, just that they didn't like the pint-sized, under-aged chick in Amina Hall. *As if I could help my size.* 'What sport do you do?' I asked.

'Table tennis.' She tilted her head. 'You?'

'I ran long-distance at secondary school. Are you good at table tennis?'

'I played for the country at the last Commonwealth Games.'

I gaped at her. 'Wow! That's impressive.'

She smiled. 'How about you?'

'I'm probably not talented enough to be here.'

'You might surprise yourself.'

'What do you mean?'

Her eyes scanned the field. 'Look around, what do you see?'

Not sure what she meant, I shrugged.

'How many female competitors are here today?'

'Twelve.'

'Exactly. That's between all the sports. Not much competition in any.'

'You don't think more will join us?'

'Nah. Half the residents of Amina Hall are middle-aged women. The others don't care. You, my friend, might just end up holding the banner for the hall.'

It took me ninety seconds to run the 400-metres race, but I came second. Next, I ran the 800 metres and since I was the only one running, I topped the podium. I remembered a famous Yoruba saying: *In the land of the blind, the one-eyed man is king.* That rang true in my case, and I had just secured campus accommodation for the rest of my studies. *Thank you, Funbi.*

'Didn't I tell you,' my new-found friend said an hour later. 'Welcome to team Amina!'

*

By now I knew I liked pretty boys, the ones almost too handsome for their own good. I dated one such boy on campus. Conceited beyond words, he fancied himself a Casanova and girls flocked to him in droves. 'Just friends,' he claimed, but I couldn't see him staying faithful, so after a month I stopped visiting him. The funny thing was, I don't think he even noticed. I decided I needed a nice, middle-of-the-road guy, attractive enough, but not so much that I'd have to fight every other girl off him. That's when Felicia introduced me to Debo, a second-year law student.

At five-foot eleven, he towered over me. Charming, with mocha-coloured skin that matched mine, his face sported one tiny vertical tribal mark carved into the top of each cheek. Debo's tribal marks fascinated me. It was a rarity to find them on someone close to my age in Lagos. Like most of my peers, I had grown up viewing tribal marks as barbaric, an act confined to the annals of history or rural dwellers. Yet, Debo's parents were affluent and educated enough to have lived in the UK. *So why had they marked him?* I couldn't help wondering if they were just deeply afro-centric or steeped in the traditional religions. Either way, it told me something about his background that didn't sit right with me, but for the moment, I ignored it.

Like I guessed he would, Dad said nothing about me travelling to England over the summer. Although disappointed, I understood his motivation and the risk he didn't want to take. Funbi kept her promise and, between my June examinations, I interviewed for the waitressing job. Within a few days, I heard the fantastic news. I not only had the job but it guaranteed accommodation on site. Ecstatic, I invited Debo round to celebrate.

'Are you spending the entire holiday at home in Ibadan?' I asked.

He waggled his eyebrows, an amused smile quirking at his lips. 'Yes, why?'

'Bisola's twenty-first birthday is in August. Her parents live in Ibadan too. I might go.'

He pulled a pen and tiny notepad out of his pocket, wrote on the paper and handed it over.

'Here's my address. If you come to Ibadan, I'd be delighted to see you.' With that, we parted ways.

I went home and told my parents I planned to live and work on campus through the summer. I worried they wouldn't support it, but I needed the job. It was the key to my Plan B; the one I was concocting to get myself to London without Dad's financial help, and I was prepared to offer a compromise. I informed them the position required me to reside on campus Monday to Friday. I'd have to work evening shifts and it would be safer than travelling home late at night. Since I'd only have occasional weekend shifts, I would be home most weekends. They bought my well-thought-out argument with little dissent.

My next conversation was with Bisola, who'd been talking about her party non-stop. 'I'd love to attend, but I can't see my parents letting me travel to Ibadan by myself,' I said.

She rolled her eyes. 'If only they knew the places you've been. I could arrange for someone to pick you and a few others up from campus.'

'That wouldn't be enough. Would you go home with me so they can meet you? That might allay their fears.' She agreed and one day that week we both popped down to my parents. Bisola turned on the charm and won them over. The trip to Ibadan was on.

*

If Dad had kept his promise, I should have been in England. Instead, I spent the summer break working through the week and going home at weekends. The weekends at home were tolerable, but the older I got, the more glaring the differences between my way of thinking and everyone else's. With most students gone, life on campus was tepid and my evenings were quiet. Funbi lived on campus since she was waitressing at the club too, but her energetic social life included a boyfriend who lived in town. I preferred the solitude at campus to living at home with all the drama of the extended family. When I wasn't at work, I read or listened to music. ABBA was my most recent find, and I loved picking apart the harmonies, line by line.

*

The day before Bisola's party, her brother picked a group of us up from campus. Two hours later, after a riotous reunion, we settled down for a quiet night. The next morning, I asked Bisola if she needed any help with the preparations. 'It's all taken care of,' she said.

'In that case, do you mind if I slip out for a few hours? I promised Debo that I'd visit if I made it to Ibadan.'

She winked. 'Sure, have fun.'

I caught a taxi to Debo's address, but as the taxi drove away, I chewed my lower lip. It had only just occurred to me that his parents might disapprove of him receiving female visitors. *If that were the case, he wouldn't have given me his address, would he? Maybe he didn't really think you'd come,* the voice in my head parroted. *Well, I'm here now.* Before I lost my nerve, I approached the iron double gates and pressed the doorbell. I kicked the tip of my stilettos in the dust while I waited for a response. Two minutes later, the side-gate unlatched, and a man leaned out. 'Yes? Can I help you?' he asked.

'Is Debo home?'

He looked like the guard. *Would he let me in?* As if reading my mind, he opened the gate and closed it behind me. 'Stay here. I'll go fetch him.'

As he disappeared into the residence, I surveyed the palatial structure screaming his parents' wealth, its front portico towering like a mausoleum.

From the distance, I spied Debo ambling down to greet me. Something was amiss. It showed in the stiff way he held his body and in the smile that didn't quite reach his eyes. 'Hi,' he said, extending a handshake. The guard looked on with curiosity. It wasn't our usual form of greeting, but I took the hand. He led me down a walkway to the back of the main residence. 'My parents gave me an apartment in the boys' quarters,' he said, as we climbed an external stairway to the building's second floor. Debo opened a door, and I walked into a well-apportioned living room, tastefully furnished in brown and beige. The words burst from my lips, 'Your home is lovely!'

'Thanks. Have a seat. Can I get you a Coke or something else to drink?'

I sat down before replying. 'A Coke is fine, thanks.'

While he was busy fetching drinks, I perused the rest of his man-cave, noting the expensive music deck in a corner of the room. A small glass table in front of the couch held a stack of national newspapers, including *The Daily Times* and *Punch*. Underneath the dailies, a half-hidden image of a topless model peeped at me from the sheets of a magazine. I snorted. *Men and their desire to ogle the female form!* The three-seater I sat on faced full-length windows dressed in creamy curtains that complemented the chocolate-coloured leather sofa. Beyond the open curtains, I glimpsed a superb view of the Ibadan skyline.

The clinking in the adjacent room stopped and Debo emerged with two glasses. I took the drink he offered. 'Thanks.'

He raised his glass in salute.

'How have you been?' I asked.

'Fine. You?'

Two-word phrases? I wonder what's going on. 'I've been well. Campus is quiet without other students.'

He nodded, brows creased as if in deep thought. I stopped talking, and we both drank in constrained silence. Halfway through the drink. I put the glass down.

'This was a mistake. I'd better leave,' I said.

That startled him. 'Sorry, I'm a tad preoccupied.'

'Do you want to tell me why?'

He ran a hand over his head.

'You might as well,' I pressed.

'It's another girl,' he sighed. 'She is a family friend. My mum wants me to marry her, so she won't be pleased to hear I had a female visitor.'

Ahh! That explained a lot. I pulled myself together. 'That's an enormous step. I accept that our relationship is new, but what do you want? Do you wish to wed this girl?'

'I can't disobey my parents.'

The audible breath that followed revealed how conflicted he was. But his last statement told me all I needed to know. *Another relationship gone awry.* Fortunately, I wasn't too invested in it yet. I stood. 'I'll be on my way.'

He nodded. 'I'll call you a taxi.'

Minutes later, I climbed into the taxi, pensive. I wouldn't have taken Debo as a mama's boy, but I knew Yoruba mothers wielded immense power over their son's choice of spouse. I wondered about his mother's motives. *A business merger perhaps?* But it was no longer my concern.

*

Four hours later, Bisola waltzed across to where I sat in a corner of her dad's living room while the party blazed around me. 'What's wrong with you?' she said, her hips swaying in tune with the music.

'What do you mean?'

'I mean your dour face. This is a party, or haven't you noticed? You've not been yourself since you got back from Debo's.'

'Yeah, sorry. I guess we broke up.'

One finely arched brow rose. 'Oh well, it's a perfect day to break up.'

'How does that figure?'

'Nothing like a party and alcohol to cheer you up.'

I mulled over that for a second. If I ever needed an excuse to drink, I guessed this was it.

'You are right. Let's get this party started.'

'It started ages ago, you idiot.' She shimmied her hips and floated away.

After two bottles of shandy, I was decidedly less morose. I couldn't fault the DJ. So far, he had played all my favourites, Kool & the Gang's 'Ladies Night', The Bee Gee's 'Night Fever', McFadden and Whitehead's 'Ain't No Stopping Us Now'. I shuffled and bumped to ABBA's 'Dancing Queen', working up a sweat. The song ended and the first line of Shalamar's 'I Don't Wanna Be the Last to Know', floated out. *Ugh! Not a break-up song.* I squeezed past the bodies and found my way to an empty chair. My feet needed a break, anyway. I sat fanning my face, pushing the stuffy air around, and scanned the room. At the far side, I spied Bolaji, another casual friend from campus, swiping sausage rolls off the buffet table. She waved, then turned her attention back to piling her plate high. Moments later, she wormed her way across the room, accompanied by a guy.

The bloke at her side gave a friendly smile. 'Meet my cousin, Bade,' Bolaji said. I smiled at the newcomer, extending a hand. 'Hi. I'm Funmi.'

He shook it before tucking his hands in his pockets. I took his measure. Twinkly eyes, medium height, two-inch afro that reminded me of Michael Jackson's before he got his Jerry curls. *He's cute.* I'd seen him gyrating on the dance floor earlier. He had showed off some adroit moves. 'Can I take the chair beside you?' he asked.

'Please be my guest.'

I shuffled my seat, so it angled towards his, while Bolaji faded into the crowd.

'Bolaji says you are a student at the University of Lagos,' he said.

'I am. Are you too?'

'No. I am on my National Youth Service year at the computer centre on campus.'

I blinked twice. He didn't look old enough to have graduated already. I took in his slight build and skin the colour of cinnamon, but it was his eyes that caught my attention. As I stared into them, I felt a zing and tingled all over.

We chatted for a while and it turned out he was five years older than me. He'd graduated from the University of Ibadan and his family lived in the city. Somehow, we got to talking about childhood memories.

'I was born in London,' Bade said.

'Wow! Me too.' *What were the odds of that?*

We spent the next hour exchanging titbits and found we had several experiences in common. He told me how he had learned to defend himself from racist bullies at his London school. His mother had bought him a giant, sand-weighted, plastic snowman for boxing practice. I laughed out loud. I'd found a kindred spirit in the middle of a desert. When my laughter died down, I caught him staring at my mouth. A spark of awareness zig-zagged between us. 'What?' I asked.

He coughed. 'I like the sound of your voice.'

He liked my voice? The one that had got me into trouble more times than I could remember?

'Actually, I have a confession to make.'

My lips quirked. 'I'm listening.'

'I overheard you and Bisola talking earlier about your boyfriend.'

Heat rushed to my face. 'Oh that; he's history.'

'In that case, I'd like to take you out sometime.'

I hesitated before responding. I was straight out of a relationship, albeit a short one. He didn't have Debo's height or classic looks. *You are done with pretty boys, remember?* His eyes were bright and alight, his smile infectious, and he seemed nice. *And that spark, the one I was always searching for, was worth exploring.*

I found myself agreeing. 'Yeah, why not?'

'How about I drive you and Bolaji back to Lagos tomorrow?'

'You've got a car?'

'Uh-huh.'

'Okay. That would be great, thanks.'

We agreed that Bolaji and I would meet him at his mother's home the following morning. I didn't know it yet, but I'd just met my future spouse.

CHAPTER TWENTY-SEVEN

London, Here We Come!

By the middle of the next semester, Bade and I were a couple. He loved partying as much as I did and fancied himself as a DJ. With his expanding collection of cassette tapes, his friends often requested his services. We travelled most weekends to parties across Lagos, Ogun and Oyo states, and when we weren't partying, he drove me around Lagos, introducing me to his friends. I went home less frequently, preferring to visit Mum at her shop. It had taken Brother Lekan's intervention, but now that Mum treated me like an adult, I enjoyed her company.

On one such visit, Mum turned her chair around, fixed that all-knowing gaze on mine and said, 'Funmi.'

'Yes, ma,' I replied.

'Funmi.'

'Yes, ma.'

'Funmi.'

'Yes, ma!'

'How many times did I just call you?'

That was a Yoruba elder's way of saying, 'Listen up! I'm about to say something important to you.' 'Three times, Mum.'

'The boy you are seeing, where does he come from?' *Ah! I hadn't seen that coming. Neat trick.* She hadn't even asked if I was dating. *How much should I reveal?* I stalled.

'His mum lives in Ibadan, but his dad has died.'

'That's not my question. Where is the family from?'

I put the good news first. 'His mum is Ijebu.'

'And his dad?'

'He was from Abeokuta.'

'Hmm. Abeokuta. The Egba don't treat their wives well.'

I resisted the urge to snigger. No other tribe measured up for the Ijebus and their children. Each tribe thought likewise, preferring their children to marry within the sub-group, despite them all sharing the same Yoruba identity.

'You need to find someone else.'

I almost smiled. Now she wanted me to find a man, any man, provided he was Ijebu. I imagined screening all potential suitors: *Are you Ijebu? No? Next!*

'Funmi, are you listening to me?'

Her voice jolted me out of my musings. 'Yes, ma.'

She peered into my eyes, trying to gauge my sincerity. 'I know you. You don't listen to anything anyone says. You will do what you will.'

I kept my face deadpan. 'I heard you, Mum.'

'Tell me his name and his mother's name.'

I gave her the details she wanted, and she dropped the subject.

On my way to the campus, I processed the conversation with Mum. The moment she made the mental shift that I was no longer a child, the dynamics of our relationship and her expectations changed. In Yoruba culture, a girl's path was linear: school, husband, then babies. Mum clearly thought I was ready for the next cultural milestone: me finding a spouse. I assumed she guessed I was in a serious relationship either because she saw less of me, or Brother Lekan had let something slip. Or maybe she'd just fished for information out of instinct.

A few weeks later, Bade said he wanted to meet my parents. 'No, you don't,' I said, 'Dad, perhaps, but my mum would eat you alive.'

'She can't be that bad.'

'She's not bad, just tough, and you are Egba. That doesn't bode well for you.'

'But I'm half Ijebu!'

'Yeah,' I laughed, 'but it's the wrong half.'

It was comical. My boyfriend wanted to meet my parents and here I was dissuading him. That same week, Mum asked if I had ended the relationship, but I neither confirmed nor denied it.

*

My maternal grandmother, Mama Iwaya, came to town to care for a cousin suffering from postpartum blues. I had seen her sporadically over the years at family weddings and funerals, the memories of her kindness a sharp contrast to my relationship with Dad's mother. Not wanting to miss an opportunity to see her, I agreed when Mum suggested we visit her. Mum and I curtsied to the elders who sat outside in the front yard, as we entered the home where Mama Iwaya was staying. The baby's grandmother, Mum's first cousin, welcomed us before leading us to the room where Mama Iwaya sat next to the newborn.

With the same gusto with which she greeted me when I was six, Mama Iwaya held out her arms. 'My daughter! Eh, see how grown up you are.' I smiled as I knelt to greet her.

She pulled up a stool. 'Come, sit beside me and tell me all about your life. Your studies, they are going well?'

I settled on the stool and answered all her questions. Mum's cousin offered a tray of drinks. I selected a can of Coke, pulling back the ring, before gurgling. The chilled drink soothed my parched throat. A few swigs later, I put it down.

Mama Iwaya adjusted her wrapper, turned to me and without missing a beat said, 'This man you are seeing, tell me about him.'

Ambushed again! Mum planned this. 'There's nothing to say Mama. I like him, he likes me.'

'What has he given you so far?'

'What do you mean, Mama?'

'Your mum says she's asked you to break it off and you won't. If it's because of all the things you've taken from him, don't worry, I will give you the money myself, so you can pay him back.'

I gave my grandmother a blank look. 'But Mama, I have taken nothing from him.'

'Nothing at all?'

I nodded.

Her eyes widened. 'Wait,' she ticked the items off on her fingers, 'no shoes, handbag, jewellery, money?'

'No, Mama.'

Mama got off her seat. She paced the length of the room and back, stood right in front of me and peered into my eyes. 'Are you well?'

'I'm fine, Mama,' I said.

She shook her head. 'I don't think so. Something must be wrong with you. I thought you modern people were smarter than that?' She untied the wrapper at her waist, re-tied it and wagged her forefinger. 'Before I married your grandfather, he promised me heaven and earth.' She paused, slapped both hands against her thighs. 'Once I married him, his promises disappeared into thin air.' She flicked her fingers in the air to show the nothingness.

Comprehension dawned. Mama thought modern dating was like courtship in the 1930s when a suitor showered his amour with gifts. She assumed my reluctance to break things off was because I was indebted to Bade.

'I can't believe you've got nothing from him,' she muttered. 'You had better go back and ask for everything you want before you marry him. If he turns out like your grandfather, you will be grateful for the advice. At least get an umbrella and a wristwatch.'

A bubble of laughter welled deep in my belly, but I tamped it down. She wouldn't take kindly to me laughing in her face. Mama, it appeared, was more vexed and concerned at my apparent stupidity than the fact that I wouldn't break off the relationship. I was certain this wasn't the result Mum had hoped for. *Oh, how ironic! Serves Mum right.* When it was time to leave, Mama reiterated her message. 'If you want anything, get it now!'

'I hear you, Mama,' I said, hiding my smirk behind a smile.

*

Home for the weekend, I had just finished helping Mum prepare supper. I walked into the parlour, balancing a plate of semovita and okra soup in one hand and a bowl of water in the other. I stooped to deposit both on the small stool resting between Dad's legs. I straightened up, prepared to return to the kitchen.

'Thanks,' Dad said. He dipped his right hand in the bowl of water, to cleanse it before eating, paused, then looked at me. 'Wait. I've got some news for you. I've got your ticket to England.'

'What!' I spluttered. 'Sorry, I meant pardon?'

He grinned as if he had just been crowned King of Bariga. 'You can go this summer.'

'Thank you, thank you!' The words gushed out of my mouth. I couldn't hug him with the food in the way. Instead, I hopped on the spot with unconstrained joy.

'Promise me one thing.'

I nodded.

'You will come back to finish your studies.'

'I promise I will, Dad.'

'Go on, you can tell everyone now.'

At the door, I looked over my shoulder. 'Have you told Mum?'

'Yes. Remember to thank her.'

'Yes, sir.'

I dashed back into the kitchen and enveloped Mum in a hug. She gave me a pat, a rueful smile on her lips. I broke the news to my siblings. They surrounded me, bopping up and down like over-inflated balloons. Later that evening, Tope and Bolanle congratulated me, although I detected a slight touch of envy in Tope's acerbic 'You still have to come back and finish your studies.'

Back on campus, I placed a telephone call to Nan. Throughout the years we had stayed in contact, and her letters always had a telephone number scribbled at the bottom. For a fee, the university allowed you to make local and international calls from one of the administrative offices. The operator dialled Nan's number and handed me the phone. 'You've got five minutes,' she said. It was my first time using a phone and all I could afford. Besides, there was a lengthy queue for the phone behind me. I lifted the handset to my ear. Brrr… Brrr… I crossed my fingers and prayed Nan's number hadn't changed since her last letter.

'Hello?'

My heart skipped at hearing that voice on the other end. I wondered why I had never rung her. 'Nan, it's me, Ann from Nigeria.'

'Ann? Is that really you?'

'Yes Nan, it is. Look, I've only got five minutes, so I need to let you know I'm coming to London.'

'What! When?' Her excitement was palpable down the line.

'I am arriving on British Caledonian Airways on…'

'Wait! Let me get a pen.'

I tapped my foot anxiously, hoping my five minutes wouldn't end before she took down the details.

She came back on the phone breathless. 'Okay, I'm ready.'

I reeled off the details and spent the last few seconds enquiring after the rest of the family. She was still telling me about Pop when the line went dead. I grimaced and handed the phone over, but my heartbeat quickened, excited for the future.

*

The rest of the academic year flew by and before I knew it, the examination cycle was back. The day I finished my last paper, I went out with Bade to celebrate. He drove me to an open night market in Sabo, near Yaba, where Mallams sold *suya*, a local delicacy that I had developed an insatiable taste for. He parked his car by the roadside and held my hand as we strolled over to where several vendors displayed their food. I picked out four skewers of beef coated in a chilli and peanut paste and watched as the Mallam roasted them over an open coal fire.

Half an hour later, parked underneath the brooding branches of the trees lining Lovers' Lane, we licked off our fingers, having thoroughly enjoyed the midnight snack. Lovers' Lane was the nickname of the secluded access road leading to the Vice Chancellor's lodge on a tiny island, jutting into the Lagos lagoon, next to the campus. Cars dotted both sides of the single-carriage road, creating a chevron along the muddy bank. We reclined our seats, lay back and listened to the gentle lap of the waves against the lagoon shore, a mere stone's throw away. 'Are you all packed and ready to go?' Bade asked.

'I haven't got gifts for Nan and her family yet.'

'Are you excited?'

'Yes, but anxious about flying alone.'

We lay there silent for a while. Suddenly, Bade levered his seat upright, rested both palms on the steering wheel and stared through the windscreen. I mirrored his movements at a more sedate pace.

'Is everything all right?' I asked.

He turned to face me and breathed deeply. 'Do you see me in your future?'

I searched his face, trying to fathom his intent. The answer was easy. I loved him and although we argued over everything, often and passionately, he understood me more than anyone I knew. We had one elemental thing in common, a deep desire for individuality, to be whoever we wanted to be without the restraints that our culture placed on us. *We could run away and be rebels together.*

'Yes, I do.'

He looked deep into my eyes. 'I love you,' he breathed. 'Will you marry me?'

Speechless, I nodded, before whispering, 'I love you too.' He slipped a hand in his right pocket and dug around. When he withdrew it, a shiny solid gold signet ring lay in his palm. 'This was my dad's. I'd like you to wear it until I can give you an engagement ring.'

My heart beat faster than I had ever known it to, faster than when I was running on the racetrack. From watching the adults getting married around me, I knew Yoruba men didn't do proposals or give engagement rings the way English men did, yet here I was. I reached out my left hand and he slipped the masculine ring on my third finger. It swivelled around, several sizes too large. A smile split my face in half. 'Thank you. I won't wear it all the time because I don't want to lose it.' He leaned forward and pulled me into his arms, his face inches from mine. I closed my eyes as his lips descended, sealing the promise.

A week later, I was back at home packing for my trip. I visited Yaba market and bought gifts: for Nan, a stunning, tan leather bag, and matching wallets for Pop and Tom. Relatives and family friends gave Mum money and requested I buy some Nigerian lace for them, as London lace was deemed superior to the local variety. Dad gave me £400 as spending money. I had never seen so much money in one place.

I clutched my handbag to my chest as we walked into the departure lounge of the Murtala Mohammed International Airport, named after the fallen Head of State in the 1976 coup. It was 19 July 1980, and Dad and Mum had come to see me off. 'Relax,' Mum whispered, 'you don't want to alert people to the fact that you are carrying all that money.'

As we approached the extended queue at the check-in desk, I pulled my shoulders up to my ears and let them drop with a shrug. I breathed in and out slowly, hoping that would do the trick. Time ticked by as the queue inched forward every few minutes. The check-in process required customs officers to frisk each piece of luggage manually. Two-and-a-half hours later, I was ready to go. At the entrance to passport control, I hugged my parents.

'We'll see you at the end of August,' Mum said. They turned and made for the exit. Just before they were out of sight, Dad swivelled round and waved. 'Have fun!'

CHAPTER TWENTY-EIGHT

Awakened Consciousness

Seven hours after take-off, the plane's wheels made a bumpy touchdown at Heathrow Airport. I gathered my belongings and followed the other passengers off the plane. At the immigration desk, the officer looked at my Nigerian passport.

'You were born in London?' he asked.

'Yes, sir.'

'What is the purpose of your visit?'

'I am on holiday.'

'For how long?'

'Six weeks.'

He stamped the passport and handed it over. 'Enjoy your stay.'

Thanking him, I tucked the document in my handbag and made my way to baggage reclaim. An hour later, I wheeled my trolley into an alley lined with people ready to welcome a loved one. I scanned the sea of faces frantically. *Would I even recognise Nan?* 'There she is,' a voice said. It was Tom at the far end of the line. Nan stood beside him, barely up to his armpit, beaming from ear to ear. It was as if time had stopped for them. They looked no different from my image of them twelve years earlier. Nan wore a flowery dress, her short, unruly curls sticking out all over her head. Tom's horn-rimmed plastic frames were almost identical to the metal ones I'd last seen on him in the 1960s. I walked into their embrace. *It was so wonderful to be back.*

*

Tom introduced me to the friend who drove them to the airport. I murmured my thanks as I settled into the back seat beside Nan. 'The weather has been good so far this summer, hasn't it Mum?' Tom said, as the car zoomed down the motorway without hitting a single pothole.

If only the Lagos-Ibadan expressway were this smooth. I tuned into the conversation. 'I thought the summer weather was always great,' I said.

'It can be unpredictable,' Nan said. 'Sometimes we get all four seasons in a day.'

I turned to look at her. 'You mean it gets cold in June? I haven't packed clothing for cool weather.'

Nan rang her fingers through her hair and fluffed her curls. I smiled. The gesture brought back childhood memories. 'Some days you might need a light jacket, but it's nothing to worry about.'

Right. First things on my shopping list: a jacket and cardigan.

The sun dipped low on the horizon, its orange embers merging into a blue line, signalling the onset of dusk. As the three-lane motorway merged into a dual carriageway, and the neon lights atop the London skyscrapers came into view, I felt a flutter in my chest. I had waited so long for this. The city unfurled as we whizzed past, beautiful and quiet. No jay walking, no beeping car horns, none of the noise typical of a Lagos street. People hurried along the pavements, crossing only at the traffic lights. At several junctions, red lights brought cars to a halt, with drivers stopping regardless of whether there were oncoming vehicles. A soft gasp escaped my lips. *How very civilised.*

Nan cut into the silence. 'As you know, when I quit fostering, the Council moved us into a flat.'

A memory flickered in the recesses of my mind. I nodded. 'Yeah, you said so in one of your letters.'

'It's only got two bedrooms,' Tom said, 'but you can have mine and I'll sleep on the pull-out in the living room.'

An hour after leaving the airport, we pulled up next to a block of flats on Birkbeck Road, in the Hornsey area. I stepped out of the car and took a cleansing breath. The air had cooled and as the chill seeped in, I rubbed my arms vigorously. The brown-stone five-storey building in front of me ran almost the entire length of the street. On the other side, a row of terraced dwellings, just like our old house, stood proud. 'Ann, go in with Mum. I'll be right behind you with the suitcase,' Tom said. I gave the driver a courteous nod before following Nan in and up a flight of stairs.

As soon as Nan put her key in the lock, a yapping sound started inside the flat. Nan turned the door handle, and a miniature poodle flew at her, jumping on all fours. 'Down!' Tom warned behind me. The fur-ball moved back a little, still dancing, its tail wagging in all directions, until it saw me. Then it bared its canines, snarling. I froze and looked at Tom. I wasn't afraid of dogs, and this one was puny, but its dislike of me was obvious and, tiny or not, it had teeth. 'Don't show any fear,' Tom cautioned. He grabbed the animal by the collar and led it into a room before shutting the door in its face. The dog protested with a furious yap, which soon turned into a piteous whine. As we moved further into the hallway, a balding, grey head emerged at the top of the stairs. I grinned at him. 'Pop!' Smiling, he slowly made his way down. 'Come here.' He opened his arms, and I rushed into them.

*

The following morning, I came down for breakfast. Nan's kitchen and living room occupied the ground floor, while the two bedrooms and bathroom were upstairs. The miniature poodle, or Diddlydoo as I took to calling it in my head, growled again, but stopped when Tom threatened to lock it in the broom cupboard. 'Don't mind him,' said Nan. 'He thinks he is a watchdog, and he's protecting me.'

Ha! The silly thing wasn't even shin high.

I grabbed a seat at the small circular dining table while Nan flipped eggs in a frying pan. It was almost like the old days. I glanced around the compact room. The cream flowery curtains drew my attention. 'I see your love of flowers hasn't changed over the years.'

Nan cackled at my comment. 'Your tongue hasn't either.'

I smiled. I didn't remember myself as a sharp-tongued brat in my early childhood, but given the amount of lip I gave Mama in Nigeria, I must have been. The linoleum on the floor caught my eye, the black and grey circular pattern an exact match to the one gracing Mum's kitchen at home. *How could two rooms worlds apart have the same covering?* I couldn't resist the urge to point out the coincidence.

'My mum has got the same carpet as yours on her kitchen floor.'

'The same what?' Tom asked.

'Carpet.'

'What?' He looked at me, his eyes a mirror of confusion.

I pointed to the floor. 'Carpet.'

'Oh, you mean carpet.' He rolled and extended the 'r'.

I had already noticed the differences in our accents and that I had to repeat myself several times to make myself understood. It seemed I would need to work extra hard at communicating over the summer.

After breakfast, Tom and I took a walk in Priory Park, across the road from the old house. It brought back memories of those occasions, long ago, when he'd sneak me a sweet. So much remained the same: Tom apparently still loved his walks and I still harboured a sweet tooth; 144a Middle Lane looked more or less the same; the pansies blooming in the park were no different to those twelve years ago; the playground was still there, albeit with a fresh lick of paint. Yet so much had changed. The sky in my childhood imagination was a perfect blue and resembled nothing like the overcast clouds that greeted me that morning. I recalled most of the houses on Middle Lane as redbrick. Now, the lower end of the terrace flashed a grey and cream combination and together with the dull sky created a rather drab landscape. Tom and I cut through a trail in the park and doubled back to the junction of Middle Lane and Priory Road, right where the fish and chip shop used to be. Alas, it was no more, replaced by a kebab shop.

As we walked back to the flat, I studied the pavements covered in polka dot remnants of stale chewing gum. Outside the block of flats, people had carelessly dumped their waste on the floor around the large unemptied garbage cans. *Mama Yaba would have a fit if she saw those.* While the streets of London were less dusty and cleaner than Lagos, they by no means met her standard for cleanliness. As I climbed the stairs to the flat, I examined my feelings. I loved being around Nan, Tom and Pop. However, so far, what I had seen of London in broad daylight did not live up to my expectations – and I wasn't sure why.

*

Nan still loved bingo, and she took me to one of her weekly sessions at the community centre on the ground floor of the block. I scanned the room, noticing no other Black people. Nan introduced me to several people from the past, none of whom I remembered. She handed me three tickets and explained the rules.

'When you hear a number, cross it off. If you mark five numbers in a row, shout "bingo".' I settled beside her, pen in hand, ready to win something.

'Legs eleven,' the caller announced. 'Duck and dive, twenty-five. Dancing queen, seventeen.'

I giggled at the rhyming lingo for each of the numbers called, as I settled into the rhythm of the game. 'Bingo!' I screamed in excitement, circling my fifth number. Silence descended, all eyes on me.

'That's blooming lucky,' Nan said. 'Here, let me see.'

I handed the ticket over. She pointed to the numbers covering three different rows. 'They ain't in a single row.'

'Oops, sorry.' The room tittered. I hung my head in embarrassment.

*

Over the next few days, a pattern emerged. When I wasn't helping Nan prepare meals, or out walking with Tom, I curled up beside Pop in the living room and read. Occasionally, I'd walk up and down Middle Lane trying to identify the old haunts. Susan's house, the backdrop to my racial awakening at five, was either on Lightfoot Road or Rokesly Avenue, but I couldn't remember which. I walked up and down both streets, staring at the houses, hoping to jog long-buried memories, without success.

'Do you know what happened to Susan and her mother from the old church?' I asked Nan one evening.

'I haven't seen them since I stopped going to the church aeons ago. They've probably left the area. Why do you ask?'

I could barely understand my emotions, let alone explain them. 'Just curious. Has the neighbourhood changed much?' Every time someone walked past me, they looked me over as if I were a curiosity.

'Not really. A few coloureds like you moved in around Turnpike Lane, but not here.'

Although I knew Nan meant no harm, I bristled at the word 'coloured'. The adjective reawakened old sensitivities and reminded me that even here I was perceived as different. My introspection continued over the following days. I had spent so many years dreaming of my return to London. Now that I was back, I felt rudderless, trying to re-capture something of the past, without knowing what. The awareness that my existence was temporarily suspended in a world of make-believe that wouldn't last left me ambivalent and at odds with myself.

*

Pop took his time coming down in the mornings and spent most of his day in a chair, his feet up on a padded stool. He was still as uncommunicative as ever, preferring to watch television or listen in on conversations. As far as I could tell, he no longer smoked his tobacco pipe, which was probably better for his health.

One morning, over breakfast, I asked Tom how to get to Liverpool Street. 'Why do you want to go there?' He paused his cup of tea a few inches from his lips. 'It isn't much of a tourist attraction.'

'It has a market where people sell Nigerian lace. I need to buy a box load of the stuff for folk back home.'

'You've got enough money for that?' He sipped and swallowed.

'Yeah. I have £800.'

'Blooming heck!' He coughed, spluttered and made a gasping sound, his face going beetroot red. I surmised the liquid had gone the wrong way down his throat. I dashed to the sink, filled a glass with water and handed it to him. He gulped some water, then gasped some more. I hovered, hoping I hadn't killed him with shock.

By the time Nan came downstairs, he'd recovered somewhat, but his eyes were rimmed red. 'You wouldn't believe how much money she's got,' he told Nan.

'Only half of it is mine. The rest of it belongs to the people I am buying stuff for.'

'It is still a lot to spend on holiday,' Tom said.

I hadn't stopped to consider the value of the money Dad gave me and I realised I had taken him for granted. One naira was equivalent to a pound and if it meant that much to Tom, how about Dad who worked for and earned it?

Tom wasn't done with me yet. On our walk to the park that afternoon, he broached the conversation again. 'You know mum and dad live on a state pension, right? You should give them some money as a contribution towards your keep.'

The thought had never crossed my mind, the idea of paying my way in someone else's house a novel one. In Nigeria, people fed their guests with whatever they had. I gritted my teeth at the implications of parting with cash I'd rather spend on myself.

'How much sounds right to you?' I asked, after an uncomfortable silence.

'You decide, but £120 seems fair.'

I did a quick mental calculation. That would leave me with £280. When we got home, I went to the bedroom, counted out £150 and handed it to Nan. I half hoped she would reject it, the way a Nigerian elder would, but she thanked me, wrapped me in her arms and kissed my cheek. I felt bad for not having thought of her needs and wanting to keep hold of the money. But I was proud that for the first time, I was paying my own way, albeit with Dad's money.

CHAPTER TWENTY-NINE

Summer of Enlightenment

When I asked about the best place for shopping, Tom recommended Wood Green Shopping City. As Nan predicted, the weather had varied over the week and that day was no exception. Despite it being the beginning of August, the chill in the air made me pull up the zip on my jacket. Even on the hottest day so far, I hadn't been able to leave the house without at least a cardigan.

Two buses later, I walked into the shopping centre and my eyes sparkled at the array of glittering shops lining both sides of the walkway. Two entire floors of shops filled with fashion, household goods and everything in between awaited my perusal. With relish, I slipped into the first shoe shop and headed for the size five aisle. Since my days of having to go barefoot, I had developed something of a fetish for shoes. I couldn't wait for the day I'd have enough money to buy a pair to match every outfit I owned. I strolled up and down the racks, picking up shoes, slipping them on and putting them back.

A pair of black, strappy, stiletto sandals covered in rhinestones caught my attention. I picked them up and checked the price tag. At an eye-watering £40, they were well out of my price range. Although I still had over £200 spending money, I needed a sizeable chunk of it to buy gifts for everyone at home. I walked around the shop looking for something cheaper, but the most attractive shoes cost more. Deciding I'd try my luck elsewhere, I left. I window-shopped for a while, trying on clothes and footwear until my feet ached. Then I found Clarks. It brought back instant memories of the social class division at secondary school, between those who wore Clarks and those who didn't. Intrigued, I entered the store and stared in dismay at shoes that were more granny than glamour.

A gentle flutter in my stomach reminded me it was way past lunch time. I found a McDonald's, ordered a hamburger meal and found an empty bench. As I munched through my lunch, I weighed my financial options. On campus, students who travelled abroad for summer came home with a new wardrobe. I had planned to purchase at least two pairs of shoes and four outfits, but my reduced budget would not stretch to that and everything else I needed to buy. I swallowed the last bite of my burger and glugged the remnants of my root beer. Shoes or clothes? The shoes won. I went back to Ravel.

Tired from a hard day of shopping, I headed home. As soon as I put my key in the lock, the familiar yapping started. I knew it would end the minute the monster saw my face, and it didn't disappoint me. Grrr…it bared its ugly teeth again. 'Welcome back,' Nan said, holding Diddlydoo by the collar as I dragged my shopping bags into the kitchen. 'Did you find everything you needed?'

'Hardly. I just about found shoes I liked and could afford. With the amount I need to spend on gifts, I won't have enough for a decent wardrobe.' I puffed, sank onto a chair and pulled out the two pairs of high heels I found after hours of searching. One black and one brown, they would service my needs over the coming year. At £30 each, they had been at the top end of affordable.

'Who are all the gifts for?'

'Friends and every single member of my dad's household, including his tenants.'

'Why do you need to buy presents for that many people?'

'That's the Yoruba way.'

'What will happen if you don't?'

'Well, let's see…my friends would probably ostracise me and my family would call me Scrooge or something similar.'

She whipped around from the task she was doing at the sink, disbelief on her face. 'You are joking, right?'

'Nope, I'm dead serious.'

Her face took on a pensive note. 'Maybe you are shopping in the wrong place. I'll take you out tomorrow.'

*

The next day, Nan led me down the High Street, until we stopped in front of a typical two-storey Victorian dwelling. Inside, Nan introduced me to Kostas, a portly man of Mediterranean colouring and his wife, Eleni, who ran their own clothing business. 'I didn't know that places like that existed in London,' I said, as Nan and I walked out of the shop two hours later. For a fraction of the shopping mall's price tags, I had purchased two tops, a skirt, a pair of denims and two dresses from Kostas's establishment. The dresses were being refitted to my exact body measurements and would be ready for collection within the week. 'They are a Greek-Cypriot family business,' Nan said. 'They supply the major chains all over the country. There are several businesses like that on the High Street.'

That week, the whole family visited Trafalgar Square, and Nan brought along Julie's two young sons. Tom took a Polaroid picture of me posing with the pigeons in a blue dress I bought at Kostas's shop.

'We brought you here as a child,' Nan said.

'Really?' I had no recollection of it.

'Remind me to show you the picture when we get home.'

Next, we walked down Whitehall, where I watched the Changing of the Guards. Nan and I posed with a guard and got another picture for the effort. The rest of the day, I stuffed my face with candy floss and ice-cream, the elixirs of my childhood. I returned home, replete but exhausted, and collapsed on Tom's bed in a happy daze.

A knock on the door moments later alerted me to Nan's presence. 'Here,' she said, walking in and handing me a black-and-white photo of Dee and me, with Tom in the middle, sitting on the concrete ledge surrounding the Trafalgar Square fountain. As Nan sat beside me on the bed, I whipped out the Polaroid picture Tom took earlier. The similarities were uncanny, with both pictures taken of the same ledge, with the water fountain and pool in the background, albeit in a different section of the square. My arms were folded in my lap in both pictures, almost as if I had instinctively tried to recreate the same scene from twelve years before. Nan gave me a side squeeze. 'You were a happy girl.'

I searched the faded picture of my childhood, noting the wide smile on my face. 'I was.' Despite the evidence in my hands, I still didn't remember the first trip, but I remembered being happy in England. *Could I be happy here again?*

*

Towards the end of my holiday, I travelled by coach to Northampton and spent a weekend with Mrs Silvers, Mum's friend of old, and the one who introduced her to Nan. Like my parents, she and her family had returned to Nigeria in the early 1970s. However, tragedy forced her and her children back to England. Her daughters were all around my age and I had a brilliant time getting to know them. They took me up to their bedroom, where

I stared transfixed at the life-size posters of George Michael and Michael Jackson plastered over every inch of the walls. I broke into giggles. 'What's with all the posters?'

'Haven't you ever had a teenage idol?' one of the trio asked.

'What's a teenage idol?' They looked at me as if I had just crawled out of a Neanderthal's cave.

On the few occasions we ventured into town, I noticed a distinct lack of Black people on the streets of Northampton. 'Is it hard being the only Black people around?' I asked.

'It can be, but we have each other,' one of the girls said.

*

On my return to London, I found my way from Hornsey down to Nunhead, to visit Brother Rotimi, a cousin, and Brother Segun's eldest brother. The 63 bus took its sweet time meandering from Kings Cross to Peckham, and I spent the minutes marvelling at how dingy parts of London, especially the south, looked. Perhaps it was the general lack of sunshine and the fact that in Lagos the houses were painted an array of every known colour in the spectrum, but London looked depressingly grey. Rows and rows of Victorian-style houses lined the streets from Clerkenwell, to the Elephant and Castle, to the Old Kent Road. In a faded redbrick, brown brick or pebble-dash grey, they heightened the gloomy atmosphere.

Growing up in Nigeria and reinforced by a considerable amount of playing Monopoly with friends, I had romanticised the images of London in my head. According to the game, Whitechapel and the Old Kent Road were the cheapest parts of London. But nothing prepared me for the reality of the squalid, concrete estates mired in graffiti that dotted the route. Contrary to what the Yorubas believed back home, the streets of London were not paved in gold.

The uniformity baffled me. *In a country that celebrated individuality, why did almost every building and every street look similar? Or maybe it was just my jaundiced eye?* As the bus ambled along, another stark reality hit me like a bolt. The people on the south side of London represented a mix of ethnicities: Black, Indian, white and everything in between. *Was there a link between the affluence of the neighbourhoods and the colour of the people who lived in them*? Given my earlier observations, I couldn't but wonder.

As the bus neared my destination, my thoughts turned to my impending meeting with my cousin. Brother Rotimi's dad, Baba Posi, named after the coffins he made for a living, was Mama's first cousin. Like Mama Yaba, Baba Posi was one of the kind relatives. Whenever Dad sent me on an errand to him, he'd ask how I was getting on with my studies before rewarding me with cash for my accomplishments. Brother Rotimi was his eldest son, and we had never met, but despite the ten-year age gap, we took an instant liking to each other. He was studying for a degree in business administration and expected to return to Nigeria and help his father run the family business. I asked him about Liverpool Street market.

'Will Nigerians ever stop buying lace?' he asked.

'Mmm, I don't think that's possible?' I had never been to a party where lace wasn't the uniform.

'I can take you there. We can meet up at Liverpool Street station.'

My eyes lit up. 'Would you? That would be wonderful. I also need to get gifts for everyone back home.'

'You can get T-shirts at wholesale prices for men and cheap knock-off perfumes for women at the market.'

I heaved a sigh of relief. I'd had sleepless nights wondering how to solve that problem. Early on a Sunday morning, I met him outside the station. He took me shopping down Middlesex

Street market which Nigerians had renamed Liverpool Street market because of its proximity to the station. Two hours later, with a new suitcase stuffed with lace, cheap perfumes, T-shirts and jeans, I made my way back to Hornsey.

*

My long-awaited homecoming had whirled past like a hurricane. Now that my last day in London loomed, my thoughts became contemplative. That night as I went to bed, I pondered the bundle of contradictions my trip had turned out to be. I had shared little of the past twelve years, with Nan, Pop and Tom. Some memories were still too raw to dwell on and I felt a powerful sense of loyalty to my family. But I told them about my studies and about Bade. Only they knew I'd promised to marry him. *Why was I able to tell them, but not a single person back in Nigeria?*

Aside from the odd looks, I hadn't experienced any racism in London, but I wasn't blind to the fact that my colour set me apart. Even Nan called me coloured and she loved me. I knew my parents loved me too, as did some of my extended family. But they didn't understand me and to them I was also different. As a Black person, could I live in England and be successful, or was I hankering after a fool's dream? The Silvers said they found being Black in England challenging, but they coped. The Kostas family, who looked like fairly recent immigrants, were running a thriving business. *But the Kostas are not Black,* the voice in my head echoed.

The following afternoon, I gave Pop a hug and patted Diddlydoo before climbing into the taxi taking me to the airport. The creature had eventually accepted my presence. Nan and Tom climbed in with me. As the taxi moved off, I waved back at the silhouette of Pop's lonely figure in the upstairs window. I would never see him again. At the departure gates, I turned for one last hug. I knew I'd be back; I just didn't know when. Although still sprightly, Nan wasn't young anymore and I might never see her again. I wrapped my arms around her, trying to infuse into the embrace every ounce of love I felt for this woman.

She squeezed me tight. 'You keep writing, yeah?'

I blinked away the tears seeping out of the corner of my eyes. Tom offered me a tissue. In return, I gave him a quick hug, before picking up my hand luggage and walking into the crowd.

Despite my misgivings about the racial aspects of living in England, the summer was the most contented I'd ever been. A big part of me wanted to stay in London, but I was not one to break promises. I'd invested two hard years in my studies, and I didn't believe in wasting my effort. I settled into my aeroplane seat, mulling on the juxtaposition between the two cultures pulling me apart. *Who was I, really? Nigerian, British, both?* The difficult years had hardened me in many ways, but beneath the brusque, uncaring facade I presented to the world, I cared about life and the people important to me. The image of a coconut floated through my head, with its tough, brown outer shell and its fleshy, white, inner core. It was known as the tree of life, every part useful. *Surely that was the key? I didn't need to be one or the other. I could be both and happy. But which of the two countries would let me?*

Years later, I heard that 'coconut' was a racial slur used to describe Black people who denied their Black heritage in favour of a white one, but what did I care? I had chosen my own interpretation, intent on having a meaningful life, one where I would be as useful to those around me as the coconut is to the world. I would do my best to meet my culture's expectations, but I would stay true to myself.

WHITE FLESH

CHAPTER THIRTY

Bliss and Misery

Back on campus for my last year, I applied for and received a government bursary and became financially independent of my parents. Bade came to visit, and we fell into each other's arms. Two months later, I was pregnant, the future I had mapped out for myself rewriting itself. I was about to embark on a brand-new journey in life, and with impending motherhood, my heart's call to England would have to wait.

One balmy January afternoon, I set off for Mum's shop. I had weathered the Christmas break without saying a word, but now my pregnancy had passed the three-month stage, I needed to tell her before I started showing. Mum's eyes rounded in dismay at the news of the one thing she dreaded. 'What is your father going to say when he finds out you are not finishing your education?' she said, plucking at an invisible thread on her wrapper.

'Mum, I'm not dropping out of school. I am seeing it through.'

'Won't they expel you from campus?' She looked up, her eyes a mirror of concern.

'Mum, it's not a secondary school. There are plenty of pregnant women on campus all the time.'

'Okay, but I still can't tell your dad. I think I'll get my cousin, Mama Palmgrove, to break it to him.'

I left her to do whatever she thought best. As long as I finished my studies, I knew Dad would be okay with it.

I took Bade home to meet my parents, and they swung into wedding planning mode. A child's wedding, particularly a daughter's, is an enormous deal for Yoruba parents, and mine went all out. I left all the arrangements, except for choosing my wedding dress, in Mum's capable hands and focused on revising for my final exams.

The wedding drama came next. Bade's family failed to turn up for a family introduction that Dad brought the entire extended family, including those in Ijebu, down for. Dad got so angry, he threatened to pull out of the entire thing until Mum mollified him. Next, Bade's cousin wanted to get married on the same day, and as the elder of the two, culture allowed him first choice. Frustrated, Bade posted new marriage banns without consulting either family. Then both sides grumbled.

Not knowing whether the families would ever get together or support the wedding, we planned to marry without them. In case Dad refused to pay for my wedding dress, I took myself off to Yaba market. There, I bought reams of white chiffon and lace and spent the next three weeks painstakingly hand-sewing an alternative outfit with a needle and thread. Such was the resilience of youth.

The families sorted their issues and the wedding plans moved forward. Fourteen-year-old Taiwo burst into my bedroom the day before the wedding, outrage painted on her face. 'Who is your grandmother planning to beat with those canes of hers?' she asked. Mama had arrived from Ijebu with a fresh bundle of canes.

'So, she's *my* grandmother now?' I replied with raised eyebrows.

For the wedding reception, Dad killed a cow which fed 500 guests. Mum outshone herself by procuring a seven-tiered wedding cake. Lolade stood beside me as my chief bridesmaid. Even Mama Yaba took part. She gave me the shoes I wore and came to the reception. She'd never graced a family event before and never did again until the day she died.

*

A month after the wedding, Funbi turned up at the examination centre with a pillow in tow. 'Here,' she said, handing the pillow to my waddling form. 'I brought this for you, for back support, so you can get some relief from these horrid chairs.' Her thoughtfulness, combined with the hormones raging through my body, almost made me burst into tears.

Four weeks later, in the middle of the night, Bade bundled me into his car and drove us to the Lagos University Teaching Hospital. With maternity and birth matters strictly the province of females, the midwife in charge took over and dismissed Bade.

For the next thirteen hours, I laboured alone. 'Roll onto your side and hitch your left leg up,' the midwife instructed as the birth loomed. Exhausted and lethargic, I complied, panting as I bore down. The midwife slapped my thigh, 'Push!' I did, but the baby didn't budge. I felt like going to sleep. Somewhere in the distance I heard the midwife say, 'You are tearing. You need an episiotomy.' As one contraction rolled into another, I didn't feel the cut, and moments later my daughter, Lara, burst into the world.

I heard the cry in the background as the nurses cleared her lungs and whisked her away. 'You've got a daughter,' the midwife said. I smiled weakly and fell back onto the pillows. As she massaged my belly to encourage the placenta to expel itself, I drifted off. 'She's bleeding. Call the consultant, now!' The midwife's yell broke through my semi-consciousness. I observed the staff scurrying in a detached haze. Someone poked a needle in my veins. The consultant arrived, and for several minutes harried conversations floated above my head.

'You were bleeding. We've stopped it, and now I need to stitch you up,' the consultant said as he positioned himself between my legs. I nodded, still dazed.

'Doctor, we've run out of local anaesthesia,' the midwife announced.

'We can do without it. Now Funmi, take a deep, deep breath.' I drew a breath and flinched as the needle pierced my skin. I lay rigid, with clenched teeth as the needle wove in and out of my flesh, breathing between each piercing pain. When he finished, I flopped back on the bed, eyes closed.

I woke hours later and remembered I had just given birth. I shifted myself into a sitting position and winced at the pain in my nether regions. Then the room spun and, starry-eyed, I hit the floor. 'Nurse!' the woman in the bed beside mine screamed.

The nurses came running and hefted me up and back into bed. 'Where were you going?' a kind nurse asked.

'My baby,' I gasped, 'I want to see my baby.'

'She is in the nursery. I will bring her to you later. Now you need to rest. You lost a lot of blood.'

'Okay,' I offered weakly and soon fell back asleep.

Sometime later, my eyes flickered open as a clinical hand grasped my wrist. The nurse taking my pulse eased me into a sitting position. The room spun slower this time. When it righted itself, I leaned back against the bedhead and peered into the nurse's face. 'I still haven't seen my baby.'

'Don't worry. Someone will bring you some food while I get your baby.' I nodded in relief and she walked out of the ward.

Needing to use the bathroom, I swung my feet over the edge of the bed, stood up and collapsed on the floor. The nurses came running again. 'You are not to get up,' the ward matron scolded as they settled me back in bed. Too weak to argue, I complied.

*

The next time I opened my eyes, I found Bade beside me. 'Hi,' he grinned. 'We have a daughter.'

My lips quirked. 'I know. I was there.' My anxiety surfaced again. 'I haven't seen her. They won't let me get up as I keep falling.'

'It's the blood loss. You need a transfusion, but they won't give you one unless I donate some blood first. Don't worry. I've seen her. She is beautiful and well.'

I relaxed and Bade left soon after to donate some blood. A perennial country-wide shortage of blood meant nobody got any until their relatives donated an equivalent amount. During the night, someone moved me into a maternity ward, and I woke the next morning with my baby beside me. Five days later, the doctor on call discharged me. Although Bade donated the required amount of blood, none of the doctors found the time to set up the transfusion. It would take a year on iron tablets and lots of dizzy moments before my blood reserves returned to normal.

*

Two weeks after I gave birth, Bade came to me with a proposal. Now I had graduated, the law required me to serve my country for a year in a scheme called the National Youth Service Corps. With the graduates paid an allowance rather than a salary, it provided the country with cheap labour. By posting graduates to regions outside their own ethnic groups, the scheme also tried to promote better relations across the various ethnicities. But the government made exceptions in extenuating circumstances, like being married with young children. 'Why don't we ask for you to be posted to Ibadan for the year. You can live with my mum and she can care for the baby while you work. We wouldn't need to pay for childcare and there is the added assurance of being able to trust the carer.'

I frowned. 'That means we'll be apart for the first year of our marriage.'

'I'll come to Ibadan every weekend,' he promised, but it wasn't enough, and not how I had envisaged starting married life. I protested vigorously, but Bade wouldn't budge, convinced that his mum, a newly retired paediatric nurse, was best placed to care for the infant rather than strangers.

The argument raged for days until my parents waded in when they came to visit. 'Didn't you promise to obey your husband when you said your wedding vows a few months ago?' Mum asked.

'Yes, Mum. But I don't have any friends or family in that city, I'll be all alone.'

'What if your grandmother, my mum, comes with you for the year?'

Two weeks later, I found myself ensconced with my baby and Mama Iwaya in my husband's family home. The first month passed in a blur, as I attended the initial six-week compulsory military camp, leaving home before dawn and returning at dusk. Then Mama Iwaya dropped a bombshell. 'As soon as you complete the six-week camp, I am returning to Lagos.'

I stared opened mouthed in shock. 'Mama, Mum said you'd stay with me for the year.'

Mama Iwaya pursed her lips, a determined look in her eyes. 'I'm sorry, but I'm not staying here.'

'But why, Mama?'

Mama sealed her lips and would not budge from her decision. She returned to Lagos with Bade at the end of the six weeks.

*

I was posted to the United Missionary College at Molete, a teacher training college for primary school teachers. My mother-in-law, Mummy, had a car and a driver since she couldn't drive. Bade offered to contribute to the driver's wages, and in return he would take me to work and pick me up in the evenings.

I found my first week as a qualified teacher disconcerting. At eighteen, I must have been the youngest member of staff ever. In a secondary school, I would have been older than most of the students. But, at the teacher training college, many of my students were old enough to be my mother. Yet they all deferred to me, called me Ma, and despite my protests, scurried to carry my bag as soon as I stepped through the school gates. This was their way of showing respect for their teacher and potentially gaining favour.

*

Trouble began brewing at home with Mummy insisting I must not call Bade's nine-year-old brother by his first name. She sent the message through Bade. Elbow-deep in dirty dish water, I swivelled around and gawked at him, the sponge in my hand running a trail of dirty water onto the floor. 'Are you kidding?' I said, 'He's only nine, for heaven's sake.'

'Sorry, I'm just the messenger,' he said. 'She says it's the traditional way.'

'If she wants traditional, let's do it right.' I had paid avid attention in Baba Yoruba's lessons. Before the British colonised the tribe, Yoruba wives gave members of their husband's family aliases or monikers. Some of my family's wives did the same with me, the 'brother', 'sister', 'uncle' and 'auntie' thing all a modern invention.

'How about I call him *Eyinfunjowo* (Teeth whiter than money) or *Duduyemi* (Black looks good on me)?' I said. The first moniker was a reference to ancient times, when the Yoruba used white cowrie shells as money.

My husband doubled over in laughter. 'Ooh, that's so funny!' he said.

I tapped my feet and waited him out. Once he finished, one look at my face and his merriment disappeared.

'You can't call him any of those. That's just bush!' I almost laughed at his outrage. 'Bush' was the city dweller's slur for uneducated people who lived in rural communities.

'Well, it's your choice,' I said smugly, 'you can have modern or traditional, but not a mixture of both.'

I have no idea what he said to Mummy, but I continued to call the child by his first name.

The next problem involved Mummy's driver, who took hours returning home after dropping me off at work, blaming it on the traffic. Convinced he was using her car as an excuse to run personal errands, Mummy stopped him from taking me to work. I found myself braving the Ibadan public transport system and taking two buses to get to work. Water shortages created additional stress. Like other parts of the country, Ibadan residents relied on municipal tankers or wells for their water. However, we lived opposite the University of Ibadan and the institution generously allowed locals to fetch water from its pumps. With an infant, our water usage was above average, and our needs required several rounds of ferrying heavy kegs in the boot of Mummy's car.

Soon, Mummy restricted my use of the kegs of water to drinking and cooking, as the kegs were damaging the car boot's floor. When it didn't rain, I resorted to searching for water for laundry in the neighbourhood after work. Eventually, a colleague living opposite work let me come to hers early so I could wash my baby's dirty nappies, leave them out to dry and retrieve them after work.

I still suffered dizzy spells from the blood loss when I gave birth. But as 'the wife' it was my duty to clean the two-storey detached, four-bedroomed house, cook for the family and clean up afterwards. Sometimes, Mummy added her laundry to the list. As my grandmother had predicted, I had no stomach for it, and I started ignoring some chores, which led to frequent skirmishes with Mummy.

When Bade arrived at weekends, he listened to two versions of the same story and spent all his time arbitrating. I hadn't signed up for a life of drudgery or misery, and I started planning my emancipation. Reflecting back on the image of a coconut, I decided I had grown a hard-enough shell over the years to face the challenge of life as a single mother if necessary. One weekend in November, before Bade left for Lagos, I issued a warning. 'When you come next week, I won't be here and I'm not coming back to you in Lagos either.'

His eyes widened in alarm. 'Please don't do that,' he pleaded. 'I have a colleague with connections at the Youth Corps headquarters. We'll change the posting back to Lagos over the Christmas break.' True to his word, Bade arranged things, and five months after moving to Ibadan, I moved back to Lagos. The National Youth Service Corps re-posted me to CMS Grammar School, close to home, and I found a day-care centre for Lara.

CHAPTER THIRTY-ONE

The Conflict Gallery

Three years after the 1976 coup, General Obasanjo handed power to the country's first democratically elected government. Under President Shehu Shagari, the country saw a vast expansion in housing, education, agriculture and industry. By the time I reached my late teens, the populace had grown used to a life of luxury fuelled by Nigeria's oil boom and access to imported goods. Rice became a staple diet, with Uncle Ben's replacing the stone-ridden local *ofada.* Refined groundnut oil graced many a stew pot instead of the local unrefined palm oil. Everyone aspired to riches beyond their imagination as politicians discussed the 'national cake' and people dreamed of when they would get a slice.

Alongside the boom, corruption flourished, and winning lucrative contracts based on familial connections, then selling them on at marked-up prices, became the norm. By the time a contract reached the person designated to fulfil it, often it was no longer financially viable. So, some projects never started, and many were jettisoned, with greedy officials covering their tracks and signing them off as completed, all for a fee.

Bade and I rented a two-bedroom flat in the Ilaje-Bariga suburb of Lagos. About two-thirds of the way down the road leading to the property, the tarmac became a bumpy, pothole-ridden dirt track, evidence that the contractor had abandoned the project. Our landlady, Alhaja, a Muslim who had performed the Holy Pilgrimage to Mecca, hence her moniker, gained her wealth from a lucrative contract selling flour. The high-end cars parked in front of our house showed just how profitable the business was. Without the overheads of owning a shop, she sold truck-loads of flour to agents who met her at the mill, paid her cash and carted the sacks away.

Our ultra-modern dream flat included an additional guest cloakroom, and a bathroom that sported an English bath and a heated water tank. Neighbours eyed us with suspicion, wondering how we could afford it. We did it through careful planning and cutting out extraneous luxuries. Alhaja didn't know this and although she was happy taking our money, later we realised she too had misgivings.

*

For the convenience of scheduling, students studying for the Nigerian Certificate in Education were made to take classes with undergraduates on the Bachelor of Education course. That meant certificate holders who returned for a degree in education would repeat much of the work. In protest, I had joined my peers in lobbying politicians and protesting outside the House of Assembly. This paid off, and during my youth service year, the law changed, allowing universities to offer a two-year degree to people who held the Nigerian Certificate in Education from their institution.

The following September, Bisola, Funbi, Sayo and I went back to study for a degree. Bade moved jobs and joined an oil company, which provided a staff bus for its employees. Our second-hand Fiat 131 therefore sat idly at home. When a new driving school opened next to campus, I took lessons and in no time passed the driving test. But driving on Lagos roads required a lion's heart, and for days afterwards, I ignored the car.

Traffic jams nicknamed 'go-slow' were legendary in Lagos. The country's increasing wealth had made cars affordable for the average family. That, combined with the poor road infrastructure, meant the traffic ground to a halt daily, creating the most impatient of drivers. Nobody gave way to anyone, and drivers drove nose to bumper to avoid letting anyone in. It wasn't unusual for drivers to leave their lane and drive on the other side until they blocked oncoming traffic. To solve the problem, in 1976, the State Governor had enacted a law only allowing cars whose registration started with an odd number into Lagos Island on Mondays, Wednesdays and Fridays and those with even numbers on Tuesdays and Thursdays. What did people do? They went out and bought a second car. Nigerians were nothing if not ingenious, and the traffic problem worsened.

One day, I braced myself and settled behind the steering wheel prepared to face up to the Lagos traffic. At five-foot one, I reached only two-thirds up the height of the windscreen. I drove towards the main Akoka road leading to the campus, into the arena of the big boys, the *molues* and *danfos*. Female drivers were a rarity, and with my diminutive size, I resembled a child. People gawked and pointed as I passed. 'You borrow your Papa's car?' someone shouted as I edged out of the side road.

To get on the main thoroughfare, I had to force oncoming vehicles to give way. As I inched forward, drivers tooted, warning me not to dare. It was all bravado, but still frightening. At the first viable opportunity, I pressed the accelerator and swung the car left onto the road. The driver behind me blared his horns. Through the rear mirror, I saw him give me the five-finger curse, but I ignored it. I had taken the first step towards becoming an aggressive Lagos driver.

*

Life unfolded in a predictable and prosaic manner until one morning, while I was having a quick shower, something hard clattered onto the bathroom floor. I paused the scrubbing and stared in horror at the birth control intrauterine device my body had ejected all by itself. With a busy life at the start of the last year of my studies, it was a while before I found the time to visit a gynaecologist. 'Before I replace the coil, you must take a pregnancy test,' the doctor said. Days later, I staggered in shock at the news that I was pregnant, and spent the afternoon fuming at my idiocy. The maternity clinic confirmed a due date a month before my final exams. *How could I have let this happen? How would I manage a toddler, examinations and a new baby?*

Mum was ecstatic. She didn't believe in birth control anyway. 'Nature will always find a way,' she crowed. Then at my down-turned mouth, she said, 'Don't worry. I will be there to help.'

Bade's philosophical, 'We'll manage, God will provide,' was no help. I wasn't sure how, with our finances already stretched to the limit. Plus, we weren't particularly religious and didn't attend church, so it seemed hypocritical to rely on God's providence when we spared him little thought.

'You really must stop combining studies and babies,' Funbi said, when I broke the news to my friends.

'I didn't plan this,' I moaned.

*

The pregnancy wasn't the only challenge. Bade and I woke on a Sunday morning to the sounds of Alhaja's screaming. We dressed quickly and ventured outside, where we found her yelling at Kunle and Iyabo, the neighbours in the flat above ours. 'You better tell your friends to return my cars, otherwise I will show you where I am from.' She stomped up to her flat, without sparing us a glance.

Bade and I approached the couple. 'What's going on?' Bade asked.

Iyabo ran a weary hand over her face. 'Robbers visited the compound overnight. They pushed our car out of the way before making off with Alhaja's flashy cars. Alhaja thinks since they left our cars, we must have colluded with the robbers.'

My eyes widened in alarm. We'd parked our car in the street, having arrived home after Alhaja had locked the main gates. *Did she think we'd done that to make it easier for the robbers to get to hers?* It seemed so, as Alhaja began an intimidation campaign. When we greeted her, she eyed us and walked away. The broken borehole pump remained unfixed. Her Juju medicine man visited often, pacing the length and breadth of the compound, chanting incantations, invoking the wrath of the gods on whoever stole Alhaja's cars. Following each visit, his offerings to the gods – little clay pots filled with bits of the entrails of sacrificed animals, palm oil and kola nuts – dotted the compound's four corners.

That none of us keeled over and died infuriated Alhaja no end, and she wanted us out of her property. While I wasn't afraid of her witchcraft, I worried about what my toddler could accidentally pick up in the compound. 'We need to move,' I told Bade, as another Christmas approached. We began house-hunting, and, with Mum and Dad's help, secured a two-bedroomed flat near my parents. Although not as attractive or modern, it was well within our means.

*

Christmas Eve saw me, Bade and Lara on the Lagos-Ibadan expressway heading to the annual family gathering. An hour into our journey, a loud pop resounded in the car. Bade gripped the steering firmly as the car careered left and right, going at 100 km per hour. Bade brought the juddering under control and drove onto the dirt track beside the express way. Hyperventilating, we both climbed out and examined the punctured tyre, its well-worn threads no match for the three-inch nail embedded in it.

Bade jacked up the wheel, replaced it with the spare in the boot, and we set off once more. Fifteen minutes later, a second burst tyre brought us to a halt. Since the country had no emergency services, we turned around and drove back to Lagos, limping along on the flat tyre. In Lagos, a roadside mechanic fixed one tyre. The other one, damaged beyond repair, needed replacing – something we could ill-afford. Late that evening, Bade visited an uncle who had a telephone. He contacted the nearest family friend in Ibadan and asked them to deliver a message to Mummy explaining what had happened.

The following week, we set out again, planning to spend New Year's Eve and the following day with Mummy. At Ibadan, we were met by an incandescent Mummy. Bade's message had not reached her, and she thought we'd deliberately shunned the Christmas gathering. Nothing either of us said mattered. I was the rebellious one leading Bade astray. Unmentionable things were uttered, and we departed on New Year's Day, the relationship fractured beyond repair.

*

Five months later, I found myself in labour at a private hospital, a perk of Bade working for an oil company. The first few hours passed quietly until orderlies wheeled a screaming woman into the ward and all the doctors and nurses crowded around her bed. In the snippets of loud conversation, I gathered this was her seventh child and several of them had been born by caesarean section. The doctors had warned her not to have any more babies, but her previous six pregnancies produced girls. To cement her place in her husband's family, she needed to bear him a son.

While all the attention in the ward focused on the wailing woman, I felt a tightening in my stomach as my labour pains kicked up quite a few notches. Through the haze, I drew the attention of a passing doctor. 'Doctor, I think I am going to give birth soon.'

'You?' he said, without stopping, 'You are nowhere near ready.'

With that, he joined the crowd surrounding the new patient. I swallowed my frustration. *Why did people in power believe they always knew best?* A spasm suffused my body, and I found myself pushing. I stopped. *Was my body really pushing the baby out or was that just me reacting to the pain?* The intense urge to push gripped again, and I bore down. Without warning, my baby's head pushed through. 'My baby's head is here!' I screamed. That got their attention, and a myriad of people in white surrounded my bed. It was too late to move me to the labour ward, and I had the baby there in the open maternity ward.

The doctor whose attention I had sought earlier came round. I couldn't resist the urge. 'I told you,' I said.

'You were right. I am sorry.' I accepted the apology. In my experience, they were a rarity.

The screaming woman gave birth that afternoon to a girl by another caesarean section. The nurses wheeled her back to the maternity ward and struggled all evening to control her blood pressure. I woke in the middle of the night to find her bed shrouded behind curtains. She'd died and it would be morning before they removed the corpse. Eyes wide open, with an elevated pulse, I lay in my bed, sleep elusive. After years of cultural conditioning that said the living and the dead had no business together, I couldn't help the anxiety. Both sad and angry on her behalf, my thoughts fixated on the poor woman, to me, another victim of the dictates of culture. To please her husband's family, she had sacrificed her life, leaving others to raise the seven young daughters she left behind. I knew the chromosomes in the male's sperm determined a child's gender. Yet scientific ignorance fuelled cultural fallacies, ensuring that women got blamed for failing to produce a male child. *Would change ever come?*

Back at home, Bade broached the issue of the traditional naming ceremony carried out on the seventh day after birth. Despite my ill-health after having Lara, I travelled the 130 km to Ibadan for her naming ceremony because, apparently, culture demanded it be done in the family home. I grew up knowing the ceremony was a rite of passage, but I saw none of my cousins born in Lagos carted off to Ijebu for it. They were named in the city where they were born. In any case, I was no longer willing to accede to culture. 'You can take the baby and bring her back afterwards, but I'm not going,' I said.

'I can't manage the baby and drive at the same time.' Bade said. He was right. Baby car seats and car seat belts did not exist. But it wasn't my problem. The next day, when my parents visited, Bade spoke to them. 'What are you doing about the naming ceremony?' Mum asked.

'I'm not going,' I insisted, my face set in that mulish look my parents knew so well. After the last altercation, I'd promised myself I wouldn't sleep in that house again.

'Why not?' Mum pushed.

'It's not a happy place for me. Right now, I don't need an environment that causes me stress. I am barely three weeks away from my final examinations.'

'Go,' Mum pleaded. 'All this strife is bad for everyone.'

'How about a compromise?' Dad offered. 'Go early in the morning and return the same evening.'

'I'll get two of your aunts to accompany you, so you won't be alone,' Mum added.

I gave in to my parents' wishes, knowing they were just trying to keep the peace. A week after the naming ceremony, my baby was admitted to hospital with blood poisoning. While it might have happened regardless, I couldn't help wondering whether the unnecessary travel had left her more vulnerable. The quick thinking of the doctors saved my daughter's life. But I was done with culture. I vowed I would never again do something culture demanded just because it did.

CHAPTER THIRTY-TWO

The Bubble and Burst

Like an effervescent bottle of champagne, the oil boom bubbled for years. Then in 1982, global oil prices crashed, wiping out most of Nigeria's foreign reserves and bringing the prosperity to an abrupt end. The result was spectacular in its devastation. To improve the country's external position, the government restricted imports. Farmers had stopped producing, unable to compete with cheap foreign goods in the boom days, and the cost of food and everyday items skyrocketed.

Despite the challenges of the previous year, I passed my final degree examination with a second-class upper award, but the economic downturn made jobs scarce. Sayo and I applied to the Lagos State Education Board and spent months visiting the secretariat, hoping to be deployed to a school. But it was about who you knew and how much of a bribe you could afford.

Discontent brewed in the wider populace, and with another election looming, President Shagari pointed the finger at undocumented West Africans living in the country as the source of Nigeria's woes. The government ordered the millions of foreigners, mostly Ghanaians in search of a better life, to leave within two weeks or face arrest. The act, part retaliation since Ghana did the same to Nigerians in 1969, attracted international outcry but didn't deter the government.

With the brief notice, Ghanaians packed all their belongings into large blue-white-red chequered polypropylene bags nicknamed 'Ghana must go' and fled the country. The bags remain in circulation to this day, a sad reminder of the brutality of international politics. However, the expulsion of foreigners did not solve Nigeria's woes. Although Shagari won the 1983 August election, a coup overthrew him that December, ushering in a decade of military rule, starting with General Muhammadu Buhari.

*

My insistence on self-reliance meant I had few connections where it mattered. It took almost six months of searching and help from Sayo's contacts at the Ministry before I got a job. In January 1984, I approached the premises of my new workplace with curiosity. Under the previous republic, the Lagos State governor, Alhaji Lateef Jakande, had taken a novel approach to solving the shortage of school places. The oil boom had only increased the demand as villagers flooded the cities, seeking their fortunes. Jakande responded by building a spate of what the media scathingly termed 'cattle sheds' in the grounds of the old missionary schools.

As its name suggested, Methodist Girls' High School III was the third one on the site. Because it was created last, all the other schools looked down on its pupils and staff, the Nigerian concept of seniority so ingrained that even here it reared its head. The original mission school, housed in proper buildings uphill, towered over the old playing fields on which sat rows of single-storey buildings. Each rudimentary structure comprised four shoulder-high walls, with a tin roof. An open archway in one wall allowed egress and entry. The gap between the top of the wall and the roof provided natural ventilation and little protection from the wind or rain on windy days. Inside each room, pupils sat in rows of desks and chairs, and those who couldn't find seats hung on the ledges. At the front was a simple blackboard for the teacher.

So, my career began, completely mundane, and over-dependent on the 'chalk and talk' method. There were no budgets for the teaching or learning aids that my lecturers had suggested, and even chalk was scarce. Everything I had learned at university became irrelevant as I taught classes reminiscent of my own days in school. Some teachers still carried canes, although they used them less often than my primary school teachers did. My students often struggled with my size. To them, I just didn't look old enough to be a teacher, nor did I carry a cane. I held my own, and they never disrespected me openly, as that would invite a caning from the principal. Still, some never took the lessons seriously enough.

Despite our cheaper rent, like everyone else, Bade and I found everyday living challenging as food scarcity became the norm. Soap, milk and other basic goods were hard to come by. Teachers' salaries were often held up because the government 'had no money'. At the end of each month, we queued for hours at the banks to withdraw cash, which often ran out before everyone got paid. Teachers so inclined resorted to trading and running their own businesses, bunking off work in favour of activities that would feed their families. To ease the hardship, the Ministry of Education occasionally allocated bags of rice and other commodities for staff in each school to share.

As if the economic difficulties were not enough, the new military government introduced a social correction programme named War Against Indiscipline. Although noble in its original intention to curb corruption, instil orderliness and a work ethic, the scheme fell victim to the vagaries of a top-down, heavy-handed approach. The police, tasked with policing social behaviours, such as not queuing for public transport and jay walking, used their own initiative to extend their remit. Soon, they were flogging women in public for wearing what they deemed inappropriate clothing. It was a brave woman who ventured out in trousers.

*

With life barely tolerable, people turned to religion for solace. New denominations offering hope and redemption to the poor blossomed, and empty church pews filled with fresh converts. After several invitations from Bade's colleague, we gave the Chapel of the Healing Cross at the Lagos University Hospital a try. The modern and upbeat service had us returning, and we became regular visitors.

Drawn by the pull of music, I ventured in on Saturday afternoon to explore enrolling in the choir. Bade was on a company-sponsored course in Italy and the kids were with Mum. I arrived an hour too early, having got my timings wrong, and found the choirmaster, a young man in his thirties, playing the piano. We started chatting and somewhere along the line his voice took on a sombre note. 'Tell me,' he said, 'do you have a personal relationship with your Maker?'

Flummoxed, I considered the question and my mind flicked back to my days in boarding school. I believed God existed since an encounter with Him Almighty in Form 2. Back then, the music had drawn me to a scripture union meeting, where after much singing, the gathering had settled down to discuss scripture. Confused, I held up a hand.

Senior Ngozi, the leader, pointed at me. 'Yes?'

Plucking up courage, I asked, 'What is God?'

Silence descended in the room before Senior Ngozi answered, 'God is a Spirit.'

But that didn't clear my confusion at all. I took in her gentle tone and relaxed body and ventured further. 'Okay, but what is a Spirit?'

A long hiss whistled in the silence. 'Stop asking silly questions,' someone else said behind me.

Senior Ngozi tried to stop the kingdom defenders, 'No, let her ask.'

But their reaction had told me all I needed to know. I snapped my mouth shut and never went back. However, on one of those days when the dratted periods returned, I'd called out in frustration and agony, 'God if you really exist, make this pain go away.' An hour later, I gasped in wonder that my pain had disappeared without the use of analgesics. Coincidence? Possibly, or the confirmation I sought. I chose the latter, but there any relationship ended.

Back in the present, 'What do you mean?' I asked the choir-master.

Over the following weeks, we explored the notion of God and Christianity, but in a manner different from the fire and brimstone I had heard preached throughout my youth. I found the idea that God loved me just the way I was comforting, while still reflecting that I could probably make significant self-improvements. I was easy to provoke, and I could bear a grudge, characteristics that kept me unhappy for large stretches of time as I plotted a suitable revenge. It was time to make changes and become an even better version of me, I decided.

*

Three years after I started my teaching career, I resigned so I could study for a master's degree. Dad still fancied having a doctor in the family and a Doctor of Philosophy (PhD) was as good a means of achieving that goal as any. Every few years, he prodded and ask me what I was doing about it, and although I was full grown, the culture taught us to obey our parents until they died. Besides that, I wanted to please Dad and make him proud. He had stood in my corner for so long.

Bade and I went on holiday for the first time to visit an old classmate of his in Chicago. En route, we stopped over at Milan International airport for a four-day detour in Modena where we met up with the friends Bade made two years earlier. In the grip of winter, we saw little of Italy, but we would always remember the trip for what happened at the airport on our way back.

In the departure lounge, we stood scanning the destination screens, when two police officers carrying rifles approached with sniffing dogs. The years of police brutality in Nigeria made us nervous. The Nigerian special police unit nicknamed 'Kill and Go' carried guns and had earned its stripes with the lifeblood of belligerent youth. So, wary, we stood back and let the dogs sniff to their heart's content. One police officer turned to us. '*Passaporto?*' he queried. I rummaged through my handbag, found the passports and handed them over. I kept my eye on him as he and his colleague walked away to what seemed like a little office within the lounge.

While Bade and I stood guard over our luggage, I watched in consternation as time trickled away. Thirty minutes later there was no sign of our passports or the police who had taken them. 'What are we going to do?' I asked Bade. 'At this rate, we might miss our flights.'

'Not much we can do other than wait,' he said.

Patience was not one of my virtues. I looked around the departure lounge. A group of four police officers stood near where the two who had taken our passports disappeared, but they ignored us. At the other end of the lounge, five Black travellers huddled, unease emanating from their hunched shoulders. Still afraid of the gun-toting police, I walked towards the Black group. When I got to them, I found to my dismay that they were French speakers. However, through hand gestures I deduced they were in the same spot of bother. The police had taken their passports too.

Mind made up, I stalked towards the police. It was as good a day to die as any. As I got nearer though, I slowed my approached. No need to hasten my own dispatch. Shoulder to shoulder with them, I asked in as confident a tone as I could muster, 'Passport?' One of the men tucked his hand in his pocket, pulled out the passports and handed them over. I stood there gaping, not believing the audacity. At that point Bade arrived behind me, tucked an arm around my elbow and dragged me away before I got myself arrested or worse. I found the experience so traumatising that from then on, I always travelled with multiple forms of personal identification. I also avoided driving in non-English-speaking countries to prevent the need to converse with law-enforcers in a foreign language.

We made our flight and in three glorious weeks of complete relaxation I gained so much weight that for the first time in my life, I looked like a woman. The difference was so stark that on my return, neighbours stopped in the street just to check it was really me. I completed my master's studies. Instead of accepting the master's award, I converted to the Master of Philosophy (MPhil) course, the first step towards the PhD, and a decision I would come to regret.

*

In 1985, another military coup had booted out General Buhari and ushered in General Babangida. It seemed the more our leaders changed, the more things remained the same. The austerity measures bit hard, and Nigerians who could leave did so in droves. Aware of the brain drain and the potential impact on the country's future, the government reacted with a media campaign titled 'Andrew, Don't Check Out'. Rather than focusing on solutions to the problems, the campaign vilified people as deserters leaving the country to sink in its time of need. Meanwhile, the media filled the newsstands with stories of the military's worst excesses. But they were soon silenced when Dele Giwa, the editor and founder of *Newswatch*, a popular journalistic magazine, was assassinated with Nigeria's first letter bomb.

I had held my British passport ever since my brother Kehinde decided to return to England. It had made sense for me and my siblings to all apply at once. It reduced the bureaucracy we each needed to cut through at the British High Commission and buttressed our claim to British citizenship. Gathering all the evidence together, including my lifelong letters from Nan and pictures that tracked our lives from infancy to adulthood, was an epic task. After months of me traipsing back and forth, the embassy issued our passports and Kehinde departed shortly after. However, much as I wanted to leave, Bade was happy in his job and we decided a cross-Atlantic relationship was not for us. Taiwo, frustrated by the meddling of several cousins who lived at the homestead, moved in with us, but she too was already planning her return to England.

Meanwhile, my reputation in my husband's extended family preceded me. At functions, there was always an elder or two lying in wait, ready to give a tongue lashing about some perceived wrong. At Bade's grandfather's funeral, a gentleman I hardly recognised took on the task. It all began innocuously enough. On an errand for Mummy, I knelt to greet the elders seated around a group of tables. 'How are you? *Pele*. How are the children?' the gentleman asked.

'They are well, thank you, sir,' I replied.

'Why are they not here?'

Mmm. Who told him they weren't here? 'I didn't want them to impede me from doing my duty, sir.' As the youngest wife in the extended family, I knew I'd be run ragged with errands and I couldn't do that and watch the kids. Bade could have cared for them, but the culture considered men with a hands-on approach to child-rearing as under their wives' influence. I didn't want 'husband controller' added to my resume.

'So, you gave your children to your mother to look after. Meanwhile, your mother-in-law who retired so she could look after her grandchildren sits there with nothing to do. Are you trying to kill her? Don't you know that with nothing to do she would wither and die?'

Like a fish, I opened my mouth and closed it, recognising the ambush for what it was. There was no point in explaining that Mum looked after the kids when I needed help. They didn't actually live with her. The other elders looked on with avid interest, awaiting my reaction. He continued the tirade. 'Your mother-in-law wants to raise your daughter. That's her right, so make sure you move your daughter to Ibadan.'

Over my dead body! I realised he was half drunk, which would be why his words made sense to only him. I gave my standard reply. 'Yes sir, I hear you, sir.'

'And why are you calling her a different name to the one your mother-in-law gave her?' *Ah! That old battle.*

'That's her father's fault, sir. He named her.'

'He did?'

'Yes sir, he did.' Bade and I had a pact. He would name any girls, and I the boys.

'Even if he did, you should have had more sense and convinced him otherwise.'

'Yes sir, I hear you, sir.'

Spent, he let me go. From then on, I became selective in which family events I attended. They'd have to catch me to lay into me and I planned to make that as hard as possible. It wouldn't matter if they complained about my absence since I wouldn't be there to hear it.

*

My higher education studies took a turn for the worse. The head of department, also my course supervisor, was promoted as dean. All his students were re-allocated to the acting head of department who decided the scope of my dissertation was not within his area of expertise. If I wanted to pass, I needed to find a topic more to his liking. Frustrated, I shelved months of research and began again. Then he was passed over for the substantive post in favour of a young northerner. Deflated, he became elusive, and provided little guidance on my work.

When I transferred to the MPhil programme, the faculty also employed me as a part-time research assistant. Besides running errands for the head of department, I taught some undergraduate classes. I enjoyed teaching adults a lot more than I expected I would, perhaps because I didn't need to convince my learners I was old enough and qualified to stand in front of them.

It wasn't long before I butted heads with the head of department, who seemed to pile my desk with more tasks before I could get any of them done. Maybe it was because I unwittingly broke the unwritten code between research assistants and the boss. I found out from friends later that I should have offered to serve in a personal capacity by running domestic errands such as fetching my boss's dry cleaning. But I hadn't done that for his predecessors, and I got on fine with them.

In the end, it was irrelevant, because my past repeated itself and I fell pregnant. Okay, this one was planned; I just didn't plan it well enough to avoid it coinciding with studies. Halfway through the pregnancy, I started getting heavy contractions and my doctor confined me to bed. I withdrew from the course, and the university would not grant me the original master's degree even though I had completed all the course work, including the dissertation. I would have to start afresh elsewhere.

CHAPTER THIRTY-THREE

The Leaving

I paced a few steps behind my son, Deolu, as he toddled down the aeroplane's aisle. At seventeen months, he'd only just found his balance a month before. Born after only thirty-seven weeks of gestation, he'd been slower at every milestone compared to his sisters. However, once he figured something out, it was all he wanted to do. His most recent game was to see how far he could run before mummy caught him. I picked up my pace, apologising as I brushed past passengers in their seats. Most of them smiled indulgently, amused at my son's antics. The pilot's voice echoed over the tannoy, asking passengers to prepare for landing in thirty minutes. I gathered my son, hushing his shrieks of protest as I returned to my seat and buckled us both in. I pulled out a toy, a temporary distraction, I knew, but for the moment it worked.

I settled back against the headrest, eyes bleary from staying up sewing into the wee hours. I had wanted to give the girls something special to make up for leaving them behind. The delight on their faces when I handed out the blue and yellow seersucker day-dresses at breakfast had been worth it. Over the years, I had become so proficient at sewing that, following my confinement to bedrest, I had started a sewing business. After the baby arrived, I stayed at home expanding the business to include adult sewing classes.

However, while I loved teaching the adults, I couldn't make the business profitable. Taiwo chased my debtors on my behalf, with the diplomacy I didn't possess, until she left for England shortly after Deolu's birth. So, I closed shop and went back to teaching, this time in an elite private primary school which recruited degree holders to its staff. The sewing remained a hobby that I took much delight in.

The tannoy sprung to life once more. 'Ladies and gentlemen…' I searched the toddler's bag for his sippy cup, filled it with the last few drops of milk and held it to his mouth. He grabbed it with both hands and settled into the crook of my arm. With Deolu occupied, I returned to my ruminations.

I remembered the day we decided to leave. Bade came back from work one evening, his shoulders in a dejected slump. In recent months, his relationship with his business partners, with whom he ran information technology services, had suffered. 'I think we should move to England,' he said, when I asked what was wrong.

'Are you sure?' I pressed.

'I am,' he said after a lengthy pause. 'Things are not working out here as I hoped, and we've given it our best shot.'

I knew he wasn't referring to just work. The fractured relationships between Mummy, the elders in his extended family and me stressed him out. Over the years, I had kicked and bucked tradition every step of the way and more or less become a pariah. Although I was long past caring, I bore the battle scars inside, a seething mass of resentment. I maintained close relationships with a few family members who saw me for what I was. The rest hated my gumption, but most left me well alone.

'So how do we do this?'

'Kehinde said there was a teacher shortage in London. How about you go with Deolu and secure a teaching position first? The girls and I can join you afterwards.'

I considered the suggestion. My brother's letter had arrived the previous week. Dad was in London too, receiving medical attention for diabetes-related complications.

'That might work. Dad could look after Deolu while I look for work.'

Once we made up our minds, things moved at breakneck speed. I resigned from my teaching job, but my boss refused the resignation, suggesting I wait until the end of August, in case my plans didn't materialise. She liked me that much.

Mum was superb when we informed her, even though it meant she would be alone in Nigeria with just Idowu. She championed all her children, no sacrifice too big.

'Cabin crew, prepare for landing.' The captain's voice broke through my thoughts. I noted the toddler fast asleep in my arms with relief. The plane's wheels touched down with ease, to the appreciative applause of the passengers. It taxied to the allocated hangar, and the crew prepared for letting off the cargo and passengers. Using a baby carrier, I strapped my son to my chest. A gentleman stepped up behind me and offered to free my hand luggage from the overhead compartment. I thanked him, took hold of the suitcase's handle and wheeled it off the plane.

*

The queue through immigration was legendary. However, unlike my last trip, I was holding a British passport, so I headed for the shorter line that said, 'UK Nationals'. There were no Black people ahead of me. I looked behind me and noticed a single Black man at the far end of the line. People in the queue for non-UK nationals eyed me with interest as if to say, 'Are you sure you're in the right queue?' I ignored them. Instead, I paid attention to what was happening ahead.

Each passenger walked up to the raised cubicle, handed over their passport and waited. The immigration officer took a quick glance at the document before handing it back. At the pace at which he was waving them through, I reckoned I would get past immigration in less than half an hour. In contrast, the non-nationals' queue moved at snail speed. In no time, it was my turn. The immigration officer took my passport from me and busied himself reading the information. After a few moments, he gave me an assessing look, glancing back and forth between my face and the passport. 'How long have you owned this passport, madam?'

'Five years, sir, but I had my baby son added to it last year.'

'Have you ever travelled with it?'

'No, sir.'

He held on to my passport and pointed to a row of three chairs arranged next to the wall behind him. 'Please sit over there. My colleague will be with you shortly.' I grabbed my suitcase and took a seat as instructed.

Ten minutes later, a lady officer asked me to follow her into a spacious waiting room. Now awake, Deolu was full of energy and desperate to get down. I eased him out of the carrier and put him on the floor. Immediately, he stood up and toddled across the room. I followed at a leisurely pace. I considered myself a detainee of some sort, although heaven only knew why.

My eyes travelled around the room. Most of my fellow detainees, comprising seven adults and a handful of children, avoided making eye contact. Two of the adult women, each with a child, wore full hijab and appeared Middle Eastern. A man accompanied one of them. One woman in a saree sat with two children and an elderly Indian couple. I presumed they were a family. My eyes landed on the last person, a Black woman like me, with a toddler. I acknowledged her with a nod, and she did likewise. I surmised we were all suspected of trying to enter the country illegally. What I couldn't understand was why I was a suspect. It made no sense.

A narrow counter with a glass shield separated the waiting area from an ante-room where the officials sat. I counted four or five heads in the room from my vantage point. I could hear muted voices and the ringing of phones, but none of the officials looked at or ventured near us. My siblings, Taiwo and Kehinde, were both supposed to meet me at the airport. I glanced at my watch. An hour had passed since touchdown. Luggage should be flowing onto the conveyor belt. I hoped mine would still be there when I escaped my captors. But I had bigger worries. I was running out of nappies and food for Deolu. It wouldn't be long before he needed a meal, and I only had one Farley's rusk left in my bag.

The door to the waiting room opened, and two Asian males entered. Tired of sitting, I relinquished my seat to one of the newcomers and paced up and down, my irritation growing by the second. Deolu still found the other children entertaining, but how long would that last? A male officer exited the ante-room. In an instant, everyone tuned in. Then he called my name. *Thank God.* I lifted a hand to identify myself, grabbed Deolu and met the officer halfway.

'Do you have any other form of identification on you?' he asked.

'Yes, I've got my full birth certificate.'

'The long one?'

'And the short one.'

'May I have the long one please?'

I let go of the toddler, searched my handbag, found the document and handed it over.

'I'll be back as soon as I can.' He left and returned to the ante-room.

'How long is this going to last?' I muttered to no one in particular.

'At least you've been called. We've been here longer,' the lady in the saree said.

Two hours passed. My siblings would be frantic with worry, and I had no means of contacting them. Deolu started whining. I gave him the last of the Farley's rusks. He wolfed it down in minutes and whimpered for more. 'Sorry, baby, Mummy hasn't got any more. We'll be leaving soon, I promise.' I swung him into my arms and cradled him against my chest. He was a docile child, except for when he was hungry or tired. Now he was both. I paced, danced, crooned, anything to delay the oncoming onslaught. But my anger was simmering; my son could feel it in the tenseness of my arms and that only made him crankier.

The immigration officer who had collected my birth certificate came back into the room and called my name again. This time he stood behind the glass pane. I gathered my stuff and met him at the counter. 'I apologise for the long wait,' he said. 'We've had a few fake passports come through earlier today and yours looked as if someone had tampered with it. But we've checked with the Lagos High Commission and they've confirmed it is genuine.'

My heartfelt sigh reverberated round the room.

'At what address will you be staying in England?' the officer continued.

'At my brother and sister's. I have their address written down.' I put Deolu down, retrieved Kehinde's last letter and handed it over. To my utter annoyance, he unfolded the airmail and began reading its entire contents. My blood boiled, but I had learned hard lessons about dealing with authority over the past eight years. If stooping to conquer was what it required, I would. I took an exaggerated breath, quelled my anger and calmed myself.

He finished scanning the letter before scribbling something down on the paper in front of him. He handed back my passport and birth certificate and with unbelievable insouciance asked, 'So, when are you leaving?' I did a double take. *Did he just ask that? Even though I carried a British passport? Is this how it begins?* The exhaustion from a protracted day of travelling, the cranky toddler and all the frustrations I'd been carrying for the past twenty-six years welled to the surface. I drew myself up to my full stature, all five-foot one of it, looked him dead in the eye and answered with every fibre of my being.

'I'm not leaving, I've come home.'

Without a second glance, I hitched the toddler onto my hip, picked up my carry-on and with stiff shoulders and a head held high, I walked away.

CHAPTER THIRTY-FOUR

Touchdown

Come on, let it go. Smile. You haven't seen your siblings in years. Don't meet them with a frown. Unfortunately, once I lost my temper, I found it difficult to rein it in. Still, taking heed of the pep talk I just gave myself, I arranged my face into a strained smile before walking into the arrivals lounge.

Taiwo and Kehinde's faces beamed when they saw us. 'What happened?' Taiwo asked, squeezing Deolu against my chest in her embrace. 'We thought you had missed the flight.'

I let out a sigh. 'Let's get out of here. I'll tell you on the way home.' After a swift hug, my brother took hold of my luggage trolley and led us out. We made a quick detour to grab some snacks for Deolu, then headed for the taxi rank. Once we settled into a taxi, I explained the hold-up at the airport.

'Wow!' was all Taiwo said.

Instead of overcast skies, a brilliant blue covered the horizon, welcoming me in a way the immigration officer hadn't. We spent the trip from Heathrow to South London exchanging pleasantries about family in Nigeria and Dad's specialist treatment in London. In a lull in the conversation, I asked the question burning in my head: 'Is your flat big enough for all of us?' They'd assured me it was, but I wanted to be sure.

'We currently lodge in a three-bedroom flat with a couple and their five-month-old baby. We each have a room. Dad shares mine and you and Deolu can share Taiwo's,' Kehinde said.

'We've applied to the Council for an apartment of our own and should hear from them within the next month,' Taiwo added.

Over two hours later, the taxi pulled into St George's Way and stopped in front of a sign that said 'Gloucester Grove Estate'. As we climbed out of the car, Kehinde flashed me a smile. 'Welcome to Peckham.'

I pulled out my wallet to pay the fare, but Taiwo nudged me out of the way. 'I've got this,' she said.

While she paid the fare and Kehinde heaved my luggage out of the boot, I perused the information map, which showed the estate comprised several blocks of flats. With Deolu in my arms, I followed my siblings through a footpath that cut through the middle of one block. It opened out into an open green space surrounded by several blocks. The shadows the buildings cast over the greenery created an oppressive air, and the picnic tables dotted around the expanse of lawn did nothing to soften the feel. 'Our block is on the other side of the green,' Kehinde said as we walked through it.

Kehinde pointed to a block signposted 'Whitstable Court'. 'This is ours.' He pulled open the door and we entered an inner lobby next to the lifts. I eyed the four-letter swear words posing as graffiti on the walls but kept my thoughts to myself. 'We are on the third floor.' He pressed the call button on the lift and a dull hum echoed through the lobby as the lift's gears and pulleys engaged.

When the lift opened, a blast of putrid ammonia hit my nostrils. I recoiled and covered my nose. 'Sorry about that,' Taiwo said, her nose scrunched. 'That would be the drunks and homeless around here.' I cringed when Kehinde deposited my luggage on the lift's floor. *I must scrub those with bleach before putting them away.* As I grew older, I had started exhibiting some of Mama Yaba's germophobia. The lift's door closed, and I resisted the urge to gag. In the confined space, the smell gave a whole new meaning to the term 'eau de toilette'.

The lift opened on the third floor, depositing us in an outer lobby with two doors. I looked around, trying to get my bearings. Kehinde pointed at the closest door. 'This door leads to our block. You can walk right around the estate from one block to another, through a series of interconnecting gangways.'

'But I'd be wary of doing so, because muggers often lie in wait for unsuspecting victims, especially late at night,' Taiwo chipped in. The hairs on the back of my neck prickled. *Where were we? In a den of thieves and drunks?* Kehinde led us down a long, dimly lit corridor with doors on either side. It reminded me of the 'face me, face you' houses in Lagos. At number 39 he stopped and inserted a key.

The door opened into a tiny interior lobby with four doors and a flight of stairs. As Kehinde moved the luggage into the lobby, Taiwo explained the layout. 'The bedrooms and bathroom are all on the ground floor. The kitchen and living room are upstairs.' *An upside-down flat. I'd never heard of one before.* Dad appeared at the top of the stairs. 'Welcome to England!' At the familiar voice, Deolu squirmed in my arms. I set him down so he could climb up to his grandfather. After depositing the luggage in the bedroom, Taiwo led me upstairs, where I greeted Dad and she introduced me to the couple who owned the flat. Tomi and his wife Tutu welcomed me into their home. 'Tomi's older sister is my neighbour in Lagos,' Dad explained. *Ah! Family connections had their uses sometimes.*

*

When I woke the following morning, Dad was the flat's only occupant. He showed me around the kitchen before settling down to amuse Deolu. 'What time did everyone leave this morning?' I asked, while preparing the toddler's breakfast.

'Most of them leave by six. Taiwo has an early morning job, cleaning a block of offices in the city. From there she goes on to her second job as a catering assistant.' I mulled over that as I settled Deolu in my lap and spooned some Milupa baby cereal into his mouth.

'Do they all work two jobs?'

'Most Africans here do because they are in low-paid positions.'

Not much change since the 1960s, then. While Dad filled me in on my brother's job situation, I wondered how things would pan out for my family. If we needed two jobs each, how would we manage the children?

Later that evening, I sat down with Taiwo to discuss my plans. 'I need to search for work,' I said.

'Yes, that's true, but you need to apply for a National Insurance number first.'

'What's that for?'

She explained why I needed a National Insurance number and how to apply for one. She pulled out a telephone book and a wad of newspapers with teaching job adverts. '*The Guardian* is your best bet out of these, but you should buy the *Times Educational Supplement* on Friday, as it contains only teaching adverts. You might also want to consider applying for social benefits until you get a job.'

'Thanks for these, but I won't be applying for benefit. Bade and I agreed that if I can't get a job within the summer break, I'll go back to Nigeria and we'll find another way to make things work.'

'Are you sure about that?'

I gulped. 'Yeah. It's what we agreed.'

'Okay. Here's an *A–Z*, which will help you find your way around the area.'

I remembered using one of those on my previous trip. 'Thanks, I'll get started tomorrow.'

Over the following days, I sent off several job applications and applied for my National Insurance number. Dad and I took Deolu to the children's playground, next to the flat, each day, but never stayed long. The estate gave me the creeps. People either ignored you or looked right through you. My siblings didn't know their next-door neighbours, and the one in Flat 41 had called the police on them because they were praying too loudly and disturbing his peace. He hadn't considered asking them to lower the noise first. It didn't help that the infamous North Peckham estate was literally across the road. 'Never walk through it,' Kehinde warned the day after my arrival. 'A policewoman was murdered there a few months ago. Now the police won't even visit the place when called.' So much hostility and fear created an oppressive environment, which didn't sit well with me. If I were to stay in England, it wouldn't be in this neighbourhood, I decided.

*

On Saturday, I went shopping for groceries with Taiwo. Through the week, I noticed my siblings only ate Nigerian meals. 'Do you get all your groceries from Peckham?' I asked my sister.

'Yes. Most of it from Sainsbury's or Safeway, but we get our meat from the indoor market.'

Half an hour later, I walked through the Peckham indoor market and dropped into an alternative universe. 'Auntie, come buy,' a butcher beckoned me. In all the scenarios I had imagined, none of them included a white man calling me auntie, Nigerian style.

Taiwo kept moving until she came to the stall where she usually purchased her meat. The vendor greeted her with a toothy grin.

'Welcome, my customer.' Taiwo selected a few cuts of meat, and the vendor placed them on a weighing scale. 'Ten pounds for that,' he said.

'Eight pounds,' Taiwo countered.

Wide-eyed, I observed the interaction. I scanned the rest of the market. It teemed with Nigerians, who haggled over the price of offal and cow-leg and kissed their teeth in annoyance. The vendors, all white and Middle Eastern-looking, returned the teeth kissing with equal ardour and managed the haggling with panache. I shook my head in wonder at the evidence before my eyes. Nigeria had colonised Peckham market!

CHAPTER THIRTY-FIVE

Settling In

On Sunday, I dressed up with my siblings and headed to church with them. Bade and I attended church regularly in Nigeria. Our faith was an important part of our lives and kept us grounded. As we left the flat, my sister offered me a scarf as a head covering. I'd forgotten they attended a branch of a Nigerian denomination that held fundamentalist Christian beliefs and forbade uncovered heads and jewellery. Conceding on the head covering, I accepted the scarf but lifted my chin. 'I'm not taking off my earrings.'

'That's okay. You don't have to,' she replied.

One bus later, we entered the church in the Elephant and Castle area. My siblings excused themselves, both having church duties to discharge. Dad, Deolu and I sat in a pew, waiting for the service to start. I scanned the rest of the congregation, noting a lone white woman several aisles away. 'Do many white folk attend here?' I asked.

'No, just the one,' Dad said. I noted her headscarf and lack of earrings and wondered what she thought of the church's top-down leadership style. My gaze took in the interior of the church, the high ceiling and traditional stained-glass windows. 'This was formerly a Church of England building. It fell into disuse and the Nigerian church bought it,' Dad whispered beside me.

'Why did it fall into disuse?'

'Most English people, especially the younger generation, don't attend church anymore.'

'That's surprising, given the British brought Christianity to Africa.' Our conversation came to a halt as the church officials filed in and the service began.

I had never visited a church of this Nigerian denomination before. The songs were well-known Nigerian choruses. No one danced or moved and, with no deviation, everyone clapped exactly the same rhythm to every single song. Accustomed to a more energetic style of worship, I found the solemnity confining.

After the service, Dad and I waited for my siblings outside. To distract Deolu, who was becoming antsy, I took his hand and walked him up and down the pavement. Two ladies walking out of the building almost collided with us. One of them stopped and touched my arm. 'Hello. I saw you inside the church earlier. Are you new?'

The other woman interjected. 'Of course, she is. Can't you see her face?'

I presumed she was referring to my earrings and lipstick. I'd forgotten their women weren't allowed makeup either. 'Yes, I'm new,' I said through gritted teeth. They must have sensed my antipathy as they both bade me a quick welcome and a hasty goodbye. On the journey home, I asked my siblings if there were any other churches nearby. It turned out there was a Baptist church on Well's Way, near the flat.

The following Sunday, I took a ten-minute stroll down to the Baptist church. The lady at the door directed me to a serving hatch inside the building where members served tea and coffee. A couple came over and introduced themselves as Andy and Samantha. After the initial pleasantries, Samantha cocked her head. 'I detect an accent there. Where are you from?' The question stirred something I didn't have time to explore. 'I was born in London, but my parents were from Nigeria,' I replied, feeling the need to stress the difference. We continued conversing for a while longer. Just before the service began, a Black couple with two daughters walked in. They made eye contact with me and I nodded in recognition.

The pastor, who looked as if he was in his thirties, introduced himself as Mark and welcomed any visitors. Then he picked up a guitar and started strumming a song I recognised. Everyone stood up and, without fanfare, people began clapping and bopping to the music. The service was lively, the music very much in tune with the contemporary Christian music I listened to. I joined in enthusiastically, feeling at home and knowing I would be back. Still, something niggled. With only two Black families, did I want to be the minority in this church? I had two choices: join a church where my skin didn't stand out, but everything else did, or the other way round.

*

'I need to earn some money now,' I said to Taiwo one evening. The cost of baby food and nappies was eating into my finances.

'What kind of job were you considering?'

'Early morning cleaning?'

She shook her head in denial. 'Don't you think you are way over-qualified for a cleaning job?'

'Maybe, but it's work and I need to earn.'

'How about sewing? You are skilled at it. A friend at church is a seamstress and often complains she can't meet the demands of her customers. She might be able to give you some contract work.'

'That's a splendid idea, thanks.'

The following evening, Taiwo's friend offered me work sewing baby dresses. I visited Argos and bought a cheap sewing machine.

When I wasn't out searching for teaching jobs, I collected batches of pre-cut patterns from my employer and for every dress I sewed, earned £5.

In the second week of August, two official looking envelopes arrived in the post. With shaky fingers, I tore them open and read the contents. They were both invitations to interview for a teaching post, one in Enfield and the other in Southwark. I danced around the dining table, waving the letters in the air. Deolu toddled over and looked at me with puzzled eyes. I crowed. 'Yeah, Mummy is dancing with no music, do you want to join in?' He jiggled up and down on the spot in excitement. I grabbed his hands, and we danced together.

The trip to the Enfield interview took hours, and the school, an imposing three-storey Victorian building, reminded me of my primary school days in North London. After the initial introductions, I settled into the interview room with the headteacher. The post was for a special educational needs teacher. 'How would you go about arranging your classroom to meet the needs of children with special educational needs?' the headteacher asked.

I had read in the candidates' pack that these were children who struggled in mainstream classrooms and were taught in small classes. But I didn't realise the job would require me to rearrange the furniture. My understanding of the needs of such pupils was non-existent. It hadn't featured as a subject in my five years of teacher training. Throughout my schooling and in the years that followed, children were classified as smart, dull or somewhere in the middle. Although I could not vouch for what happened in the private sector, no one had special provision in any of the state-owned schools I had taught in.

I made up an answer. 'Well, I could put the troublesome children in the front row. That way I could monitor them and stop them from messing about during lessons.'

My interviewer's eyes narrowed, and her lips flattened into a grimace. She scribbled on her pad, then looked up. 'Anything else?' she asked.

'No, not really.'

'How would you manage the behaviour of the children in your class?'

'I would expect them all to abide by the school and class rules and if they didn't, I would punish them according to the school's policy.'

She asked a few more questions about how I would plan lessons and assess the children. Her placid face gave no sign as to my progress, but my gut told me I wasn't doing well. The headteacher wrapped up the interview. She escorted me to the front lobby and informed me she would be in touch within twenty-four hours.

'How was it?' Taiwo asked that evening.

'I don't think it went well at all.'

'Why?'

'I sensed she wasn't happy with my answers about managing children's behaviour and the interview ended too quickly.'

'They treat young ones differently here to the way we do. You can't beat a child here.'

'So how do they manage children's behaviour if they never flog them?'

'I can't say. What I know is that parents in church have got into trouble with social services because they disciplined their children by beating them.'

'Wow! Are there any teachers in your church that I could talk to about this?'

'I am afraid not.'

'Are you saying that in a congregation of over 200 people, there isn't a single teacher among them?'

'What can I say?' She spread her hands out in apology. 'We've got plenty of cooks, cleaners and security guards, but no teachers.'

*

My instincts were correct. The next day, I received a phone call telling me I was unsuccessful. I consoled myself, knowing that I had one more interview lined up. But, to succeed, I needed more knowledge. The Baptist church had a Sunday school. Perhaps someone there could give me advice. On Sunday, I spoke to the Sunday school teacher, who took me up to the room the children used. I took in the layout, the different sections for writing, reading and play, and the interview questions started to make sense.

The next interview was at the Southwark Council office in Peckham, within walking distance from the flat. This time around I felt more confident answering questions, but I was still flummoxed when she asked me how I would ensure children had appropriate learning resources. At the end of the interview, the interviewer sighed, put her pen down, brought her palms together and folded them in her lap. Here goes, I thought.

'I can't give you a permanent job because of your inexperience here.' I sighed and closed my eyes, processing the implications. 'However, I am happy to put your name down on the supply teaching list.'

My stomach did a cartwheel. *What did that mean*? As if reading my mind, she continued. 'This means you can cover temporary vacant posts from school to school. That will allow you to learn how things work here and prepare you better for future interviews.' She handed me a booklet with the details of all schools in the borough and told me to phone the Council daily for information on vacancies. I thanked her and took my leave. I walked home in contemplative silence. Technically, I had a job, but it didn't guarantee me work. Could I rely on that to feed and clothe my family until Bade got settled?

The following afternoon I phoned Bade at work in Nigeria. 'Well done!' he said. 'We can move forward with the plan.'

'But the job doesn't guarantee employment,' I moaned.

'True, but it's still a brilliant start, and we can build on it,' he said.

Two weeks later, leaving Deolu in the care of Dad and my siblings, I flew to Lagos to bring the girls back to England with me. I spent a frenzied week packing up more of our belongings and saying goodbye to close friends and family. Mama was in Ijebu, and I chose not to travel to bid her farewell. Over the years, I came to accept that she did what she thought was right. While I felt no great love for her, as my grandmother, she was my duty. I respected her as such, and after I got married, I supported her financially and visited her sporadically.

Mum stood over us, her face a mix of stoicism and pride as she said prayers, wishing us every good thing she could dream of, and it was a long list. I couldn't imagine what she was feeling with two-thirds of her family gone or leaving. At the airport, I turned to give Bade a hug. He was staying behind to sort out the rest of our business and would join us in a few months. 'I'll see you soon,' he said as we waved our goodbyes.

*

During the week I was away, Dad and my siblings moved into their own three-bedroom maisonette in a different block on the same Gloucester Grove estate. A week after I left, my daughters and I walked into my siblings' new living room. Deolu flew into my arms and we spent the next few minutes in a tearful reunion. While we ate dinner, I made a mental list of all the immediate tasks ahead. I needed to apply for a Council flat of our own. 'You should apply for child benefit for the kids,' Taiwo said, when I told her my plans. 'It's for families with kids, regardless of their work status or wealth.'

'Okay, I'll look into it,' I said. My pride wouldn't let me take handouts or rely on benefits, but a universal entitlement was different.

The next day, I went to the nearest church school to register the girls. The school could only offer Lara a place. 'What about my other daughter?' I asked the administrator. *Surely, they weren't expecting me to keep her at home?*

'Try other local schools. Meanwhile, we will place her on our list in case a vacancy opens here.'

Next, I tried Gloucester Primary School, virtually next door, the one my siblings told me to avoid. They offered Leye a place. Dad agreed to take her to school and pick her up, while I did the other school run. He would also look after Deolu while I worked. We spent the rest of the day down Peckham High Street, shopping for uniforms and clothing for the cooler months ahead.

Three days after our arrival, I picked up the phone at seven in the morning and rang the Borough's teaching supply services. 'Yes, we have a vacancy this morning,' the voice on the other end of the phone said. 'Please report to Peckham Park Infants School.' I jotted down the school's address, noting its starting and end times. *Yes! I had a job. The future looked promising!*

CHAPTER THIRTY-SIX

The Unknown Unknowns

The triple-decker building housing the Peckham Park Junior and Infant Schools loomed tall on Friary Road. I made my way to the Infant School's office where I met the headteacher, Mrs Bondy. 'Thank you for coming,' she said. 'We have a Year 1 class for you today.' That meant nothing, but I kept my ignorance to myself. She led me to the annexe next door. We walked into a large hall with several rooms leading off it. 'Here's your class,' she said, turning the door handle, and we stepped into a classroom unlike any I had ever seen before.

Child-sized rectangular tables, arranged in clusters of two and three, topped with little pots full of pointy-tipped colouring and lead pencils, greeted me. Mrs Bondy rattled off what I needed to know. 'The register is on the teacher's desk. I'll leave you to get acquainted with the room. If you have any questions, talk to Nicky in class 2N next door. Please pick the children up from the playground when the bell rings at nine.' I thanked her, and she left me to the day's business.

I reached for the register. A quick flick through reassured me it was like any other, with diagonal strokes marking each morning and afternoon session. *Phew! At least some things were familiar*. I explored the rest of the room, noting an easel covered in paper, with a shelf, on which rested several paint pots. I eyeballed the two shallow trays, one filled with water, the other sand, next to the easel. *What were they doing in a classroom?* A dirty-white Victorian enamel sink hung on the wall near the trays. Below it, a wire rack nestled, its function, unfathomable to me. The classroom looked attractive, with children's drawings and paintings displayed beautifully on boards on the wall.

At the centre of the back wall, wide cabinets filled with red trays caught my eye. I pulled some trays out and found a wide range of learning resources, all unfamiliar except for Lego. Additional plastic trays holding children's workbooks sat on top of the cabinet. In the left corner of the room, an attractive rectangular rug, complete with patterned cushions and a square book box created a cosy reading nook. Wired book racks around the perimeter of the rug kept the space cordoned off from the rest of the class. I pulled open the tall cupboards resting against the last wall and found an assortment of paper and card stored in different-sized trays and containers.

My brain worked furiously, like one of Bade's computer processors. I had never seen a set-up like it, and now all the questions at my interviews came crashing back. A brief glance at my watch showed I still had a few minutes before the bell rang. Time to pop next door. I knocked on Nicky's door and introduced myself. 'It's my first day as a teacher in a British classroom,' I said, 'so any advice would be most welcome.'

'Where are you from?' she asked in a melodious Welsh lilt. The question grated. Everyone I met wanted to know where I was from, but I hid my irritation because I needed more than a little help.

'Nigeria.'

'Oh. Right. I suggest you get to know the children today. Keep them busy with a range of activities.' She walked me back to the class and pointed to the water and sand trays. 'Get them working in groups of four or five and rotate them around the activities through the day. Have some on the floor here with the large wooden bricks.' She pulled out a tray I had missed, 'And here are some simple worksheets. Some children can work on these while you read with others.' The bell rang while she was still speaking. 'Follow me and I'll show you your class in the playground. We can catch up at lunch time and chat some more then.'

Overwhelmed, I took a deep breath and followed Nicky into the playground. 'We've got a new teacher.' The message whispered through the queue of children lining up in front of me. I tried to project an air of one in command despite the blood racing through my veins.

'What's your name, Miss?' a little Black girl with two pigtails asked.

'I will tell you when we are all in class,' I said. 'And what's your name.'

'Rachel.'

'How old are you, Rachel?'

'I'm six, Miss.'

Six! I had never taught a class that young.

*

In class, I introduced myself, opened the register and started calling out names. 'Your name is funny, Miss,' a blue-eyed, blonde boy interjected from the back of the class. The rest of the class tittered. I ignored the comment and continued with registration.

Two hands shot up. 'Miss, can we help take the register to the office?' *Some things don't change.* I still remembered being Mrs Simpson's little helper.

Following Nicky's advice, I set the class to work in distinct groups. I plonked myself down at a table with a group of pupils and pulled out some reading books. Within minutes, the noise rose to an unacceptable level. I was used to silent classes, where children only spoke to answer questions. I leaned back in my chair, observing children crawling all over the place. A group of boys working with the large bricks had built a racetrack. 'Vroom! Vroom!' their voices rumbled, chasing cars up and down the ramps. A cluster of girls at the water tray plunged their fingers in the water, then flicked it into each other's faces. 'Miss!' one of them shrieked. Ronnie, the blue-eyed blonde who thought my name was funny, was busy flicking pencils at another group – pencils that Nigerian children guarded with their lives. *How did children learn anything with this crazy style of organisation? Whatever happened to sitting at desks in rows, facing the teacher? I wished I had eyes in the back of my head like my grandmother used to claim she had.*

I clapped my hands to get everyone's attention. 'Please keep the noise down.' The hubbub reduced briefly, then rose again. This time, I raised my voice above the din, for emphasis. 'Please talk quietly!'

'My mum says teachers shouldn't shout,' someone said behind me. I turned around and met Jared's condemning glare. A few other heads nodded, agreeing with him, but the chatter dropped to an audible hum. I wondered how many times the children would berate me before the day ended.

The classroom door opened, and Nicky's head appeared. 'I forgot to tell you that the children have playtime at ten-thirty, followed by assembly. You should let them go out now. From the playground, they go straight into assembly.' Before I could speak, the children scrambled to their feet and lined up at the door. 'Next time, make sure they tidy up first,' Nicky whispered, her eye scanning the untidy mess the children had left behind. I let the class out, stopped for a quick bathroom break, before heading back to the classroom to prepare for the next session.

After assembly, I rotated the children around the activities, and they settled down to work.

'Miss, it's hot. Can you open the window?' Ronnie said.

I arched my eyebrow. 'What's the missing word at the end of that sentence, Ronnie?'

'Miss, you talk funny.'

'The missing word, Ronnie?'

'Please,' he muttered with obvious reluctance.

I walked up to the sash windows and examined them to see how the mechanism worked. I fiddled with what looked like a lock resting on the windowsill. The lock unscrewed easily, but no matter how hard I tried, I could not push the lower pane up.

'Stupid teacher. She can't even open the window,' Ronnie uttered, loud enough for the entire class to hear. I winced, pausing my window-opening antics, and took a moment to gather my wits. It was a day of many firsts. No one had ever called me stupid to my face, let alone a child.

I turned with deliberate calmness and gave him the full benefit of a frosty stare. 'That's very rude, Ronnie. You need to apologise now!'

'But it's true, you can't open the window.' He folded his arms, a mutinous look on his face. The class looked on with avid interest, wondering who would win the battle. But there could only be one victor if I wanted the children to learn from me.

'That does not excuse your rudeness.'

Ronnie stared at me, his chin thrust at an angle, daring me to do my worst. I remembered a Yoruba proverb which said, 'If a child refuses to allow his mother to slumber, he too will not sleep.' With feigned nonchalance, I crossed my arms. 'If you won't apologise, you will have to miss your lunch-time play and stay indoors here, with me. The choice is yours.' I matched his stare with one of my own.

'Fine, I'm sorry.' The words dripped with insincerity, but I let the belligerence go, choosing to pick my battles with care. There would be plenty more ahead.

*

Three-thirty could not have arrived sooner. With more elation than any teacher ought to feel, I led the class to the playground and handed the children over to their parents. As I stood watching the last kid leave, I rubbed the back of my neck, easing out the knots under my fingers. *How did British teachers do this*? The little munchkins had run me ragged. How could I survive every day without a trusty old cane? I remembered Ronnie's insult. He'd given me a dose of what my elders in Nigeria must have felt when they thought I disrespected them.

I went in search of Mrs Bondy. Assuming she still wanted me back, I needed a crash course in behaviour and classroom management. 'How did the day go?' She asked, putting the phone down as I walked in. *How to answer that?* I chose honesty. 'I don't believe I taught anybody anything today.'

She laughed. 'At least you realise that. Tomorrow you will do better.'

I relaxed and explained how different teaching in Nigeria was.

'Well, for a start, we never hit children here,' she said, placing a heavy emphasis on the last word.

'I understand that. So, how do you manage unacceptable behaviour?' The class had ignored my requests and for most of the day done whatever they wanted. That had to stop.

'You start by negotiating class rules with them, then…'

She lost me at 'negotiating'. *British people negotiated with children? No wonder the kid said I was stupid. He probably thinks all adults are stupid.*

'What if the children want to negotiate unacceptable rules?'

'Your job is to lead them through making the right set of rules, followed by an agreed list of sanctions for disobeying them and rewards for obeying them.'

'If I have to reward them for behaving well, isn't that bribery?'

'You could see it as bribery, or more accurately as an incentive.'

I had never seen a Nigerian adult negotiate with a child – the idea was a complete anathema. What did children know? But if that's how the British did it…

'I'd better think of ten rules for tomorrow.'

'The children in your class are only six, some not even that. They won't remember ten rules. Maybe five. Keep them short, simple and positive. By the way, I need a teacher for the next six weeks at least. Are you interested?'

'Yes, I am. Thank you.' I didn't hesitate despite the challenge. I needed this job, and thirty Ronnies wouldn't stop me. Still churning ideas in my head, I left for home. So much to learn, so much I didn't know. Would I succeed or fail?

*

The next few weeks passed in a blur, with me receiving mentoring sessions from Mrs Bondy almost daily. I was confident that I was in charge in my class and not the other way round, but so many things remained a challenge. All the staff called each other by their first names, including Mrs Bondy. But years of conditioning meant I could not utter her first name. She wasn't just the boss, she was old enough to be my mother. I wanted to be like everyone else, but every time I tried, her first name stuck to the back of my throat like a pesky little fish bone. So, she remained Mrs Bondy and an uncomfortable silence pulsated in the room, long enough to make me squirm whenever I called her that.

At work, I barely kept one step ahead of the class, having to read up about the curriculum each day before I taught it. It didn't help that the national curriculum had only been introduced in September and teachers were just starting to create matching schemes of work. With no textbooks to follow, I had to research every topic from scratch. I thought the Nigerian government was haphazard. It seemed the British system was equally confused. Why the British government thought one primary school teacher ought to teach over ten subjects competently was beyond me. I took delight in teaching my class Yoruba songs they'd never heard. But how did one teach music appreciation? I concluded that since the children sang with gusto, that showed how much they appreciated it.

Teaching physical education (PE) was my nemesis. What did I know of teaching a child to dribble a ball? Only boys dribbled balls in Nigeria and most got whipped for wasting their time on such a frivolity. How did one teach children to do a forward roll safely, when I feared they would break their necks in the process? The only PE I knew was running, and my children grew tired of it. 'Miss, can we use the climbing frame?' they clamoured each week. In Nigeria, normal people did not climb walls. I eyed the giant metal grille with apprehension, refusing to be responsible for the death of a child. But the children would not let up, since they saw other classes using the frame. Eventually, I approached Mrs Bondy, and she arranged for me to observe another teacher. After that, I allowed the children to use the frame, but always with a prayer on my lips.

*

Less than a quarter of the children in my class could read. I promised myself that if I did only one thing right, it would be to get them all reading. It would be a hard promise to keep. 'We don't do it like that here, my dear,' Mrs Davids said in a patronising voice when she dropped into my class to work with a group of low-achievers. Mrs Davids was the oldest member of staff and, so far, all I'd ever got from her was veiled criticism.

'What?' I asked in confusion.

'Those,' she said, pointing to the alphabet and three-letter-word flash cards in my hand. 'That's old-school. We use real books to teach reading in this school.' I tutted silently. Given her age, I was certain she learned to read with flash cards.

'But the children don't recognise the words in the books. They just parrot what has been repeated to them.' It had taken me days to realise this.

'True, but they will learn to, once they are familiar with the story.'

'So, I should just keep on reading them stories, and somehow, by magic, they will learn to read?' I couldn't help the scepticism in my voice.

'Just don't let the headteacher see you with those cards.'

I frowned. *Was she saying don't do it, or do it, but don't get caught?* I decided she meant the latter. My sanity depended on it.

CHAPTER THIRTY-SEVEN

Home, Anything but Sweet Home

Autumn blew in on a chilly October morning, and the goose-bumps on my skin as I hurried to work told me it was time to prepare for winter. Just before the half-term break, Mrs Bondy called me to her office for a chat. I tried to force my limbs into a relaxed pose as I perched on the edge of the easy chair she offered. Mrs Bondy left the high-backed office chair behind her desk and moved to the comfy one opposite mine. She leaned forward, her eyes intense. 'You need to spend more time in school at the beginning and end of each day, preparing for your class,' she said. 'Of all my teachers, you arrive last, just before the bell goes, and you are the first person to leave.'

I nodded and swallowed. She was right, but bar a miracle, I couldn't see a way around my dilemma. I explained myself.

'Lara's school day starts a few minutes before ours. Her school won't let me drop her off any earlier. Also, after school, I have to leave early to pick her up and by the time I get there, I am half an hour late as it is.'

Mrs Bondy turned my words over in her head. 'Have you considered finding a neighbour whose child attends the same school and sharing the task with her?' she asked. 'For example, if she does the morning round, you could get to work much earlier and leave early for the evening pick-up. The alternative is to pay someone to do both rounds.'

Now why hadn't I thought of that? I thanked Mrs Bondy for her suggestion and promised to act on it.

When I brought up the idea over dinner, I found out how unhappy Lara was at school. 'The kids at school call me African Foufou,' she said, 'and they won't play with me.'

'Why didn't you tell me?'

She shrugged. A single iridescent tear dropped on to her half-empty plate. She brushed her arm over her eyes to wipe away the evidence of her pain. I leaned closer and rubbed a soothing hand over her head. She was my stoic one. I turned to her sister. 'Leye, have children been calling you names at school?'

'Sometimes, but I tell the teacher and she sorts them out.'

I focused back on Lara. 'Have you told your teacher?'

'Yes, but she does nothing. She just tells me to ignore them.'

In the ensuing silence, I processed the information. The church school, chosen for its Christian ethos, had ignored my child's distress, whereas the county school with the poor reputation had done something about it.

'Tomorrow, I will book an appointment to see your headteacher,' I told Lara.

That night I lay in bed reflecting on the past month, the heavy burden of guilt at not noticing my daughter's unhappiness weighing me down. I couldn't believe the simplicity of Mrs Bondy's solution to the school-run problem. Yet it hadn't occurred to me. In a moment of clarity, I realised that as an adult in Nigeria, life had become somewhat easier. With fewer challenges, I had fallen out of the habit of problem-solving. To do better than just survive the hostilities of my current environment, I needed to draw on those skills again.

I met with Lara's headteacher, and she promised to look into the issue. She gave me the names of a few mums who lived on the estate. One of them agreed to take Lara to school and back for a fee.

Meanwhile, my first pay cheque was delayed because I didn't have a current account, and the school wouldn't pay it into a savings account. The bank required two non-family references, which, given my circumstances, proved challenging. By the time a friend of my siblings and Mrs Bondy agreed to vouch for me, I was dangerously low on funds. The child benefit I applied for hadn't materialised either. I took the children shopping for winter clothing, but with only enough money to cover their needs, I dropped by the second-hand shop for mine. It wasn't until my bottom kissed the pavement that I learned I had bought fashion boots, their pretty little kitten heels no match for the black ice lining the pavements.

*

Bade arrived in the middle of November. The girls were excited to see their dad; Deolu not so much, judging by his scowl when I deposited him into a cot bed, and Bade climbed into Deolu's favourite spot beside me. Two weeks later, Mrs Bondy dropped into my classroom at lunch time. 'Would you like a temporary, fixed-term contract to replace your current casual supply one?' she asked.

'I would love one, but when I first applied, the Council assigned me to the supply teaching pool because I lacked experience of teaching in England.'

'Well, that's changed. Are all your qualification certificates available?'

'Yes, they are all at home.'

'Wonderful, bring them in tomorrow and I'll start the process.'

All day long, I floated on air, ecstatic at the prospect of a short-term contract. I wouldn't need to worry about changing jobs until the end of next summer.

Meanwhile, Lara still complained about being bullied at school. I had a chat with Mrs Bondy and the headteacher of the junior school on the same site. Both schools had a space, so I moved Leye to mine and Lara to the junior school. Just before we broke up for Christmas, Mrs Bondy asked me to take my certificates to County Hall in Waterloo, which housed the Inner London Education Authority. Within a fortnight, my temporary contract, placing me in the school until the end of the academic year, arrived.

*

One Sunday, after service, Yemi, the other Black woman in the congregation, approached me. 'How did you get your teaching job?' she asked. I explained the process and asked why she wanted to know.

'My husband and I have lived in the country for five years. In that time, I have earned a living cleaning offices, but I qualified as a teacher in Nigeria,' she said.

'Ah. Why didn't you search for teaching jobs when you arrived?'

'I am Black, and I didn't train here. I thought I wouldn't get one.'

'You are here legally, right?'

'Yes, we are.'

'Then I suggest that you apply, but before you do, spend a week observing teaching in your daughters' school.'

It was advice I doled out to every Nigerian would-be teacher who asked me. I could not in good conscience let another human experience what I did on my first day. She followed my advice and within three weeks swapped her cleaning job for a teaching post. I wondered how many more over-qualified Nigerians worked in menial jobs because they assumed the system would discriminate against them and therefore hadn't tried to find better employment.

After Christmas, the Council allocated us a flat near Borough tube station. In the preceding months, they had tried forcing me onto the North Peckham estate. Twice, I refused. Then they offered one in the Bermondsey area. The day I tried to collect the keys, they rescinded the offer. 'There's been an administrative error. There is no flat in Bermondsey, but you can have a three-bedroomed property on the North Peckham estate right now,' the housing officer said, without the slightest hint of guile.

Did she think I was a fool? 'No thank you, I'll wait,' I replied. All five of us in a single room was excruciating, but I'd rather be cramped and safe.

*

Bade and I huddled under an umbrella while we map-read our way from the bus stop on Great Dover Street to our new dwelling on Manciple Street. So far, January had been miserable, with a constant daily drizzle. Five days earlier, the Burns Day storm had blown in, leaving dozens of casualties in its wake. After a five-minute walk, we turned a corner and found Strood House, five storeys tall, in all its dilapidated glory.

The dirty white paint peeling off the external facade of the sash windows told a story of neglect and rot. We climbed to the first floor, noting the neat little puddles of urine in the square corners of the stairwell. But none of this prepared us for what came next. The door to the apartment was slightly ajar when we arrived. Bade rapped his knuckles against it and called, 'Hello'.

'Hello,' a voice answered from within. I followed Bade into the tiny hallway, past a closed door on the left. The hallway curved to the right. We walked past two more doors, one on each side of the corridor, through an open doorway into a spacious room. But it wasn't the size of the room that drew my attention.

Every single door was riddled with holes; small round holes, slitty holes, golf-ball sized holes. A door, presumably belonging to the room we were standing in, leaned against a wall, disfigured like the others, its hinges still attached. A connecting door to another room looked equally bruised. Gaping, I surveyed the rest of the room. A metal electricity conduit pipe dangled precariously from the ceiling. Underneath the carpet of household rubbish covering the floor, a hypodermic needle winked at me. It looked as if the Burns Day storm had dropped in for tea and forgotten to tidy up.

At the window, I noticed a glazier, busy replacing broken windowpanes. At his feet, shards of glass glinted in the sunlight, creating tiny prisms of reflected light. 'I've been 'ere all morning sorting them windows,' the glazier said, in a cockney accent. 'I ain't gonna finish today, so I'll be back tomorrow.'

Still trying to find my misplaced voice, I nodded.

'What happened to the doors?' I managed.

'I ain't got no bloody idea. Found 'em like that. They just kicked them squatters out. The Council will send someone out to replace them doors.'

Squatters! That explained a lot, although not the different-sized holes in the doors. The room we stood in looked like the living room with its tiled Victorian fire surround. The fireplace had been replaced with an ugly electric fire. Bade pushed the interconnecting door. It led to a double bedroom. I glanced at the living room's door again. It was grim, with slivers of splintered wood poking out all over.

Bade and I ventured out in different directions, exploring the rest of the flat. I opened the door on the left and eyed the Victorian, high-level water cistern with its rusting metal chain. Without thinking, I looked down. Ugh! I shouldn't have done that. A grey-black sludge clung fast below the toilet bowl's water line. It hadn't seen a brush in years. I backed up and went searching for Bade. The next door led to a double room with another interconnecting single room. I found Bade eyeing the work counter in the kitchen. The metre-long worktop had one cupboard underneath and a space for a fridge. Two additional wall cupboards provided all the storage space. A space beside the cupboards looked large enough for a free-standing cooker. 'The bathroom is through here,' Bade said, sliding open a door to reveal a sink and bath. *Why would they place the bathroom right next to the kitchen with just a partition between them?*

We found the answer to that riddle at church the following Sunday. Properties built at the turn of the century for the working class had no indoor bathrooms. People used public baths instead. To modernise the old apartments, the Council had carved a bathroom out of the kitchen.

*

Bade and I walked back to the bus stop in silent contemplation. I wondered if he was remembering the modern two storey, three-bedroom house we had last rented in Nigeria, with its split-level living and dining area, complete with vaulted ceiling. I was in two minds, desperate to get out of our current situation, but not into a flat unfit for human habitation. Yet if I refused it, we could be on the waiting list for months to come.

'What do you think?' Bade asked, settling into a seat on the bus.

'I don't know,' I said. I shared my thoughts, listing the pros and cons.

'Let's visit the housing office and discuss the state of the flat with them,' I suggested.

The housing officer was unrepentant. 'We'll give you £250 to decorate the flat, but that's it.'

'What about the doors and the dangling electricity pipe?'

'We'll fix those before you move in.'

I sighed in relief.

'Do you want it?' the officer said.

'Can I sleep on it?'

'Fine, but you need to let me know tomorrow. We have an extensive waiting list.'

At home, I described the state of the flat to my siblings and Dad. 'On the plus side, it is in a nicer neighbourhood than Peckham,' Kehinde said.

'That may be the case, but given the hypodermic needle I saw, there must be drugs on the estate,' I replied.

'True, but there are drugs in every neighbourhood,' Taiwo pointed out.

I grappled with the decision all night and left for work in the morning undecided. I returned home and met Bade at the door, coming back from posting off another job application.

'Have you decided?' he asked.

'No, not really. How about you?'

'I think we should accept it. Your siblings have helped long enough.'

I picked up the phone and dialled the housing officer. 'We'll take it,' I said.

CHAPTER THIRTY-EIGHT

Why, Oh Why?

Almost five months after I started working, I was still waiting for the child benefit allowance, so I wrote to the Department of Social Security. Like a defence attorney, I cited every relevant bullet on their information leaflet, explaining how I met the criteria and why I should have received the allowance ages ago. 'When should I expect it,' I enquired, 'given that I have contributed four months' worth of taxes to the British economy?'

Our church congregation rallied around our cause like troopers. The pastor, Mark, asked for volunteers to help us decorate and move into the flat. With the stipend from the Council, Bade and I bought the decorating supplies and carted them to the flat on a Friday. The next day, we set out early, planning to get to the flat well ahead of our volunteers. At the top of the stairs, our animated chatter ended abruptly when we noticed the front door ajar with a white sheet of paper taped to it. My heart beat louder than an African drum, as Bade prised the paper off and we read its contents. It was from the Metropolitan Police, telling us we were burgled overnight.

In stunned silence, we entered and assessed the damage. The burglars had stripped the flat; the decorating supplies, the wallpaper stripper we had hired and the wallpaper pasting table we borrowed from Mark, all gone. The Council had delivered new doors the previous day. Unhung, they were gone too, but the most devastating discovery in the kitchen brought us up short. The only evidence that the flat ever owned a central heating boiler was a trail of dangling wires and pipes.

Distraught, I called Mark from a pay phone to stop folk coming down. We had no money to replace the supplies, and getting the front door locks fixed was the priority. After calling out a locksmith, I returned to the flat. In abject misery, I sank down to the living room floor and stared into space while Bade strode from room to room. Then I started a monologue with God.

'God, they say you are all seeing and all knowing. Where were you today? On holiday? Taking a break? What were you thinking? You know how much money I have left in my purse. Why would you let this happen?' I waited in the silence for a response, a bolt of lightning, anything. A knock on the door startled me out of my repose. It was Mark. Not quite the answer I was expecting from God, I barely acknowledged his presence as Bade showed him around the empty rooms.

Mark came back and slid to the floor beside me. 'What now?' he asked.

'I don't want the flat. I am returning the keys to the Council on Monday.' The words tumbled out in a flash of mutinous rage. Bade shook his head without saying a word. He was wise, my husband.

'You can't do that,' Mark said. 'You've already signed the contract. If you return the keys, they will say you made yourself homeless and they are under no obligation to rehouse you.'

I didn't want to hear that. For the past six months, I had maintained a fragile grip on reality. Now, the dam of emotions burst, and I sobbed like a child. Mark rose beside me and disappeared. Bade took his place, holding me as I cried my heart out.

Spent and exhausted, I noticed a scratching coming from somewhere in the flat. Curious, I picked myself off the ground and followed the sound. It came from the toilet where I found Mark, on his knees scrubbing out the filthy toilet bowl, while I'd indulged in my pity party. A tough lesson in humility and service, it snapped me right out of my funk. I set about cleaning other parts of the flat with the supplies we'd brought along that morning, and as I scrubbed, I prayed. 'God, those burglars mustn't die until after they become Christians. You hear me?' It seemed appropriate poetic justice, that they might turn from their wicked ways. The alternative was to curse them, which is what I really wanted to do. Instead, I took all my rage and vented it on the inanimate surfaces I was cleaning. The physical exertion helped return me to a state of equilibrium. The locksmith came, changed the locks, and we left.

A letter arrived the following week, telling me I would receive my child benefit, including five months of back payments immediately. It brought no joy, just disillusionment, that had I not been persistent, I would still be without the money. *How many people, in similar circumstances, lacked the ability to fight the system?* I had grown up believing modern Britain was built on equality and fairness, but I was discovering an underbelly where access to such privileges depended on knowledge, wherewithal and personal resolve.

The following week, Bade got a job as a software engineer. The news brightened the dank February days and brought some much-needed cheer. His office in West Drayton, on the outskirts of London, meant considerable travelling costs. The child benefit had arrived at an opportune moment.

*

Early on Monday, I turned up at the housing office with a police crime number to report the theft of the doors and boiler. 'We'll have to order you a new boiler,' the housing officer said.

'How long will that take?'

'I don't know. Check back every few days, but it could take weeks.'

'Weeks! I have young children. We can't stay in the flat with no heating or hot water for weeks.'

'I'm sorry I can't be of more help. I have to warn you though, if you don't stay in the flat and squatters re-enter it, it will be your responsibility to clear them out.' My eyes bulged. But he was dead serious. The Council would give no more help.

Bade and I devised a plan. We would sleep at the flat each night, but the children would remain at Painswick Court. I would return to Painswick Court early each morning to get the girls ready for school. Bade hadn't taken out insurance when he hired the wallpaper stripper. The hire company agreed he could pay back the cost, plus interest, on a monthly basis. It would take us a year to clear the debt. On Mark's advice, we contacted social services who gave us second-hand beds, wardrobes and a sofa. In return, we gave them a donation. On our first night at the flat, Bade and I huddled together on the bed, fully clothed and tried to sleep. Even with our winter coats on and a duvet thrown over our shivering bodies, the biting cold seeped through to the bone. The following night we bought two tiny fan heaters, but without doors to keep the heat in, we need not have bothered.

We still needed to decorate the flat and buy the white goods which social services could not provide. We tried buying a fridge and cooker from Dixons on credit. With the forms completed, the helpful sales assistant picked up the phone. 'I won't be long, I just have to ring this through,' he said. Minutes later, he shook his head. 'I'm sorry, but credit has been denied.'

We shuffled out of the store, heads hanging low and tried Currys. Same result. 'Let's ask my bank for a loan,' I said to Bade. *Perhaps we would fare better.*

I filled out the bank's loan application form and waited. The information leaflet said the bank would let us know with a phone call within five days. Eight days of silence passed. With a familiar sense of foreboding, I called the bank. Initial pleasantries over, I asked the question eating me inside out. 'This is the ninth day since I dropped off the application form. Can you tell me why you did not contact me within five days, as published in your information leaflet?'

'I'm sorry madam, a letter is on its way to you now,' the voice at the other end said.

'I can't wait for the letter. Can you tell me the outcome now, please?'

'I am sorry, but the bank has declined your application.'

'May I know why?'

'I'm afraid I am not at liberty to disclose that.'

'Who can disclose the information?'

'You'll have to talk to the bank manager, madam.'

I booked an appointment there and then.

'Please take a seat,' the bank manager said, welcoming us into his spacious office. Bade and I plonked ourselves down on the comfy sofa and waited. The bank manager turned to me.

'May I ask where you are from: Nigeria or Ghana?'

I bristled. *Not that question again*. 'Nigeria. Why do you ask?'

'Well, I'm sorry to say this, but in recent years, we've had a spate of single women from Nigeria and Ghana taking out loans before disappearing into thin air.'

Ah! So, I am paying for other people's transgressions.

'Well, I am not going anywhere.' I explained our circumstance to him.

'It would help if you were on the voters' registration list and if your husband also opened an account here,' he said.

'What is the voters' registration list?'

He explained. I wondered why my siblings hadn't mentioned this, then realised they probably didn't know about it either. Their church forbade the use of credit or getting into debt of any kind, so it may never have been an issue for consideration. The bank manager made Bade fill out an application form, took copies of both our passports and approved a loan for £500.

As Mark couldn't reschedule volunteers from church to help decorate, half of the loan went on an interior decorator. Church folk helped in other ways, with donations of crockery and minor household items. Through Mark, an anonymous benefactor gave us £500, half as a loan and the other half as a gift. The move took place two weeks later. It had taken the Council three weeks to replace the doors and boiler. Alex, a church member, donated his time and van and helped us move. Our families would become friends for life.

*

I started to notice subtle changes in my daughters. Deolu hadn't started talking yet, although he had just marked his second birthday. The girls, however, were bilingual and fluent in English and Yoruba. In the past, they would have responded in either language; now, they would only speak English. When I encouraged them to speak Yoruba, they point blank refused. It didn't help that Bade and I both processed our thoughts in English. It had been our first language, after all, so it was easy to let it slide and, gradually, the family stopped speaking Yoruba.

The next battleground was their hair. 'Mummy, can I perm my hair so it's straight and silky like all the girls in my class?' Lara asked. Her sister sidled up to her, waiting for my response.

'I'm afraid not,' I said, remembering what my first perm had done to my head. There was no way I was putting lye on my children's scalps, even though they now made kits for kids.

'Why not?' she pressed. 'You have a perm.'

Having gone through a childhood where everyone had tried to muffle my voice, I had raised my children to speak their mind. Unfortunately for me, they were both smart-mouthed. 'Perms are created using chemicals that are not safe for growing children,' I replied. Because I said 'growing children', not 'people', my daughter did not have a flippant comeback. But she was not happy and hair-plaiting time on Saturdays became an unpleasant affair.

Lara detested the one chore I gave her. 'My friends don't have to help their mothers with dishes,' she moaned.

'Do I look like one of your friends' mothers?' I asked, with classic Yoruba sarcasm.

At eight, she was a year older than I was when Mama had started my training. While I had no intention of overburdening her with daily chores, I still wanted her to contribute to the family's welfare. It was the African way, and I needed the help. My daughter, however, had other ideas.

I woke up on a Tuesday morning and started getting the children ready for school. Each morning, I handled all three on my own since Bade left for work early. Once Deolu was out of the bath, while I was getting him dressed, Lara would use the bathroom next. Then she would watch Deolu while I helped Leye, before we all had breakfast. That morning, having finished dressing Deolu, I called for Lara but didn't get a reply. 'Lara, hurry up!' I yelled. Still no reply. I carried the toddler into the children's bedroom and found Leye alone. 'Where is your sister?'

'I don't know.'

'What do you mean you don't know?'

'She's not here.'

I searched the connecting bedroom where she slept, but she wasn't there. A quick sweep of the living room, bathroom and toilet and I came up empty. I stood, frowning, in the empty hallway, unease creeping up my spine. *How could I have lost a child inside the flat?*

The doorbell rang. With a single stride, I reached for the handle and opened the door. There, standing on the threshold, was my daughter and a strange woman. I stood there gawking, the lack of comprehension stamped on my forehead. 'I found her in the park nearby, on my way to work,' the woman said. 'It's not safe for a child out alone at this time of the morning, so I convinced her to show me the way back home.'

With new understanding, I looked at my daughter, who stood limply, head cowed, holding a plastic bag. 'Thank you so much. I am so grateful to you.' I reached for my daughter and drew her into the flat. 'Thank you, God,' I whispered in the emptiness as I shut the door.

*

I led Lara into the living room and collapsed onto the couch. I sat dazed for a few moments before dialling my school, telling them I had a family emergency and would not be coming in. With the immediate issue dealt with, I turned to my daughter, who was still standing in a corner clutching the plastic bag to her chest. 'What's in the bag?' I asked. Wary, her big, brown eyes watched my every move, but she said nothing. I held out my palm. 'Give it to me.' She handed it over and I peered inside. It contained leggings, sweatshirts and cans of baked beans. *Humph! So, this was a planned runaway.*

I wiped a weary hand over my face. I wanted to howl, but my instincts told me the situation required delicacy. Deolu whimpered beside me, and I realised the other two hadn't eaten. 'Right, let's get some breakfast,' I said, bustling all three into the kitchen.

'Are we going to school today?' Leye asked, as I pulled out cereal boxes and bowls.

'No,' I replied, my head still in the fridge, searching for the milk. I hissed as I caught sight of the bottle on the shelf I had just searched twice. *The morning's events must have addled my brain.* 'Mummy has things to sort out with your sister,' I said as I poured the creamy fluid over their bowls.

We ate in silence while I contemplated my next move. After breakfast, I rang Bade at work. There wasn't a lot he could do, but just hearing his voice soothed my jangled nerves. With Leye and her brother playing in their bedroom, I settled down with my eldest, determined to find out why she ran away. 'I don't want to wash dishes,' she said, in response to my query. I searched her face, trying to fathom what was going on behind those brown eyes. Her body had lost some of its rigid stance now she realised I wasn't going to kill her. *How long had she been planning this escapade? It took some sass. She'd clearly put some effort into it. Admirable, if one thought about it dispassionately. Why hadn't I tried that in Nigeria? You know why: Mama would have whipped you till kingdom come.* I cocked my head. 'Are the dishes the only reason you ran away?'

She nodded. *How to respond?* I remembered it wasn't a chore I'd enjoyed either. I considered the chores of a typical eight-year-old in Nigeria, what I did at her age. Balancing UK expectations against those of Yoruba culture, I didn't think washing-up was onerous, given it was her only chore. Yet, I couldn't have her running into danger.

I explained things from my perspective. 'I know you don't enjoy doing the dishes, but I need your help with them. Your friends may not do chores. Some may have mums who don't work, so they can do it all. Your dad and I work so you and your siblings can have a better future.' There was no point adding that our salaries also supported both our extended families in Nigeria. 'Do you understand what I am saying?' She nodded. I pressed on, going by pure instinct. 'If you live with mummy and daddy, you must help with the chores, and doing the dishes is the easiest of them all. I love you and I want you to be safe. But, if you really don't want to live here, I'd prefer to call Social Services on your behalf, so they can place you somewhere safe. I don't want you running away again because it's dangerous out there alone.'

I paused and assessed how she was taking it so far. Her eyes were focused on me. *She is paying attention. Good.* I buttressed my point. 'Remember, there are no guarantees that whoever you are placed with won't expect you to do some chores. Every family is unique. Spend the rest of the day thinking about it. Then, at 3 p.m. I need to know your decision because I want to ring Social Services before they close for the day. Is that okay with you?' Again, she nodded.

I let her be, with no idea if my strategy would work. She had been a strong-willed toddler, a deep thinker, astute in reading situations and knowing how to make the best of them. While her younger sister used flattery to get what she wanted, Lara threw tantrums if she had an audience she thought she could influence. Her tantrums would disappear as soon as her audience did. I'd heard of Nigerians losing their children to Social Services, but it was safer to hand her over myself, rather than let her run away again, and she would too. I hoped it wouldn't come to her leaving, but if it did, maybe someone would steer us through the crisis.

My heart pounded as 3 p.m. loomed. It was time for my daughter's decision. Would she choose us or the unknown? 'What have you decided?' I asked.

'I want to stay.'

'Are you sure? You will still have to do dishes.'

'I'm sure.'

Phew! Tragedy averted.

*

Mrs Bondy was my go-to person whenever I needed counsel. The next day, she listened as I recounted the previous day's events. 'Do you think I am asking too much of her?' I asked. 'If for whatever reason we had to return to Nigeria, I wouldn't want her to be an outcast or disadvantaged like I was.'

'Only you can be the judge of that. Different cultures, different expectations. She is bound to see the differences between her circumstances and those of her friends though, and she will wonder why and may resent it.'

With my boss's words echoing in my thoughts, I cut back on how much I asked Lara to do at home. But not completely. She was African, after all. I even considered buying a dishwasher, but there was nowhere to put it in the flat. A few years into the future, Mum visited us in England. When her eyes lit on my dishwasher, she called my name three times. Immediately, I was twelve again.

'You are spoiling your daughters and doing them a disservice by using a machine to wash the dishes. What kind of women will they grow into?'

'Mum,' I said, 'what would you prefer: that your granddaughters are spoilt or that one of them is missing because she ran away to avoid doing dishes?' The stupefied expression on my mother's face was my reward. I had never seen her so lost for words. The Yorubas have a proverb, 'My child is dead, is better than my child is lost.' Spoilt daughters were the lesser of the two evils.

CHAPTER THIRTY-NINE

Prejudiced or What?

Just before my contract ended in the summer, Mrs Bondy visited my class once more. 'I have a vacancy for September,' she said. 'If you are happy here, I can give you a permanent contract.' I accepted the offer and enjoyed the summer with a new-found peace.

In September, another startling discovery challenged my perception of British fairness. I was earning far less than I should, given my qualifications and nine years of teaching experience. An old family friend asked me to act as a referee for her teacher training application. Reading through the form, I realised the starting salary for new graduate teachers was higher than my current earnings.

'I think I am grossly underpaid,' I said to Maria, (Mrs Bondy), the next morning. We were finally on a first name basis.

'Why, what makes you say so?'

I told her about the application form.

'Okay. Put that in a letter and I will send it to the local authority on your behalf,' she said. I did as she asked. A few weeks later, Bade discovered that with over ten years of post-graduate experience, he was earning the same wage as the new graduates in his team. *What were the odds of both of us being underpaid despite being in different industries?*

The following January, the local authority completed a fresh salary assessment, adding £3,000 to my annual wage. A good thing it was too, because Bade and I had decided to buy our own home and move out of our drug-ridden neighbourhood. Like Maria did, Bade's line manager took his case to the human resources department, but it would take years to resolve his income discrepancy. The company gave him a promotion and a salary rise that still didn't reflect the responsibilities of his job and experience. To redress the balance would require acknowledging someone got it wrong. No one wanted to do that. Instead, he received another pay rise six months after the first, which still left him at the bottom of his new pay scale. It seemed we had to strive to receive anything that was rightfully ours, and the more we talked to people, the more our experience appeared commonplace among ethnic minority migrants.

*

We entered the house-hunting whirl with astounding naivety now that I look back on it. Several viewings later we were no closer to finding a big enough dwelling to our taste. Neither Bade nor I liked Victorian houses, and the modern ones we viewed were too small. 'Why are you buying a house in England when you haven't built one in Nigeria yet?' Yemi asked after church on Sunday. 'Shouldn't your priority be where you will live when you return home?' I opened my mouth, then paused. *How do I explain that I don't view Nigeria as home?* I let the question slide with a self-deprecating smile.

One day, the estate agent's voice took on a different nuance. 'I've got just the right house for you, in New Cross,' she said. We arranged a viewing, and on a Saturday, met the estate agent at her office before trailing her car to the property. I had passed my British driving test the previous year, and we had bought a second-hand Nissan coupe.

My eyes lit up when we turned into a cul-de-sac, in a brand-new development with modern houses. The excitement built as we crossed the property's threshold. An archway connected the open lounge and dining area to a fitted kitchen. It was slightly bigger than our current one, came with fitted appliances, including, joy of joys, a dishwasher. Upstairs, we found the bathroom, and three bedrooms: a double, a single and what the estate agent described as a box room. It was the first house I could see myself living in, Bade likewise.

Things moved quickly after we put an offer in. Thanks to Prime Minister Margaret Thatcher's enabling policies, we got a 100 per cent mortgage and didn't need a deposit. However, somehow, we had not factored in the cost of moving or solicitors' and agents' fees. Our Nigerian broker friend had failed to point these out, or we hadn't paid attention. Either way, the bill when it came, left us gasping.

*

We moved mid-summer, less than two years after our arrival, and invited friends from church around. House-proud, I showed my guests around my home. Deolu's cot bed occupied the box room. The girls shared a bunk bed in the single room, and we used the double. I led my guests back to the living room, and the doorbell rang, announcing more guests. As we exchanged hugs and kisses, one of them exclaimed, 'Wow! new car, new house, what are you guys trying to prove?' I flinched, and an uncomfortable stillness filled the room. Someone broke the silence by requesting directions to the bathroom.

Later, I processed the remark. *Why did our church friends think we were flaunting our achievements?* If I were being cynical, I would suggest that now we were no longer a charity case, some were struggling to relate to us. We'd owned two cars in Nigeria, so a new car and a house weren't anything untoward from our perspective. Yes, we'd upgraded the Nissan, whose roof leaked. But we'd bought a Pronto, a barely recognised Malaysian brand, the cheapest we could afford with a decent specification, on a hire purchase agreement.

I had tried unsuccessfully to develop deeper relationships with some church folk with whom I thought I had a few things in common. The first had been Sarah, a nurse. I rang her often and expected reciprocal calls. When she didn't call, I reached out and said, 'I called you last, so you should be making this call.'

'Why do you say that?' She countered. 'It's not telephone tag. If I want to speak to you, I will call, but I don't have to just because you called last.'

That had me flummoxed. I had grown up under a cultural premise that said, 'I visit you, you visit me'. I explained my reasoning.

'We don't do that here,' she said.

I wondered what else I had got wrong. Since we were having the conversation, I raised other issues.

'I noticed you bristle when I ask you questions about my children's health. Is there a reason?'

'Yes, there is. When I am with you, it's my free time and I don't want to be reminded of work. When you ask me health-related questions, I feel as if I am on duty. You are not my patient, so legally and professionally, I shouldn't be giving you advice.'

Another eye-opener. 'I am sorry,' I said. 'I didn't realise that.' In Nigeria, your first point of call was always your friends and family. People didn't distinguish between personal and professional roles, and you wouldn't visit a medical practitioner if you had one on tap for free.

I hoped the frank discussion would strengthen the relationship, but I was wrong. Our chats became more infrequent until

I stopped trying altogether. Two years down the line, I had no close friendships and at least one of my casual friends didn't think much of us buying a new house. On the bright side, my salary increase came through, just in time for our first mortgage payment, and what a surprise it was. The Council paid me an entire year's worth of back pay, filling the big hole in our finances that the extra moving costs created.

*

Three months after we moved, Bade came home with a bombshell. His company was moving to Hampshire. 'What? When?' I exclaimed. It took him four hours to get to work and back. I wasn't sure where Hampshire was, but anything further than zone six was bound to lead to longer travelling time and higher travel costs.

'Within the next year,' he replied. 'They are offering a relocation package to cover house-moving costs.'

'But we've barely settled in.' I had just spent an entire weekend labouring over the bathroom. I had discovered the truth behind the British do-it-yourself bug. Compared to Nigeria, the price of British labour was astronomical. Bade, no fan of DIY, refused to take part in my home-improvement project. 'Get a professional to do it,' he said, like a typical Nigerian male of his time.

I ignored him and single-handedly tiled the wall next to the bath.

The relocation package included the company paying for three trips for staff to scout for a new home. The following spring, Bade and I spent over two hours driving the forty-six miles to Fleet, the quintessential British town where the firm would be based. With my eyes peeled to the windscreen, I navigated the town's streets and parked up next to the estate agents with whom we had arranged three viewings. We had asked to see modern houses, similar to our current abode, but they all cost at least £10,000 more.

After the viewings, I asked the estate agent the question plaguing my mind. 'How diverse is Fleet's population?' In an entire afternoon of driving, I had seen one Black man and one man of dual heritage.

'We have a few Asian and Black families. The older generation, like my dad, still uses the old language, but most people are open and friendly.'

I assumed that by 'old language', she meant racist, but I didn't ask.

On the way home, we drove past two more Black people: a woman holding a little girl's hand. 'What do you think?' Bade asked.

'I don't know. I can cope with being the only Black person for miles, but I wouldn't put the kids through that.'

'Okay, next time, let's try Basingstoke. It's just ten miles from Fleet, and as a bigger town, it ought to be more cosmopolitan.'

As summer loomed, I started sending job applications for the following academic year to schools within travelling distance of Fleet. One day, my eye caught an interesting advert in the *Times Educational Supplement*, placed by Hampshire County Council, for newly qualified and experienced teachers. I rang them, and the job pack, when it arrived, detailed the interview process, which included the Council allocating successful candidates to the right school. I sent off my application, and we decided to give house-hunting in Hampshire another try.

*

This time, we took the children with us and headed to Winchester. On the way, we stopped to view more properties in Basingstoke. We navigated an unending series of roundabouts and glimpsed more Black folk than we did in Fleet. However, the lacklustre houses we viewed did not warrant uprooting the family. We drove to Winchester for the night.

That evening at dinner, my roaming eyes registered the fact that we were the only Black people in the hotel's restaurant. If we planned to live here, we would have to be comfortable being conspicuous. My eyes connected with those of a lady at a nearby table. She smiled and whispered, 'Your children, they are beautifully behaved.' I smiled back and said thank you. *Was that just a nice observational compliment? Did she only ever see badly behaved Black children, or did she think Black children couldn't behave well?* I admonished myself. *Now who's being sensitive?* But still, I wondered.

After breakfast the following morning, we took a stroll down the ancient, cobbled High Street. The sun came out to play, creating a joyous sense of abandon. The children had never been out of London and their excitement bubbled as they skipped over the cobbles. At the Great Hall, we gaped, enthralled by the replica of King Arthur's Round Table. The girls had learned about Henry VIII at school, so they too caught the wonder at standing in a hall that had survived the expanse of time.

Hunger beckoned soon after, and we headed for the children's favourite eatery, McDonald's. 'Daddy, look! Black people!' a little girl squealed in excitement and pointed pudgy fingers at my children. Everyone on the street turned and gawked. I cringed as I watched my daughters shrivel right in front of my eyes. Fortunately, Bade had Deolu in his grasp. I put an arm around each girl. 'It's okay,' I murmured. 'Ignore them. Just keep walking.' We walked through the crowd, staring unseeing and found our destination. Minutes later, I chewed and swallowed my burger without registering the taste, my mind locked on the last scene. I couldn't blame the child. Her exuberance simply reflected her daily existence in which seeing a Black family was a rarity. *But how much of that could we endure, and how well would my children cope?*

In the end, it was a moot question. My interview experience throughout Hampshire and Berkshire left me bitter. In one school in Reading, a little boy sitting outside the headteacher's office looked up as I approached and said, 'Hello, Black lady.' To him, I wasn't just a lady. I was a Black one. To my surprise, Hampshire County Council wrote saying although I was successful in their pool interview, they were advising me to approach schools directly for a post. I'd even had to chase them to get that piece of information. Since this was contrary to what they published about the interview process, I concluded it was about my race.

Living in Hampshire, we decided, was not worth the risk to our family. The negatives far outweighed the positives. Also, the travel time was the same, with direct trains from New Cross to Waterloo, and from Waterloo to Fleet. So, for the next five years, Bade commuted by train. The company stopped paying the outer London weighting, so he earned less and had to pay more on transport, but for our children he made the sacrifice. Never once in those five years did he complain about the four-hour daily commute.

CHAPTER FORTY

Who Am I?

Since the return to England, I had tried my hardest to fit in, but nothing reminded me of my failure more than the incessant question 'Where are you from?' On a cerebral level, I recognised it as pure curiosity. However, my instinctive response was almost always negative. It triggered all the old insecurities and made me feel as if I didn't belong. 'I'm from London,' I would say in denial. My inquisitors, keen to identify the origin of my roots, would query, 'Yes, but where are you originally from?' My accent had lost the heavy Nigerian drawl, but people could still detect what someone aptly described as 'a little something foreign'.

I made friends with Jenny, my white neighbour, two doors down. Jenny and her husband were my age, although they had no children. I admired Jenny's sense of dress. She always looked chic, yet I wouldn't have picked the clothes she wore off a rack. 'Where do you shop for clothing?' I asked one evening while sharing a cuppa in her living room.

'BHS.' She gave a wry smile at my half-opened mouth.

'I would never have guessed. I shop there all the time, but I haven't noticed the designs you wear.'

'It's all about your personal style and what you naturally gravitate towards.'

I asked if she would go shopping with me and she agreed.

Before the trip, I considered what my personal style was. I could only sum it up in one word: 'Nigerian'. After I got married and gave birth, I realised that there were different cultural expectations of how I should dress. As someone else's mama and a wife, society expected me to be even more conservative: no sleeveless dresses or tops, skirts above the knee, plunging necklines or trousers. Despite my rebellious streak, under General Buhari's right-wing War Against Indiscipline, I'd had no option but to conform, and, years later, still dressed the same. I wondered if my fashion style was akin to walking around with a sticker on my forehead proclaiming 'Not from around here'. *If I re-invented myself, would the questions stop?*

On a busy Saturday evening, Jenny and I walked into BHS in the Surrey Quays Shopping Centre. My eyes caught a rack full of clothes in pastel colours and I made a beeline for it. I fingered the hem of a paisley, brown gathered skirt. My penchant for sweet things had left me decidedly chubbier. The elasticated waist guaranteed comfort and ensured that with my expanding waistline, it would fit for years to come. 'No,' Jenny shook her head and beckoned me to the next rack which held a selection of shorter, A-line skirts with geometrical, almost psychedelic, patterns.

'Mmm, it's not what I would normally buy,' I said.

'Exactly.'

Then she nudged my elbow and pointed. 'Look!'

My eyes followed her fingers and collided with two octogenarians admiring the skirt that had held my devotion only moments earlier. I blinked twice as realisation hit. My personal style was granny clothing!

*

With new awareness, I set about rehabilitating my self-image with a vengeance. Under Jenny's guidance, I updated my wardrobe and took makeup lessons. I even ventured into high street stores other than BHS.

I had noticed that unlike the impromptu visits that Africans bestowed on unsuspecting relatives, the British only visited when invited. To be properly British, I needed to do some inviting, and who better than my boss who had shown me much kindness? But first I needed to learn how to prepare British meals beyond the frozen Iceland food that fed my family daily. I stocked up on cookery books, including *Mary Berry's Complete Cookbook* and *Delia's Complete Illustrated Cookery Course.*

Maria accepted my invitation with grace. 'Are there any foods you and your partner don't like?' I asked.

'We eat most things, provided they are not hot or spicy,' she said. I guessed she preferred her food lukewarm, just like some of my colleagues did their tea. I consulted my cookery books. For starters, I chose melon with Parma ham. It didn't require much work. Making a note to avoid anything with spices, I ignored the curries and for the main, settled on honey roast potatoes, carrots, peas and steaks. For dessert, I turned to Iceland's frozen black-forest gateau. Baby steps… The only challenge I had to worry about was keeping the steaks and vegetables at an optimum temperature, so they were neither too hot nor cold. To solve the problem, I prepared the vegetables a little in advance and kept them warm in the oven and cooked the steaks last.

Maria and Paul arrived at eight after I had fed my children and sent them to bed. I served the first course, and we settled down to delightful conversation. 'Thank you, that was lovely,' Maria said, putting down her cutlery. Paul echoed the sentiment, and I beamed from ear to ear. I got up to clear their plates and serve the main course. 'This is twice-peppered steak with vegetables,' I announced, placing a plate in front of each guest while Bade topped up their wine glasses. I thought Paul's eyes rounded in appreciation as he surveyed the steaks, every inch studded with red and black whole-peppercorns. I waited as both my guests sliced into the meat and Paul bit down on a morsel. Head down, I cut into my steak.

Suddenly, Paul bolted upright and made a gurgling sound. I stared in horror as his face turned a mottled red and the veins in his neck bulged. Maria grabbed a napkin off the table and handed it to him. He spat out the chunk of steak in his mouth, spluttered and coughed. Bade and I hovered behind him. 'What's wrong?' I asked, 'Has the food lodged in his throat?'

'It's the heat from the food,' Maria said, as she fanned his face with her napkin.

'Heat? I don't understand.' The food hadn't felt too warm in my mouth.

'The chillies. Remember, I said he doesn't eat spicy food?'

'Oh, my God! I am so sorry. I didn't realise you meant chillies when you said "hot".' *And I'd gone and studded them like a prized collar*. When Yorubas referred to the heat in chillies, they used the term 'peppery', hence my confusion.

'Can you open the patio door? The fresh air outside might help cool him down,' Maria said.

Bade scrambled for the patio door keys, and I sneaked a peek at Paul's face. He looked worse, tiny pearls of sweat beading on his forehead. Bade opened the door and Maria led him out.

'I am so sorry,' I murmured over and over, as Paul hacked intermittently.

'Don't worry, I'll walk him round the garden for a bit. Go back inside,' Maria said.

Bade and I returned indoors and waited.

Well, that went well, didn't it? I rested my head in both palms. I'd nearly killed my boss's partner. Ten minutes later my guests returned, Paul looking a little less red. I offered to remove all the offending peppercorns.

'No, don't worry. I'll just eat the veg,' he said.

We settled into awkward conversation and tried to salvage the rest of the evening. While we ate, I hoped no more surprises awaited. I imagined digging into the gateau and hitting a solid block of ice in the centre. To my relief, there were no misadventures with dessert, and by the end of the evening my guests were laughing over the earlier mishap.

It took months before I braved inviting someone else to dinner, but this time, the evening was a success. With new-found confidence, I experimented with foods from all over the world. Nigerian meals dropped off the family menu and I stopped going to Peckham to shop. We started eating out once a week with the children, albeit at McDonald's, with the occasional trip to the Chinese diner. I was well on the way to becoming an assimilated Brit. The few relationships I had with Black folk outside the family fell away, except for one. People rarely asked me where I was from anymore, and Nigeria only got a mention at weddings when I turned up in traditional attire. But even that garnered too much attention. Soon, my *iro* and *bubas* were consigned with the rest of my African heritage, to the back of my wardrobe, or so I thought.

*

While I was busy finding myself, my eldest was inching into puberty and her sister wasn't far behind. I knew they were developing into strong-willed characters. They'd had a minor skirmish with Dad, who had stayed in England for two years before returning to Nigeria. Once when he was visiting for the weekend, I arrived home to Dad's 'You wouldn't believe what your kids said to me today.' My lips curved into a knowing smile. It never ceased to amuse me the way Yoruba people denied their children when they were naughty. 'What happened?' I asked.

'I was in the middle of berating them for leaving their toys all over the floor when Leye put out her hand and stopped me. "Grandpa," she said, "You can tell us what to do when we come to your house, but this is our house. Here, you can't tell us what to do." If they hadn't been my own grandkids, I would have thought someone coached them just to mess with me.'

I burst into laughter. 'Yes, Dad,' I said, 'they are becoming very British.'

When my daughters wanted to challenge me, they would ambush me together. 'Our friends all get pocket money; can we have some?' they asked. Before their very eyes, I turned into a 'Nigerian woman'.

'What are you talking about? Pocket money for what?' I planted my hands on each hip and leaned in. 'Do I not feed and clothe you? Do you not have enough crisps to snack on in the house? Pocket money *ko*, pocket money *ni*.' I hissed and walked away.

That evening, after the kids were in bed, Bade broached the subject. 'Your daughters would like some pocket money.'

Ha! They were my children now. 'I don't know what they want to do with pocket money. I didn't get pocket money until I went to university.'

'You are comparing your era to theirs?'

I slipped into bed and turned the bedside lamp off, still fuming. *Pocket money, my bottom.* We didn't use swear words in my family.

The following day, still aggrieved, I related the story to Maria.

'It's just pocket money. Why are you so riled up about it?' she asked.

'I buy them everything they want and need. I just don't understand what they need it for, except for sweets.'

'Look at it this way. Their friends get some, so they feel left out. There are advantages to giving them pocket money. It would teach them to manage money and you can dock it when they misbehave.' My ears perked. *Now she was talking.*

I gave in to my children's demands and offered them £5 each, weekly. Docking their pocket money also became my favourite sanction. That was until one day, Leye stopped me mid-flow with, 'It's okay, I'll give you my pocket money. You don't need to shout.' After I finished scraping my mouth off the floor, I realised I needed to concoct a whole plethora of fresh sanctions.

*

I considered myself a modern woman and unlike my mother's generation, no topic was off limits in our family. Whatever my children wanted to talk about, I was more than ready, even when the questions were uncomfortable. I gave them a Christian book about sex. One evening they sidled up to me in the living room. 'Mum,' Lara said, 'this book says people shouldn't have sex until they are married. Is that what you did?'

Dear Lord! With studied calmness, I closed the book in my hands and looked at my daughters' expectant faces. The album full of my wedding pictures proved otherwise, and they knew it too.

'No, I didn't. However, I didn't practise my faith then. You will have to make your own choices based on your own conviction.' That I did not lie, or hedge, seemed to satisfy them, and they left me alone for a while.

My daughters' last question had been about my values and had been relatively easy to answer. The next few questions challenged my behaviour, which was steeped deep in traditional Yoruba values I didn't know I was holding on to. 'Why do you call us from upstairs to fetch you a drink, when you are downstairs and can walk to the kitchen yourself?'

Whaaaaaat? I stopped myself yelling just in time and thought about it.

The answer lay in a single Yoruba prayer: 'When you grow old, you'll have plenty of people to send on errands'. As a child, each time you ran an errand, the adults blessed you with the prayer. You grew up convinced of your unequivocal right to send other children on errands. You had done your bit in your youth. Now it was their turn. I explained the reasoning behind my actions to my children. To my surprise, they accepted my explanation and offered a compromise. 'How about we get you a drink every time we come downstairs, regardless of whether you want or ask for one? In return, you could reduce the number of times you call us from upstairs to get you a drink.' It was a fair deal, and I agreed.

The next two questions were not so clear-cut. 'Why don't you hug us like other mums do?' they asked. 'It makes us feel you don't love us.' This was deeply personal, something I'd never considered. Again, I examined myself. Once I had landed on African soil, except for when I met relatives I hadn't seen in a long while, hugging was not a normal part of daily existence. This wasn't just about my family; I had noticed it in other Yoruba families too. In addition, after spending decades bottling up my emotions, expressing them openly was new territory.

I explained how I grew up and apologised to my daughters. 'I am sorry I made you feel that way. If you need a hug, ask me, and I will try to hug you more.' They accepted that but had one more question. 'Why do you give us the smallest piece of meat when we are the ones who need the protein to keep growing?'

My unfiltered reaction? *How impudent!* In reality, I didn't have a decent response to the question. I was simply repeating what my ancestors did before me. From then on, they got their fair share. Mothering in England, I discovered, required a high level of adaptability and compromise, especially if you were navigating across opposing cultural divides.

CHAPTER FORTY-ONE

My Mother's Daughter

My children's questions had started me on a deeper journey of self-discovery that proved I was more African than I had fooled myself into believing. In many ways, I was exhibiting the same behaviours I had detested in the adults around me while growing up. I also realised that I said no to my children too often and all for only one reason. Growing up, the same was said to me. I needed to figure out which parts of me were African and which parts were British. Somehow between those two extremes, I had to forge an identity of my own which epitomised a clear set of values I could apply to raising my family.

The next step in my enlightenment had me figuring out which values I wanted to keep and which to discard. I sat down and made some notes:

Yoruba	**British**
What I disliked: Totalitarianism Insistence on cultural compliance and conformity Co-dependency	*What I disliked:* Lack of regard for the elderly Hypocrisy – equality and fairness on paper, but not always in practice

Yoruba	British
What I liked: Respect and care for the elderly Politeness Close familial connections (caveat: nuclear and immediate siblings only)	*What I liked:* Egalitarianism Individuality Personal independence and accountability Self-reliance

I liked the Yoruba emphasis on respect, provided it was warranted. I had no time for irresponsible elders who demanded respect. On the British side, I abhorred the horror stories about the elderly being mugged or ill-treated by uncaring staff at nursing homes. I wanted my children to respect authority but have the confidence to challenge the status quo. I wanted them growing into self-reliant individuals who could make informed decisions and stand by the consequences of their actions, regardless of peer pressure.

It was a complicated balancing act, navigating between the two cultures, especially as Leye was getting mouthier by the month. The first test of my resolve came when she screamed 'shut up' at me while I was telling her off. We both froze in stunned surprise. With checked fury, I inched into her personal space. 'Did you just tell me to shut up?' I jabbed a finger at my cheek. 'See this face. It is Black. You do not tell your Black mother to shut up. Ever! You hear me?'

She had the grace to look crestfallen. 'I'm sorry Mummy.'

I let it go, hoping she received my message loud and clear.

*

The next skirmish involved both daughters cornering me in the living room. 'Mum, can we ask you something?' Lara said. I shifted on the sofa to face them. A gaze darted between them.

Something is up. 'Go on,' I said.

'Can you stop buying our clothes and let us buy them ourselves?' Leye, now eleven, asked.

My Nigerian instincts kicked in. 'Why? What's wrong with the dresses I buy you?'

Silence. I raised my eyebrows, waiting for a response.

'We don't like the styles,' Lara, the older of the two, said.

I see where this is going. They'd asked me to buy them mini-skirts, and I had refused. Now, they wanted my hard-earned money to buy whatever they wanted. Uh-uh. Not happening.

Clothes shopping was a summer event, and my philosophy was to provide for my children's needs, not their wants. After I got the girls to discard whatever they had outgrown, I replaced those with new items. I learned the trick from Lolade, my old school friend, whose father had done the same with her. The girls' eyes tracked mine. Leye twiddled her fingers and Lara bit her lip, both signs they were nervous about my response. Nonetheless, when they presented a united front, I knew they had thought it through, and I'd have a battle on my hands. I managed the pupils in my class through negotiation. *Why not do the same at home?*

'Lara, grab my measuring tape from upstairs, please.' I ignored their startled eyes. They liked to think they had me all figured out. To maintain an air of mystery, I enjoyed surprising them sometimes.

Lara came back with the tape trailing behind her. I took it from her. 'Here's what we'll do. I'll give you both a fixed amount of money for shopping and I will tell you the minimum number of items you must buy with it. Together, we will measure the minimum skirt length allowed. Are you okay with that?' Their eyes lit up as if I'd just announced they could have ice-cream for breakfast, lunch and dinner. They both nodded. I placed the tape at Lara's waistline and trailed it down to the middle of her shin. 'How about here, twenty-six inches?'

'Mum! That's way too low.' She pointed above her knees. 'This length is what the girls wear at school.'

'You call those skirts? Those are belts pretending to be skirts. How about we settle for the middle?' I moved the tape up four inches. 'Twenty-two inches?'

She sighed. 'Okay.'

I pointed at Leye. 'You too?'

She nodded. Although I didn't know it, my daughters gave in so easily because they'd figured out a better solution to their problem. They bought skirts with elasticated waists and rolled them up at the waistband to shorten the length.

There would be many more negotiations. When could they wear makeup, date boys, go to the pub? They had to get my sister Taiwo to wade in on the latter. Having never been inside one, somehow in my psyche, a pub was the equivalent of a Nigerian beer parlour, where according to Mum, Nigerian men met with prostitutes. I didn't want my children anywhere near them. It took me a while to identify the source of that particular hang-up and change my perspective.

On their first solo shopping trip, I parked myself on a bench inside Lewisham Shopping Centre, while my daughters let loose. Hours later they came back, Lara with several more items than the minimum stipulated. She'd found the cheapest items possible and consequently bought more. Leye, however, bought the most expensive items she could afford and spent the rest of her teenage years nicking clothes from her sister and me. No amount of negotiating would resolve that particular problem.

*

Since my arrival, Nan and I had kept in touch by phone, but now that my family was fairly settled, I wanted her to meet them. One Saturday, Bade and I bundled the kids into the car and drove to North London. A rush of nostalgia hit me as we neared Nan's house. I pointed out my childhood haunts, the park, and the fish and chips turned kebab shop, to my children. 'Uh-huh,' they nodded blithely at my commentary, a 'whatever' expression plastered on their faces. I stopped chatting, their indifference a brutal antidote to my wistfulness.

As I introduced Nan to my husband and children, she hugged each one before leading us to her lounge, where we spent some time catching up. 'Tom is out, and the poodle died soon after Pop,' Nan said in response to my questions. A few minutes later, she rose from her couch and shuffled to the kitchen. I followed behind her, my eyes tracking her movements.

Although she had weathered the years well, age had finally caught up with Nan. I wondered how old she actually was, but I refrained from asking. Apart from the ever more visible laughter-lines crinkling in the corner of her eyes and the puffy ankles, she looked the same. However, her hands shook as she filled the kettle with water and I could see the effort she put into lifting it. I helped her serve my family tea and biscuits, and we resumed the chatter. The visit didn't last long. I could see Nan was tiring. We said our goodbyes, and I promised to keep in touch. Once more she hobbled behind us to the door where we kissed goodbye. On the way home, with my thoughts fixed on Nan, I realised she was running out of time. While most of my life still lay before me, hers was drawing to a close.

In the months that followed, each time I went to call her, I paused, then put the phone down. *What if she had passed? Was I ready to deal with that?* I just knew I wouldn't cope with the news of her demise, so I put it off. Before I knew it, the months became a year, then two. One day, determined to overcome the fear, I dialled Nan's number. After four rings, Tom's voice came over the airwaves.

'Hi Tom. It's me, Ann,' I said. A moment of silence followed.

'Oh, Ann. How are you? We haven't heard from you in a while.' Pause. 'I'm sorry to tell you…'

My heart stilled as his words washed over me, and the news registered. I offered my condolences at the end of the brief conversation and spent the rest of the day wandering around my house, aimless and morose. It was my first brush with the death of someone who mattered to me. My dithering had lost me precious time with her, and now, it was too late. My mind drifted back to my childhood, to the countless joy she gave me. She'd had a tremendous impact on my life, and I didn't think I ever told her that. As I reflected on the past, hers and mine, a peace settled amidst the sorrow and regret. She was gone, yes, but she would always be with me.

*

We were halfway through the 1990s, and, via a teachers' bursary and with Maria's blessing, I had spent the last three years studying part-time for a master's degree. It had been a hard slog managing work, the family and studies. Maria and her deputy, Lucy, helped every way they could. On days when I had late afternoon classes, Maria gave me the time off, unpaid, and taught my class. Lucy picked my children up from school and cared for them until I got back. I could never thank them enough.

The day I received the news that I had passed my dissertation, Maria called me to her office. 'I'd like you to apply for the deputy headteacher post I just advertised,' she said.

Dazed, I stared, the thought having never crossed my mind, although I knew Lucy had been appointed as the headteacher of another school.

'I was considering moving into lecturing,' I said. Like my first degree, my master's focused on higher and further education.

'You can do that when you retire. You've got a lot to give to teaching. Lecturers are not well paid, and you will earn much less than you do right now.'

I hadn't known that. Six years on, I was still discovering new stuff about Britain. I thought it was like Nigeria, where the higher up you taught, the more you earned, with university lecturers at the top of the pay scale. But financial considerations aside, this was an immense responsibility.

'Mary is applying for the post. I don't want to vie against another colleague for it.'

'Mary hasn't decided. She's also considering a move to Somerset. In any case, it doesn't matter. People get appointed on merit and anyone meeting the person specification and job description requirements can apply.'

I processed that. In the six years since I joined the staff, I had become the school's science leader. Ironic, I know, given how badly I did in science at school. I'd done a good job with the role, I knew that. Still, deputy headship? It wasn't in my plans at all.

'Are you sure I am right for the post?'

'Absolutely. I wouldn't suggest it otherwise.'

'Okay. Thanks. Can I think about it?'

'Sure.'

I agonised over it for an entire fortnight. Conflicted, I weighed the pros and cons. I loved teaching adults. I had enjoyed lecturing when I did it part time in Lagos, and I got a buzz whenever I designed staff training sessions as the science leader. Teaching younger children required indefatigable commitment, but that warm glow that overcame me when a light bulb switched on in a child's head was priceless. There was the pay, of course. My family would not benefit from a drop in income. However, how would my colleagues relate to me if I became part of management and I was no longer a comrade? 'You should talk to John at church,' Bade said. 'He helps people with job applications, and it might give you some clarity.'

John gave me useful pointers on how to improve my curriculum vitae. 'Even if you don't submit the application, you will be better prepared for future jobs,' he said. I applied on the closing date and waited.

'You've been shortlisted,' Maria said three days later. The following Friday I attended the interview. Later that night, Maria called me at home. 'Congratulations! You got the job.' My career was about to go down a path I never envisaged.

COLOURLESS WATER

CHAPTER FORTY-TWO

Now unto Others

Weeks into my new role as deputy headteacher, Maria called me to her office. 'The local authority is funding a school effectiveness project, and I'd like you to lead our school's team,' she said. With all the skills and knowledge gained during my previous studies, I led the team successfully and my confidence bloomed.

On the last day of the project, a tutor approached me. 'Have you thought about applying for headship?' she asked.

'Me? I've only been a deputy for a year,' I said.

'That doesn't matter. You are ready.'

She had planted the seed, although I didn't act on it straight away. A year and several interviews later, aged thirty-three, I watched as the premises manager hefted up a sign with the logo I had just designed for Crawford Primary School. At the bottom of the board, against the blue background, right next to the word 'Headteacher', my name shone in white letters.

At the pinnacle of my professional career and with all the self-assurance that it brought, I was no longer afraid of potential encounters with Yoruba culture. My favourite Nigerian foods featured often in the plethora of meals I cooked. I even found I couldn't go without pounded yam and okra stew for more than a fortnight. The outfits at the back of my wardrobe came out for cultural days, birthdays and weddings. 'Mum,' Lara joked, 'the older you get, the more Nigerian you become!' There was a truth to that.

*

My children continued to challenge me. 'Why do you still use an anglicised version of your surname on your voice mail message?' I didn't have a cogent reason other than the anglicised version was easier to pronounce. But they disagreed. 'If we can learn to say McDonald, they can learn to say our names.' Point taken, I recorded a new message. It felt strange pronouncing my name correctly on the new recording, after years of mangling it for the benefit of my Caucasian friends and colleagues. Ironically, years earlier when Maria had tried to pronounce it right, I'd dissuaded her from trying.

The girls, now in their late teens, developed an avid interest in discovering their African heritage. I taught them what I knew, and they learned the rest from friends from similar backgrounds. Often, they would come and say things like 'Sola's mum said it's a shame you didn't teach us to speak Yoruba.' There was no end to the reach of Yoruba culture. Here I was, still facing censure from virtual strangers who thought they knew best.

'Hey,' I'd counter, 'you stopped speaking Yoruba of your own accord.'

'Yeah, but you should have made us.'

Deolu, who had grown up while I was in the throes of my anti-Yoruba phase, understood nothing of the culture and had no desire to learn. 'He's white,' his cousins said, much as mine said of me years before. All in all, I considered myself an amalgamated Yoruba Brit. It was the best I could do.

*

Amid my growing acceptance of the African in me, I continued to have sporadic bruising encounters with Yoruba culture. I rejected several requests to house people coming to settle in the UK or on holidays from Nigeria. I would only welcome those I thought could accept the non-Yoruba me. Every refusal earned a black mark, but I knew letting such people into my home would spell disaster. Bade, gentler and more welcoming, struggled with the refusals, but conceded that I was probably right.

Two years into my new job, Dad died suddenly. His death came as a shock, and I grieved the loss deeply. Bade and I flew to Nigeria for the funeral. At the airport, distracted, I handed the customs officer my form with my left hand. The hand reaching towards mine stopped halfway. The officer hissed, 'Eh, what is the matter with you? Woman, you are on African soil now o!'

'Sorry, sir,' I begged, swapping the offending document to my right hand before offering it again. He plucked it from my fingers and waved me through. I had learned the hard way that feigned humility got me a lot further than protest.

At the wake-keeping, I read a Bible passage. I was two verses in when the glazed expression on my relatives' faces told me that they did not understand a word spoken in my posh English accent. I tried reverting to my Nigerian one and found I didn't remember how. By the time I got to the end of the reading, I had created a hybrid that was neither English nor Yoruba. I had to laugh at myself. My extended family came to offer their condolences. Tacked after each greeting was, 'You went to England and forgot us, ehn? We are here o. Don't forget us o.' I understood their gripe. But since I couldn't support them all, I had made the brutal choice of cutting everyone off, only offering help, via my parents, to kin who were very needy. In essence, it cemented my reputation as hard-nosed and uncaring.

As for my in-laws, who hadn't bargained on a wife they couldn't tame, it was payback time. Except for immediate family and the handful I was very close to, the vast majority snubbed the funeral. The row of tables and chairs specially reserved for them sat empty while my siblings' in-laws overfilled their allocated space. The almost empty chairs proclaimed the discord. 'Look,' they said, 'we don't like her.' It hurt, but I took it in my stride. It was the price of individuality.

*

As my thinking about race deepened, I considered how being bi-cultural impacted my life. Years of professional study helped me understand that Mama's inability to reform me stemmed from living my early childhood in a different cultural context. Four-fifths of my pupils were Black, many of those Yoruba, and I wondered how they fared, navigating the quagmire between Yoruba and British culture. Perhaps I had a real opportunity to help them in ways others couldn't. It was time for the coconut to nourish others.

The first opportunity came when Toyin, a newly arrived eight-year-old from Lagos, walked past me in the school hall. She fell to her knees, greeting me the African way, while everyone around gaped. I drew her to her feet and led her to my office. Remembering what a visit to the head's office in Nigeria entailed, I switched to Yoruba. 'Don't worry,' I said, 'you are not in any trouble.' I explained that in England, she didn't need to greet me like that in school. A confused expression replaced the anxious look on her face. *Aw, poor girl. She had so much to learn.*

Just how much she had to learn became obvious six weeks later. 'I've got a problem with the new girl, Toyin,' her class teacher said.

'What's the matter with her?' I asked.

'Wish I knew. She arrived a model pupil, almost too angelic. Spoke only when spoken to, didn't move out of her seat, did her work. Now she's in all kinds of trouble.'

I'd seen the phenomenon in my teaching days at Peckham. 'Send her to me,' I said.

Toyin arrived in my office with none of the fear I had witnessed on her first day. Blithely, she took the chair I offered, her right foot tapping the chair leg repeatedly. 'Your teacher is not happy with you,' I said in English. The tapping continued. I switched to Yoruba. 'Do you think because you haven't seen a cane, there are no rules here?'

The impact was instant. She sat up, alert, eyes wide, foot still. 'We have rules, we just don't beat them into people. Would you prefer a beating?'

'No, ma.'

'So why have you been doing things your teacher told you to stop doing?'

She wrung her hands in her lap, her eyes pleading. 'I'm sorry, ma. I won't do it again, ma. Please don't tell my mum, ma.'

'Well, you'd better not let me hear anything negative about you from now on. Apologise to your teacher and behave yourself.'

'Yes, ma. Thank you, ma.'

A smile flitted over my face. Only a Nigerian would thank you for admonishing them.

The incident showed I needed to help my Yoruba parents understand the differences between the cultures and prepare their children better for life in Britain. The number of Nigerian children referred to Social Services because of corporal punishment was rising in the borough. Young Black males were arrested, often because they appeared shifty and wouldn't maintain eye contact with police officers. Who was teaching these children to switch their behaviours in response to the cultural cues around them? Who was telling them 'Keep a steady gaze on the police officer, but keep your eyes on the floor when granny tells you off'?

The next incident involved five eleven-year-old boys who burst into my office with 'Miss, the supply teacher is racist!' It took them a moment to calm down and explain. 'The supply teacher put only Black boys on the wall.'

In the playground, 'on the wall' was the usual sanction for misdemeanours and involved time-out, standing next to a wall.

'How does that make him racist?' I asked.

'He is white, Miss, and all the boys on the wall are Black.'

'Ah! Did he let off any white boys who misbehaved?'

'No, Miss?'

'So, the only reason the boys on the wall are all Black, is that they were the only ones misbehaving?'

'Yes, Miss.'

'He's not racist then, is he?'

'No, Miss.'

With sagging shoulders, they filed back out to the playground. What a complicated issue race was. My misinformed pupils thought they'd uncovered a scandal. The next spate of assemblies focused on the meaning of racism, but could one really unpack that in an assembly? The truth was, they would find out soon enough in real life.

*

My school was multi-cultural in every sense, with thirty-four languages spoken across the school population. I wondered how the school could support families better, and to find out, I sent a questionnaire to all parents. The returned responses were fascinating. Parents from India and Pakistan wanted to know why we taught their children about sex. Those from South Asia wanted to learn better English so they could support their children with homework. The African parents of the youngest children didn't understand why their children came home with sand in their hair. 'We sent them to school to learn, not play,' one wrote. *Now where had I heard that before.*

Feeling the need to tailor my response to the specific needs of the different communities, I carried out additional meetings with parents grouped by cultural or ethnic similarities. Thereafter, the school introduced a raft of programmes to support each group as best we could. But the bid to promote stronger cultural integration caused offence. Amid the real successes, a lone dissenting voice appeared in a letter. 'Why are you operating a form of apartheid and grouping parents by ethnicity?' the couple queried. I invited them in for a chat. 'We don't identify with any of those groups,' they said.

'You don't have to join any group. I am happy to meet with you on your own if you prefer.' Unhappy with my explanation and offer, they complained to the Director of Education, who paid an impromptu visit. One whistle stop tour around the school later, he left, satisfied that I was not engaging in nefarious activity. Still, the complaint made me pause and re-evaluate. It seemed, with race relations, whichever side you were on, you were bound to offend the other side.

Then one bright morning, my office phone rang. 'Are you free to speak with a very irate parent?' my office manager asked. Minutes later, the gentleman walked into my office. While he did not look threatening, his stiff shoulders and tight lips showed his displeasure. I welcomed him and spent the next five minutes listening to his concerns. I promised to investigate the issue and get back to him in due course. Hoping that was acceptable, I waited for him to speak. 'Can I speak to the boss now?' he said.

I blinked and did a double take. 'I'm the headteacher,' I replied.

'No, the boss, boss, you know, the one in charge?'

'That would be me.'

It took a minute for the words to register. When they did, his face glowed. 'You are?'

I nodded with a wry smile.

He leaned forward, his right elbow on his knee, a knuckle under his chin. 'How did you do it?' he asked.

I feigned ignorance. 'Do what?'

'Become the top man?'

I shrugged. 'Worked hard, went to school.' I opened my palms, not sure how to explain the last thirty years.

He stretched out his hand. 'Let me congratulate you. Well done and keep up the good work for our people.' He rose and left, leaving me staring in his wake. *Were there so few Black people in positions of authority as to render a Black man speechless, when he came upon one?*

*

I began paying more attention to the racial elements in all my interactions. Southwark Council had one other Black headteacher, and at meetings and conferences, I found myself in a noticeable minority. At the beginning of a meeting, the Black service personnel would flash me a look, one that said 'Shouldn't you be over here with us, serving tea and coffee?' Halfway through the day, as they registered that I really was with the 'suits', their demeanour towards me would change to one of curiosity and wonder. I hated that it reinforced the superficial differences between me and my colleagues, and it pointed to the significant underrepresentation of Black people in positions of power.

One more incident became a turning point. A parent with whom I'd had a difficult history requested an appointment. I wasn't keen on the meeting, but to get it over with, I gave her my first free slot. 'How can I help you?' I asked as she sat down in my office.

'Thanks for giving me your time,' she said. 'I am interested in a promotion at work. Part of me wants to go for it, but a voice in my head says I'm a Black woman, they won't give it to me, so why bother? Then I thought of you. You are Black and successful. If you could get to the top of your profession, maybe I can too.' *Wow! There I was thinking she came to complain about something.*

We started chatting and comparing childhoods, hers in the West Indies, mine in Africa. The similarities were uncanny, even down to walking barefoot to school. There was one notable difference. Her coming to the UK as a young girl in the late 1960s bagged her a front-row seat to witness our parents' generation's humiliation because of their colour. She therefore left her house every day seeing signs of racism in neon lights. I realised that the harder she looked, the more she found and reacted to it. In contrast, I had been fortunate enough to grow up in a country where, despite the hardships, the colour of my skin was not a determiner of my future success. I believed I could achieve anything I wanted, and that philosophy propelled me to reach new heights.

Months later, I ran into her in the playground. 'Did you apply for the job?' I asked.

'No, I didn't,' she said.

I smiled and went on my way, more than a little sad that she had denied herself the chance out of fear and resignation.

I was privileged, despite my skin colour, but how could I use it for good? The upside to my desperate desire to be British in every sense was that it forced me to learn all I could about the culture. While I was no guru on the subject, I understood far more than most of the marginalised Nigerian women around me. I began giving talks within my sphere of influence through church events and meetings. The questions came tumbling out. 'My daughter in boarding school in Somerset wants a razor to shave her armpits and legs. Should I send her one?' It seemed an innocuous request from a daughter to her mother, except that Yoruba females did not shave, and her mother didn't understand why her daughter wanted to.

'My son is always in trouble at school, so I have taken all his toys and TV away permanently,' one parent said.

'Since his punishment is permanent, what incentive has he got to behave better?' I asked.

'My son won't listen to me. They say I can't beat him. I don't know what to do with him, so I am going to send him to Nigeria,' another said.

Chills ricocheted down my spine. 'Please don't,' I entreated, telling her why I thought it was a terrible idea.

Little by little, I started helping parents navigate the unwritten cultural rules they accidentally stumbled over. 'You should write a book about it,' my sister-in-law said, one evening after a session with a group of parents at her church.

'You know, I just might,' I said, as the idea took hold.

CHAPTER FORTY-THREE

Something Inside

Clackety-clack, my fingers clicked away on my computer keyboard, my focus finely honed on the document on my screen. It was a mid-afternoon in July, a week before the end of the year and my stint as headteacher. Brrr-Brrr, Brrr-Brrr, the ringing cut through my concentration. I blinked, shifted my focus from the screen and picked up the phone. It was the school office. 'Miss, we need you down here in the hall.' Click. I looked at the dead phone in my hand. The parents' newsletter I was drafting would have to wait.

I stood up, walked out of my office onto the mezzanine floor balcony, which hovered above the school hall and stopped short. The entire staff and pupils sat silently below, staring at me. I could even spot a school governor or two. Like the Biblical Moses looking down at the hordes of Israelites before parting the Red Sea, I surveyed the school community laid out before me. *How had they filled the hall without my hearing a thing?*

I took the steps going down with care. Over 400 pairs of eyes charted my every move. *Now isn't the time to slip and fall.* At the bottom of the stairs, Kayley, my deputy, waved me to the chair prepared for me. One by one, class representatives came up and handed me a book the entire class had made for me, filled with messages of love and drawings. As I turned the pages, tears filled my eyes. I'd had an amazing six years and loved almost every moment. But the next adventure beckoned. In six weeks, I would start my new role as one of Her Majesty's Inspectors of Schools.

As the presentations continued, my mind flipped back to the interview process. Halfway through it, I'd vacillated. Why did I want to work for Ofsted, an organisation most of my colleagues hated? But why complain if you're not willing to be part of the solution? A chance meeting at an event where I'd been the keynote speaker for a group of aspiring headteachers kept me on course. At the end of my speech, a greying gentleman walked up to me. He shook my hand and with a piercing gaze said, 'Go and make a difference.' I later found out he was a retired inspector. His words inspired me, and I took them as a positive omen, a sign that it was meant to be.

The last class presented their book. Kayley stepped forward with a humongous bouquet. I accepted the gift as the whole assembly burst into applause. I thanked the pupils, staff and governors and told them how much I would miss them.

'And now for the grand finale!' Kayley said.

The school choir, my pet project, filed into the front of the hall. Thanks to my days of dissecting ABBA songs, I'd taught the soloists to sing with confidence and the rest to harmonise in unity. I had led them through various performances at special events, and now they were preparing to sing for me. A soloist stepped forward and lifted her voice. *Arghh! Labi Siffre's 'Something Inside So Strong', the one song guaranteed to make me bawl, the lyrics almost a commentary on my life, on Black lives everywhere.* Kayley shoved some tissues into my hands. The rest of the choir waded in on the chorus: 'Something inside so strong…'

As I wiped my tears, I remembered Dad telling me my education would be his only legacy. He would have been as proud of me as Mum was. An ever-constant champion in my corner, she'd moved back to England following Dad's death. Mama too had gone the way of elders. She'd said I'd tell my children's children stories about her. She was right. Stories of her abounded among the younger generation in my family and I wasn't the only one telling them. My siblings were too.

I didn't know what my future held or how many more proverbial glass ceilings I'd happen upon. But I knew if I hit my head against glass hard enough, it would crack, and my bruises would heal. It had been a long journey of discovery and somewhere along the way, I found myself. I am Black, I am Yoruba, I am British, I am me, Coconut.

A LETTER FROM FLORENCE

I want to say a huge thank you to you for choosing to read *Coconut*. If you enjoyed it and want to discover more inspiring memoirs, just sign up at the following link. Your email address will never be shared, and you can unsubscribe at any time.

www.thread-books.com/sign-up

To protect their privacy, with the exception of my parents, siblings, grandmother and great aunt, the names of all the people in this memoir and some of their identifying details have been changed. I have also used an abbreviated version of my African names throughout this memoir. I accept that other people who feature in this memoir may have a different recollection of events. Such are the peculiarities of the human memory.

People often ask why I started writing my memoir. Was it for the catharsis? Was it because of how far I had travelled from my relatively humble beginnings? I suppose those are partly the reasons. But I think the main reason is the avid interest in history and culture that I have had all my life. Where better to start than with my own history and culture? My early childhood shaped me profoundly and made the subsequent move to Africa challenging in ways my parents did not anticipate. I was not prepared for the culture shock I experienced or its impact on my physical and emotional wellbeing.

Today, shifting economics, war and pestilence are making new migrants all over the world, leaving more people than ever navigating life across two or more cultures, and often in very hostile environments. Modern migrants will have to work out their place and answer that complicated question: 'Who am

I and why does society treat me this way?' The answers in all likelihood will have many facets, and that's okay. It took me a while to accept that I was many things at once, and to find my place. But the most important thing I learned was to recognise and embrace the many 'helpers' I've had along the way. They came from all ethnicities and colours, each one of them reaching out a hand, easing my path.

So, if like me, you are out there taking a stand against a system, a culture, a political structure, you are not alone. I hope and pray that you will walk with integrity to make your mark and create a path for others to follow.

If you are parenting or mentoring young people across multiple cultures and are not already aware of the potential conflict this can create for them, I hope my experiences shed some light on the matter.

And, if you are one of those helping hands, reaching out to comfort, befriend and guide a migrant, I thank you for making the world a better place.

I hope *Coconut* touched something in you, and if it did, I would be very grateful if you could write a review. I'd love to hear what you think, or about your journey navigating multiple cultures, or helping others to do so.

You can get in touch on my Facebook page, through Twitter, Goodreads or my website.

Many thanks
Florence

ACKNOWLEDGEMENTS

I would like to thank:

My Maker, with whom all things are possible.

Dad, your legacy lives on. Sleep well. Mum, whose capacity to love and adaptability remain a source of inspiration. Thank you for touching the lives of countless children, mine included. Ena Akers (Nan) and her family, who filled my early childhood with love.

My wonderful editor and publisher Claire Bord – thank you for believing in me and pushing me to produce the best work possible. The rest of the team at Thread and Bookouture: Peta Nightingale, Kim Nash, Alex Crow, Alba Proko, Alexandra Holmes, Hannah Deuce, Nina Winters, Chris Lucraft, Marina Valles, Mark Alder, you are amazing. Katherine Mackrill and Jane McIntosh for the editing and feedback. Meryl Evans for the wonderful feedback and expert advice. Rafaela Romaya for the amazing cover design. Maisie Lawrence, your first DM was the prompt I needed.

Abi Dare, for helping me find my writer's voice, Kelly Morrell and Dujonna Gift-Simms for the amazing pictures. Old school mates at GSGS,Gbagada and Unilag for sharing your youth with me. My beta readers, Lola Olajide, Taiwo Wright, Seye Olajide, Dotun Okubadejo and Fola Akindeji for the wonderful feedback.

Those who guided my spiritual growth: Yemi Akisanya, Diran Ajayi, Mike Pearce, Dele and Vivienne Oke – God bless you. Ann Lewin, Rosie Medhurst, Kathy Lowers, Ray and Ruth Dobson, Usha Sahni, and all those 'helping hands' along the way – may others watch over your children as you watched over me. The Kibaya and Wisniewski families for the prayers and years of friendship.

My extended family: the Ogunoikis, Efunkoyas, the Late Brigadier Odunaiya and Mrs Abimsola Odunaiya, Dr Niran and Mrs Kehinde Talabi, Mr Gbenga and Mrs Taiwo Katibi, Tomi and Tolu Solola for accepting me and putting up with my foibles – I appreciate your love and kindness.

My extended nuclear family in the UK, the Olajides of Basildon and Rainham, the Wrights and the Ogunades. You rock and I love you loads. Thank you for the Christmases filled with joy and camaraderie. Deji and Dotun Okubadejo, your love and friendship over the years means so much to me; I love you.

My children, sons-in-law and grandchildren, I love you. Thank you for pushing me to be more. May you grow and become everything you are meant to be.

My husband, and stalwart for forty years. I love you. Thank you for your love, companionship and for letting me fly.